FIGURING THE EAST

FIGURING THE EAST

Segalen, Malraux, Duras, and Barthes

MARIE-PAULE HA

STATE UNIVERSITY OF NEW YORK PRESS

Published by
State University of New York Press, Albany

© 2000 State University of New York

All rights reserved

Printed in the United States of America

No part of this book may be used or reproduced in any manner whatsoever without written permission. No part of this book may be stored in a retrieval system or transmitted in any form or by any means including electronic, electrostatic, magnetic tape, mechanical, photocopying, recording, or otherwise without the prior permission in writing of the publisher.

For information, address State University of New York Press,
State University Plaza, Albany, NY 12246

Production by Laurie Searl
Marketing by Anne Valentine

Library of Congress Cataloging-in-Publication Data

Ha, Marie-Paule, 1953–
    Figuring the East : Segalen, Malraux, Duras, and Barthes / Marie-Paule Ha.
       p. cm.
    Includes bibliographical references and index.
    ISBN 0-7914-4385-X (hc : alk. paper) — ISBN 0-7914-4386-8 (pb : alk. paper)
    1. French literature—20th century—History and criticism. 2. Orient—In literature. I. Title.

PQ305.H25 2000
840.9′325—dc21
                                                           99-029215

10 9 8 7 6 5 4 3 2 1

To my father
and in memory of my mother

Contents

Acknowledgments	ix
Introduction	xi
1 Reading of the Asian Other	1
2 Segalen's "Quexotic" Quest	21
3 The Other in Malraux's Humanism	47
4 Duras on the Margins	71
5 Another Barthes	95
Conclusion	119
Notes	123
Works Cited	141
Index	155

Acknowledgments

I am greatly indebted to Steve Weninger who has untiringly read and reread the numerous versions of my work and offered insightful comments on its content as well as its prose. I would also like to express my gratitude to Mireille Rosello for her teaching and friendship over the years. A note of thanks goes to John Covolo for editing a few chapters of my manuscript.

A shorter version of chapter 3 has appeared in *Symposium* 48.1 (1994). A somewhat different version of chapter 4 was first published in *Romanic Review* 84.3 (1993). I want to thank the editors and publishers of these journals for permission to reuse this material.

Introduction

For many reseachers and students in the field of post-colonial studies, the main contribution of Edward Said is his inauguration of the area of study that has come to be known as colonial discourse. In *Orientalism*, through an examination of a variety of works belonging to different disciplines such as philology, history, literature, and travel narratives, Said shows how the West produces and reproduces knowledge of non-European peoples and cultures. One of the principal tasks of colonial discourse criticism is to examine the multiple ways in which the West deploys its discursive power to construct the Orient by making statements about it, describing it, teaching it and ruling over it. Besides the study of the Western modes of representation of non-European peoples, post-colonial critics also turn their attention to the "Other" that is spoken for and about in Orientalist discourse. Since the publication of Said's pathbreaking work, a series of debates ensued as to who is subaltern and whether the subaltern can articulate a specific position.[1] Another result of this new orientation is the development of critical theories to read or reread works by colonized and post-colonial writers. For reasons that have yet to be investigated, the focus of post-colonial literary studies in the west is confined mainly to Europhonic writings while relatively little attention has been paid to their non-Europhonic counterparts.[2]

In the last ten years or so, Orientalist criticism has advanced a step further as critics have begun examining Orientalist formations from the perspective of objects of the discourse. The historian Arif Dirlik, for instance, has explored the question of whether Orientalism, rather than being the autonomous creation of the West, did not also presuppose "in its emergence the complicity of the 'Orientals'" (109). In his study, Dirlik shows that through a process of "self-Orientalization," the Chinese have, in fact, incorporated Euro-American perceptions of Asians in the construction of their self-image and national consciousness. A similar reading has been put forth by Hiroshi Yoshioka in his analysis of the image of the samourai in the Japanese creation of their national identity. Rejecting the received idea that the samurai embodies an "authentic" and "original" Japanese spirit, Yoshioka contends that the samurai "is but an invention constructed as the result of the relationship between Japan and the West during the last 120 years. And it was invented not only by Westerners but also by the Japanese themselves" (104). Such analyses aim to demonstrate that Orientalism is a discourse that was not simply imposed by the West on a muted and passive Other, but was re-appropriated by Asians themselves to serve the political and ideological interests of certain classes in their struggle for legitimacy.

One way to understand the highly complex and multi-faceted functioning of Orientalist discourse is to attend to the philosophy of language elaborated by Mikhail Bakhtin. For my purposes what I find most insightful in his thinking is the view that the entire field of living human thought is intersected by dialogic boundaries and that every utterance is filled with dialogic overtones. The dialogism comes from the fact that there is no speech that does not also come from other speech as well as from the speech of the other. As Bakhtin argues in "The Problems of Speech Genres," our speech is always filled "with others' words, varying degrees of otherness or varying degrees of 'our-own-ness'" (89). No utterance is ever self-sufficient since each utterance invariably "refutes, affirms, supplements, and relies on the others" (91). As a result, our thoughts become fully articulate only in their interaction and struggle with the thoughts of others. Since there is no Adamic speaker, the object of our speech has always already been "articulated, disputed, elucidated and evaluated in various ways. Various viewpoints, world views, and trends cross, converge, and diverge in it" (93).

As a form of discourse, Orientalism, like any other language, also finds itself constantly appropriated, re-worked, and re-accentuated in the utterances of others. And these others, we have noted ealier, can be the others that Orientalism speaks for and about. A similar dialogism, I contend, also infuses the Eastern writings of the authors I examine in this book. There is no doubt that Victor Segalen, André Malraux, Marguerite Duras, and Roland Barthes assimilated a great many Orientalist ideas and references that permeate their perception and representation of the Other. Yet it is equally certain that they did not draw on the language of Orientalism without at the same time supplementing, re-accentuating, and filling it with other thoughts and languages. Besides being the ones they acquired in their home culture, these other thoughts and languages are also those of the Other with whom they engaged in both their lives and works. Their Oriental works emerge from an aggregate of various kinds of competing discourses—philosophical, anthropological, artistic, literary, political—that resound with contending voices, alien accents, and diverging viewpoints. In the process, Orientalism as a discursive formation may find itself deformed in the texts of these writers.

Besides elaborating the very complex relation of the four authors under consideration to Orientalism, I also use the Bakhtinian notion of heteroglossia to formulate what I call an "off-center" reading of texts that have been hitherto ensconced within the literary Olympus of metropolitan high culture. This reading consists in foregrounding the colonial and exotic intertextual references in the works under consideration and analyzing textual features that generally have been regarded as marginal or minor—elements such as setting, landscape, and extras. My objective is to re-establish the dialogic relations between the metropolitan and colonial worlds, which are often assumed to form separate spheres of cultural production.

Like any selection, there is unquestionably a certain degree of subjectivity and arbitrariness in my choice of authors and texts. Besides the one obvious reason that all four writers have developed special relations to East Asian cultures, which have inspired some of their best works, my interest in them is also induced by the different ways each of them deals with the Other through the mediation of Orientalist discourse. Of the four authors at issue, Segalen experienced the deepest tension in his dual role as advocate of a pristine exoticism and as medical officer in the navy, the primary military branch enforcing French imperial power. The irresolvable contradiction between his exotic quest and the colonial conquest in which he participates as a willing or unwilling party also informs his novel *René Leys*. I suggest that while an inherent impossibility resides in the very core of the narrator's "quexotic" quest, this impossibility is also vital to his exoticist project which must remain unrealizable in order to escape commodification, a fate that awaits all exotic Others in an age of colonial mercantile expansion.

In my reading of Malraux, I re-inscribe his Eastern texts within the colonial context that mediates his relation to the cultural Other. The re-articulation of the Orientalist frame of his Asian novels brings out the multiple contradictions that surround the author's Oriental engagement. On the one hand, his work abounds in uncritical Orientalist and colonial stereotypes of the Chinese and the "savage" Moi tribesmen, but, on the other hand, many of his protagonists find themselves at odds with the colonial power whose entrepreneurial spirit is inimical to the ethics of "true" adventuring. Yet it is in his unfinished novel, *Le Règne du malin*, which recounts the (mis)adventures of the would-be king of Sedangs, David de Mayrena, that one attends to the most interesting evolution in Malraux's cross-cultural intervention. In marking the demise of the epic which is the narrative genre par excellence of *la mission civilisatrice*, this posthumously published text opens an altogether new vista onto the view of the Other in Malraux's humanism.

Partly because of her status as a "white Indochinese," Duras develops deeply ambivalent relations to both the colonial establishment and the colonized. My engagement with her Asian novels takes as its point of departure the reflection on the significance of her little discussed colonialist treatise *L'Empire français*, which she co-authored with Philippe Roques in 1940. The celebratory and triumphalist tone of the book, extolling the virtues of *la mission civilisatrice*, stands in stark contrast to the virulence with which the narrator denounces the abusive power of the colonial administration in *Un Barrage contre le Pacifique*. Indeed, Duras's Asian works display a constant shiftiness vis-à-vis the colonial hegemony which she criticizes and re-affirms at the same time. While there is an unremitting effort in the texts to undermine all lines of divide—social, racial, gender—that structure the colonial space, the effectiveness of the transgressive moves initiated by Duras's protagonists remains limited as well as problematic.

Barthes's Eastern engagement no doubt poses a grave challenge to readers given the fact that for a long time he himself had been one of the most lucid and vigilant critics of Orientalism. For many Barthesian commentators, his Oriental texts, such as *L'Empire des signes*, *Alors la Chine?* and *Incidents*, present a disconcerting displacement from his former targeting of Orientalism as an object of criticism to his later practicing of Orientalism as a textual strategy. While recognizing the presence of Orientalist topoi and references in *L'Empire des signes*, I show that there are strategic attempts by Barthes to disengage himself from the Orientalist framework. Rather than reversing the Self/Other paradigm, he skirts around the dichotomy by reaching out for another space, a third space, to bring about a "retournement" (with its multiple meanings of going back to, turning around, changing, sending back) of Orientalism.

CHAPTER ONE

READING OF THE ASIAN OTHER

La religion des lettrés, encore une fois, est admirable. Point de superstitions, point de légendes absurdes, point de ces dogmes qui insultent à la raison et à la nature.

—Voltaire, *Chine (De la)*

Laques, pots du Japon, magots et porcelaines,
Pagodes toutes d'or et de clochettes pleines,
Beaux éventails de Chine, à décrire trop longs,
- Cuchillos, kriss malais à lames ondulées,
Kandjiars, yataghans aux gaînes ciselées,
. . .
Mille objects—bons à rien, admirables à voir.

—Théophile Gautier, *Albertus* LXXVII

EAST AND WEST

"Oh, East is East, and West is West,/ And never the twain shall meet." In these often quoted lines, Kipling projects such definite notions of what he and his readers mean by "East" and "West" that he feels no need to elaborate. However, even the most cursory survey of their common usage shows that these two terms have vastly different denotations and connotations, depending on, among other things, a given historical period, a particular field of study or discourse, a specific political and ideological agenda, or the region and cultural group from which one comes. According to the given contexts, "East" and "West" can be used as references to geographical spheres, cultural and racial categories, economic and political regimes or ideological systems. Even in their usage as geographical designations, which may seem the least problematic, the parts of the world known as "East" and "West" do in fact assume ever shifting boundaries. For example, in *Webster's Encyclopedic Dictionary* (1989), the East (equated with the Orient) is said to consist of the parts of Asia collectively lying East of Europe whereas the French dictionary *Petit Robert* (1979) incorporates within the sphere of the Orient not only Asia but also some countries of the Mediterranean basin or even parts of Central Europe.

A similar polysemy is evident in the other usages of the two terms. In his 1829 preface to his collection of poems, *Les Orientales*, Victor Hugo speaks of the imprint of "Oriental" colors on his thoughts and poetic reveries. In his view, the Orient not only stretches from China to Egypt but also includes Hebraic, Turkish, Greek, Persian, Arabic and Spanish cultures within its domain for, in his words, "Spain is still the Orient; Spain is half African, Africa is half Asiatic" (209). The Hugolian mapping of the Orient may not be as outlandish or outdated as one might think since in her collection, *Nouvelles orientales*, published in 1963, Marguerite Yourcenar draws from a similarly vast range of countries in her selection of Oriental tales. As she explains in an interview: "The collection *Nouvelles orientales* includes not only stories from the Far East ... and Hindu tales ... but also several stories set in Greece and the Balkans. Thus Asia and the Near East meet in these pages" (85).

If for Hugo and Yourcenar, Greece is part of the Orient, for Paul Valéry, in contrast, the Greek spirit constitutes nothing less than the essence of Europeanness. In his famous essay "La Crise de l'esprit" ("The Crisis of the Mind"), where he discusses the fate of Western civilization in the wake of the Great War, Valéry asks the question of what it means to be European. In a section entitled "Mais qui est donc Européen?" ("But who is European?"), he distinguishes three influences in the making of the European essence, namely Roman, Christian and Greek. Rome gives to Europe its political form, Christianity its moral conscience and Greece its spirit: "while the Roman conquest had only captured the political man ... the Christian conquest aims at and progressively reaches the depth of his conscience ... it is from Greece that we acquired these virtues (the subtlety and solidity of our knowledge, the purity and distinction of our arts)" (47–49). Valéry ends the section by concluding "any race and land that has been successively Romanized, Christianized and submitted spiritually to Greece is absolutely European" (53).

This long-standing narrative of European genealogy has been, however, strongly contested by the economist Samir Amin in his *Eurocentrism*. In the chapter entitled "The Construction of Eurocentric Culture," Amin demonstrates how the myth of Greek ancestry arose with the invention of "Western" history presented as "a progression from Ancient Greece to Rome to feudal Christian Europe to capitalist Europe" (89–90). For him, Eurocentrism constitutes an essential dimension in the ideology of capitalism. As such, the manifestations of the Eurocentric attitude are not limited only to European countries, but are propagated to all societies in the developed capitalist world which would include North America, Japan, Australia, New Zealand, and Israel. In the work of the anthropologist James Clifford, the concept of "the West" is given an altogether new reference that is no longer tied to fixed geographical or cultural spheres. In *The Predicament of Culture*, Clifford defines the West in terms of modern forms of power: "When we speak today of the West, we are usually referring to a force—technological, economic, political—no longer radiating in any simple way from a discrete geographical or cultural center. This force ... is disseminated in a diversity of forms from multiple centers—now including Japan, Australia, the Soviet Union, and China ..." (272).

Yet another usage of the term "the West" is to be found in Xiaomei Chen's book, *Occidentalism*, which discusses the strategic deployments of "the Occident" in the ideological skirmishes between the Maoist regime and its critics in China. On the one hand, the Chinese government disseminates a highly negative image of the West associated with exploitative capitalism in the "official Occidentalist" discourse which is used to justify political suppression at home; on the other hand, to counter the official Occidentalism, the opponents to the Maoist regime construe an "anti-official Occidentalist" discourse which presents "the Western Other as a metaphor for a political liberation against ideological oppression ..." (8). In this latter version, the "West" connotes freedom, equality, and justice, rights that the opposition feels are denied to the Chinese people by their government.

This brief discussion of the polyvalent uses of "East" and "West," whose significations vary dramatically according to the disciplinary traditions as well as the historico-cultural, national and ideological contexts in which they occur, shows that East and West are hardly two monolithic and unchanging realities as suggested in Kipling's poem. The traditional positioning of East/West as geographical and cultural oppositions rests on the conflation of two fallacies analyzed by Barbara Johnson, namely the fallacy of positing the existence of pure, unified, and separate traditions and the fallacy of spatialization: "It is as though cultural differences were simply modeled after the spatial or geographical differences that often give rise to them" (42). Since this book proposes to examine the figures of the East in the works of a number of Western writers, it is important to bear in mind the problematic nature of any discourse claiming to represent the world in facile East/West binarism.

EAST ASIA IN THE FRENCH IMAGINARY

The East that I discuss in this book is confined mainly to the Far East, specifically to countries such as China, Indochina, and Japan. My focus on those parts of the world is partly informed by my own biographical contingencies of being a Chinese born and raised in Viet-Nam. But more importantly, such a choice is prompted by the current state of critical scholarship on the Western representation of the Far East, which is surprisingly limited, not to say scarce. Such neglect is all the more perplexing given the fact that in the last twenty years the question of the representation of non-European cultures and peoples by European writers has become a highly popular theme among many literary and cultural critics. Yet most of their studies concentrate on works set in sub-Saharan Africa, North Africa, the Middle East, the Caribbean, and India.[1] Interestingly enough, these same preferences also inform the field of post-colonial studies in the United States. Indeed, the extensive critical attention which Anglophone and Francophone Maghrebin, sub-Saharan African, Australian and Caribbean writers receive in North America stands in curious contrast to the critical neglect befalling their Europhone Far-Eastern counterparts.[2] How can such a discrepancy be accounted for? Should it be explained in terms of geopolitical choices, cultural affinities, questions of canonicity, or academic fashion? While it is beyond the scope of this study to explore such salient issues of field formation, my book is projected as a step to remedy this neglect by analyzing the works of a number of French authors writing about the Far East.

China and Japan have long exerted a strong fascination on Europe and its thinkers. In his highly erudite two-volume work, *L'Europe chinoise*, René Etiemble has traced the defining moments of what he calls "L'enchinoisement de l'Europe" (the sinifying of Europe) from the time of the Roman empire to the end of the Enlightenment. He shows how Europe's reception of China and her culture alters during different periods in Western history. From the initial incredulity that met Marco Polo's "tall tales" of the Kingdom of the Great Khan to the notorious "Querelle des rites" between the Jesuits and the papal party, China aroused both intense fascination and suspicion among Europeans during the seventeenth and eighteenth centuries. While thinkers such as Leibniz and Voltaire prove to be enthusiastic sinophiles, some of their contemporaries such as Fénelon, Montesquieu, or Rousseau are better known for their virulent sinophobia. Etiemble explains these conflicted attitudes towards China in terms of philosophical and/or political agendas.

Besides the China of the *philosophes* associated with the legendary sage Confucius, there has always existed a more material China which found its way to Europe by merchant ships. In the seventeenth and eighteenth centuries, the trade of what was then known as "les Iachines" (Chinese goods) became highly profitable with the mounting popularity of "chinoiseries" such as Chinese porcelain, lacquerware, and silk among Europeans.[3] In the second half of the nineteenth century, these "chinoiseries" continued to make their way into salons and inspired works of art. Théophile Gautier and his daughter, Judith, the Goncourt brothers, and Pierre Loti, for instance, were all fervent collectors of oriental objets d'art. In their texts, the seme of the exotic Orient is often evoked through such bric-à-brac, as exemplified in Gautier's poem cited in the epigraph to this chapter.

Next to China, Japan is the other East Asian culture that has held considerable attraction for Europeans. The vogue of "Japonisme" derives from a more recent date, having started during the second half of the nineteenth century when European artists and writers discovered Japanese prints and curios.[4] Painters of the impressionist and naturalist schools developed a strong interest in Japanese woodblock print technique.[5] Like its Chinese counterpart, Japanese culture continues to maintain a firm appeal to twentieth-century Western writers. In the French context, besides Segalen, Malraux and Barthes whose works are discussed in the following chapters, one finds frequent references to these two Far Eastern cultures in the works of Paul Claudel, Saint-John Perse, Jean Paulhan, Henri Michaux, Marguerite Yourcenar, Julia Kristeva, Philippe Sollers and other Telquelians.

The fascination for the Far East was, of course, not limited to artists and writers, but also entered the consciousness of the average French citizen, especially from the 1890s onward. Because of the more concerted efforts of the Third Republic to formulate and put in place a systematic and coherent colonial doctrine, the French public became increasingly aware of the reality of the nation's overseas empire through the printed media as well as the numerous *expositions coloniales* organized by the government in different cities. The most successful colonial exhibition, partly because of its size and scale, was the one held in Paris in 1931, which attracted an estimated eight million visitors who were afforded the chance to meet French subjects from all over the empire and to stroll through replicas of native villages and monuments such as the famous Angkor Wat.[6] Besides these exhibitions, another medium that greatly contributed to bringing the colonized Other home was the press, one prime example being the vastly popular magazine, *L'Illustration, journal universel*, whose circulation surged from 120,000 copies in 1926 to 200,000 in 1939. In its various issues, its readers could find not only articles on a vast variety of topics about the colonies, but also numerous maps, photos of the natives, and drawings illustrating the lives of indigenous peoples, their customs and rituals, their houses and, crucially, the presence of the French overseas. China and Indochina were among the Asian countries most frequently covered in the magazine.[7]

FRENCH COLONIAL AND EXOTIC LITERATURE

With few exceptions, traditional literary critical scholarship that has studied the engagement of canonical authors such as Claudel, Segalen, Malraux, Michaux, or Barthes with the East has restricted itself to aesthetic and philosophical concerns. Critics have shown, for example, how these writers drew inspiration from Taoist and Buddhist ideas and how they integrated Chinese and Japanese poetics in their works.[8] What has been often left out or occluded in such readings is the ideological and political context that frames the Western writer's relation to the East. For if we look at modern history, the last quarter of the nineteenth century and the first part of the twentieth century constitute the most important period of French colonial expansion in both Africa and Asia.[9] The turn of the century saw France engaged in the final pacification of Indochina and in several skirmishes with China that ended with the obtaining of concessions in the Chinese capital and major cities such as Canton and Shanghai.[10] Writers such as Claudel, Segalen, Saint-John Perse, Malraux, and Duras, who resided in either China or Indochina during a time when these countries fell under Western domination, could not have remained totally indifferent to and unaffected by such historical developments.

Indeed, the issue of European colonialism saturates, in ways manifest or latent, the writings of all four authors under consideration in this book. Segalen, as a fervent amateur of exoticism, expresses throughout his work his strong dislike, if not hatred, of Western colonial expansion, which he perceives as a dangerous threat to the survival of the exotic. Both Malraux and Duras had a first-hand knowledge of the violence and corruption of the French colonial administration in Indochina. While Barthes never had direct experience of colonial politics, French imperialism does figure prominently in his early writings, particularly in the essays published as *Mythologies*.[11]

Why then have there been so few critical works[12] that closely examine the colonial and exotic intertextual references in the Eastern writings of these authors? One of the reasons is due to the notoriety traditionally attached to colonial and exotic literatures, pariah genres within French metropolitan high culture. In France, there persists to this very day an uncertainty about the relation between the two genres. For many readers, the two terms "colonial" and "exotic" are almost interchangeable. In her survey of French colonial literature, Martine Astier Loutfi speaks precisely of the frequent merging of the meanings of the two words: "'colonial' is often used as a synonym of 'exotic,' 'tropical'" (46). The blurring of usages is no mere accidental confusion, but a consequence of a close parallel between the evolution of exotic writings and the history of colonial expansion. Ever since its emergence at the end of the fifteenth century,[13] the notion of the exotic has been closely tied to European imperialism as Jean-Marc Moura points out in *Lire l'exotisme*: "From the end of the fifteenth to twentieth centuries ... the exotic dream is profoundly influenced by the advances and the retreats of colonialism" (13). In his study of the Orient in the literature of the seventeenth and eighteenth centuries, Pierre Martino likewise discusses at great length the connection between the development of exotic literature and colonial expansion noting that "under the Ancien Regime the history of colonization starts at almost the same time as the history of literary exoticism" (43).

Yet, in the history of the two genres, their respective practitioners have incessantly insisted on marking their differences. For example, Segalen, champion of the exotic, makes it clear in *Essai sur l'exotisme* that "Le colonial est exotique, mais l'exotisme dépasse puissamment le colonial" (the colonial is exotic, but exoticism goes far beyond the colonial) (81) while Louis Malleret, a colonial writer and critic, reminds his readers that "while it may be hard to conceive of a colonial literature that is not 'exotic,' one has to recognize that not all literatures with an exotic impression have a colonial cachet" (38). In their theoretical writings,[14] colonial novelists repeatedly signal their distance from the exotic genre. The latter appears to them as superficial, subjective and given to the sensational. Colonial literature, in contrast, is said to shoulder the far more serious mission of studying the native subjects, their lands and culture and the relationship between colonizers and colonized.

In contrast to its British counterpart, which counts within its ranks eminent literary figures such as Joseph Conrad, Rudyard Kipling, George Orwell, or Joyce Cary, French colonial and exotic literature has received scant critical attention.[15] In the French context, writers and critics of colonial and exotic literature are acutely aware of the problematic status of their object of study. In *Essai sur l'exotisme*, Segalen makes it his main task to purge exoticism of all the dirt and "scoriae" that have been heaped upon it. Yet apparently this rehabilitation campaign does not seem to have achieved the desired goal, since almost eighty years later, in his introduction to *Rêver l'Asie*, "La Littérature exotique comme miroir nécessaire," Lombard still feels the need to reiterate the problematic image of the genre: "Without being a literature 'maudite,' it is nevertheless clear that (these works) are always considered as low quality. Critics hardly discuss exotic novels ... which they consider fastidious and poorly written" (12).

A similar ostracism befalls colonial literature, which has always been treated as "littérature de seconde zone" (a second-class literature)[16] or "production mineure" (minor production).[17] In his preface to the anthology, *Indochine: un rêve d'Asie*, Quella-Villéger comments on the prejudice against colonial novels:

"The novelistic production relative to South East Asia was never given a place in serious literary history as it was despised by academics and considered a priori to be mediocre" (iii). Indeed, there is near total silence on colonial and exotic literature in today's standard French literature survey manuals such as the vastly popular Lagarde and Michard series or Henri Mitterand's *Littérature textes et documents XXe siècle*.[18] Even when a colonial writer is mentioned at all, he or she is not identified as a colonial writer and his/her colonial texts are generally omitted from the discussion. Such is, for example, the case of Claude Farrère, who wrote a number of colonial novels. In Henri Mitterand's aforementioned series and the Pléiade collection of *Histoire des littératures 3*, Farrère is introduced as a writer of "littérature d'anticipation scientifique," the forerunner of today's science fiction; no mention is made of his colonial corpus.

What accounts for this inadequate treatment of colonial and exotic works? There are several related factors behind this unfavorable reception—political, historical, social, and literary. Unlike her neighbor across the Channel, France as a nation has always had a very ambivalent attitude towards colonial expansion. In Flaubert's *Dictionnaire des idées reçues*, under the rubric of "Colonies (nos)," we read: "causing distress when speaking about them." This description, as Raoul Girardet notes, accurately reflects the sentiment of the majority of the French concerning their government's overseas conquest during the Second Empire. It was not until the 1880s that, under the leadership of Jules Ferry, the Third Republic came up with a more systematic colonial policy. Even then, support for the imperial venture was hardly unanimous, since critics from both left and right believed that, rather than squandering valuable resources in the uncertain conquest of distant lands, their government should invest its energy and effort within metropolitan France to rebuild the nation after the catastrophe of 1870.[19]

If the French populace appeared to be unsure of the advisability of its government's colonial policy, its perception of colonials proved to be even more disparaging. There was a long tradition of treating the colonies as the dumping ground for the metropole's "human dregs," undesirable elements such as criminals, trouble-makers, or prostitutes, who failed to adjust to "normal" social life.[20] In Farrère's novel, *Les Civilisés*, the Indochinese governor succinctly summarizes this negative view of the colonies and their settlers: "in the unanimous view of the French nation, colonies have the reputation of being the last resource and the ultimate refuge of the déclassés and the ex-convicts. In witness whereof, the metropole keeps for itself all its best citizens and exports only the dregs of its society" (91).

If the colonies were thus looked upon with suspicion in political and social terms,[21] their literary and cultural productions were likewise subjected to a similar deprecation. One of the major criticisms levelled against colonial literature (which also helps to explain its "minor" status) is that colonial writers allowed their political and ideological preoccupations to take precedence over the aesthetic concerns in their works. In *Littérature et colonialisme*, Loutfi develops the thesis that colonial novels were devoid of aesthetic qualities: "the very theory of 'colonial novel' was founded on specious arguments in which the aesthetics served as mere pretext for the defence of colonialism" (71) as the colonial authors "were interested in the novel more as a vehicle of an ideology than as a work of art" (72). This same criticism is echoed a decade later by Mathieu, who explains the "minor" status of colonial literature in similar terms: "Minor and disparaged because it is too enmeshed in a compulsive propogandistic will" (11).

These judgments rest, in fact, on two premises that are themselves quite debatable, namely that "true" works of art are non-ideological and that the aesthetic is incompatible with the ideological. If ideology is understood in the Althusserian sense of "ideological state apparatuses,"[22] one of which is precisely literature, could there be an artistic or cultural production outside any ideology? Indeed, Kipling's novels, which Loutfi cites approvingly, are certainly not free of imperialist tenets. Furthermore, Loutfi and other critics seem here to limit the colonial genre to those works that are described as purely propagandistic. In other words, a novel can be considered as colonial only if its author's intention is to promote imperialist views, which automatically devalues the work in question. Such a reasoning oversimplifies the way a given hegemony functions as it rests on the questionable assumption that it is always possible to decide once and for all whether a certain position is colonial or not. In fact, what constitutes a pro- or anti-colonial stand varies according to a specific historical period and political context.[23]

The equivocal way that the critics approach French colonial and exotic literature is cogently illustrated by Lombard's remark in "Prélude à la littérature 'indochinoise'": "It is no doubt true that if one sets aside Malraux (and Camus in the case of Algeria), none of these 'colonial' authors has achieved in France the repute of a Conrad or a Kipling across the Channel" (128). How should one interpret Lombard's bracketing of Malraux and Camus in his comment on colonial writers? Are we to consider these two authors separately because they are canonized by the metropolitan literary establishment even though their works are about the colonies? As to the "absence" of a French Kipling or Conrad so often lamented by critics, the problem may not be that no great French colonial writers ever existed, but rather that such authors would be dissociated from the colonial domain to be consecrated in the literary Olympus of the mother country.

An alternative that may resolve this impasse is to adopt a more inclusive approach to the study of the relation between literature and empire as found in Anglophone colonial studies. In her survey of British colonial literature, Elleke Boehmer distinguishes three kinds of writings, according to their relationship to imperialism: colonial, colonialist and post-colonial. What interests us here are the first two groups. To the category of "colonialist literature," Boehmer assigns works that are specifically concerned with colonial expansion, written by colonizing Europeans about non-European lands, and informed by the "imperialists' point of view" of the "superiority of European culture and the rightness of empire" (3). Loutfi's definition of colonial literature as extolling the virtues of colonization would fall within this grouping.[24] In Boehmer's scheme, "colonial literature" refers to writings "concerned with colonial perceptions and experience" (2). In this group, she includes works that may not make direct reference to colonial matters, but that contribute to the perception of Britain as an imperial power. As examples of this category, she cites Charles Dickens's novels and Anthony Trollope's travelogues.[25] While I am not sure that it is always possible to pigeonhole books so neatly and unproblematically, I think that Boehmer's inclusive conception of "colonial literature" helps to blur the narrowly defined cultural boundaries segregating colonies from the mother country. This in turn can bring about a deterritorialized reading of texts that have been hitherto ensconced within the confines of metropolitan high culture as is the case with the works to be discussed in the following chapters. Instead of approaching these texts centrally, I broach them from the periphery, focusing on what traditional critics consider as their "minor" or "marginal" sides.

OFF-CENTER READING

If there is one work that has contributed most powerfully to the contemporary questioning and rethinking of cultural narratives, it is Said's *Orientalism*. In spite of its problems (one being its representation of the West as a monolithic power), Said's book has inaugurated "*l'ère du soupçon*" in the studies of cultural representations. He has taught a whole generation of critics to interrogate and challenge the ideology and the politics that inform writings, studies, and visions of other cultures. More importantly, *Orientalism* has alerted us to pitfalls in our encounter with the Other as well as in the construction of our own personal and cultural identities.

One of the most useful and productive lessons to be learned from Said's work is its loosening of the disciplinary boundaries traditionally governing our appreciation of texts. His own practice of cross-disciplinary reading provides us with a theoretical frame to reread and rethink cultural productions in more "wordly" terms by re-placing them in their specific social, political and historical conjunctures.[26] Such a cross-disciplinary approach also underlies my own engagement with the Eastern texts here as my reading brings to the foreground the colonial and exotic intertextual space that structures them. For I believe, like Said, that any Western narrative of the East is always already informed by the vast reservoir of aesthetic, economic, sociological, historical, philological, and literary texts that are constitutive of and constituted by what Barthes in *S/Z* refers to as "codes culturels" or "la grande voix de la petite science" (211) (the major voice of minor science) (205).[27] Writing is the weaving of these voices or codes.

In *Orientalism*, one of Said's key arguments is that given the West's investment in Orientalist discourse, there can be no neutral contact between the West and the Orient. When a European or an American[28] scholar engages in the study of the Orient, "he [*sic*] comes up against the Orient as a European or American first, as an individual second. And to be a European or an American in such a situation is by no means an inert fact. It meant and means being aware, however dimly, that one belongs to a power with definite interests in the Orient" (11). Obviously, an awareness of power relations likewise informs all readers in the "opposite" direction (that is, the contact of colonial and post-colonial subjects with the West) for the latter's cultural and personal history has been profoundly shaped by a century or more of imperial domination. As a non-European post-colonial reader, my engagement with Western texts, in particular those that purport to represent colonial and exotic subjects, proves to be unstable, if not bifurcated. My reading experience, which is one of the reader-as-object-of-the-text, seems to contradict the lesson of Wayne Booth in *Rhetoric of Fiction* urging total identification by the actual reader with the implied reader of the narrative.[29]

Without discounting major differences between the two situations, a post-colonial reader's relationship to Orientalist literature is not without some parallels to that of the female reader vis-à-vis main/"malestream"[30] literature. In *The Resisting Reader: A Feminist Approach to American Fiction*, Judith Fetterley points out that when reading American fictions, often male-centered, a female reader "is co-opted into participation in an experience from which she is explicitly excluded; she is asked to identify with a selfhood that defines in opposition to her; she is required to identify against herself" (xii). This sense of exclusion and non-identification also informs the post-colonial reader's encounter with colonial and exotic works, for the originally intended audience of colonial and exotic literature was metropolitan. The readers inscribed in these texts are assumed to share a specific cultural and class habitus in Pierre

Bourdieu's sense,[31] which in turn defines what is familiar, as opposed to what is strange and unusual. In short, as Umberto Eco demonstrates, each text selects and creates its own Model Reader, who in the case of colonial and exotic writings, is usually not isomorphic with the colonial or post-colonial subject.

One way to understand the functioning of the split post-colonial engagement with Orientalist texts is provided by Barthes's analysis of reading in *S/Z*. Barthes contends that the "I" reading a text is never a blank slate, anterior to the text, but is constituted by "une pluralité d'autres textes, de codes infinis" (16) (a plurality of other texts, of codes which are infinite) (10). In other words, all readings are always already structured by a series of codes that both codify the texts and derive from them. In his analysis of *Sarrasine*, Barthes masterfully unravels the textual weaving of the different codes or voices that enter into the composition of each lexeme of Balzac's novella. Of the five types of major codes identified by Barthes, the two that I find most useful for my discussion of the post-colonial reading of colonial and exotic texts are the semic and cultural codes: the "seme" or "signified of connotation" is "un connotateur de personnes, de lieux, d'objets, dont le signifié est un *caractère*. Le caractère est un adjectif, un attribut, un prédicat" (196) (a connotator of persons, places, objects, of which the signified is a *character*. Character is an adjective, an attribute, a predicate) (190); cultural codes are "citations ... extraites d'un corpus de savoir, d'un Livre anonyme dont le meilleur modèle est sans doute le Manuel Scolaire" (211) (citations ... extracted from a body of knowledge, from an anonymous Book whose best model is doubtless the School Manual) (205). Barthes further adds that all codes are culturally informed and reading is a matter of decoding the voices that are woven into the very texture of a work.

Using the Barthesian notion of codes, I show here how the seme of the exotic in a text functions differently for its intended metropolitan audience than for post-colonial readers. If the exotic is generally defined as that which appears as deviating from or foreign to the self, the reverse may not be true. That is, the unfamiliar is not necessarily the exotic. For example, in the United States, a description of an inner city neighborhood will probably seem alien, but definitely not exotic, to a suburbanite. My point is that the impression of the exotic does not come "naturally" to a person, but is a culturally coded perception. In other words, a given community of readers learns to identity certain adjectives, attributes, sounds, or names as "exotic" in the same way as a French middle-class educated reader comes to read "Faubourg St. Honoré" in Balzac's Paris as the seme for wealth. In fact, a description that is coded as exotic may not necessarily refer to something unfamiliar to the readers. For example, metropolitan readers of Orientalist literature continue to find Loti or Fromentin's evocation of North Africa exotic even though the Algerian landscape may have become quite familiar to them through frequent readings of similar works. Yet this familiarity does not prevent them from decoding those texts as exotic. In *Essai sur l'exotisme*, Segalen is highly critical of the overdetermined coding of the exotic, which produces clichés such as "le palmier et le chameau, casque de colonel, peaux noires et soleil jaune" (the palm tree and the camel, the topee, black skins and yellow sun) (22). Turn-of-the-century French readers had been conditioned by their cultural background to interpret these words as constituting an "exotic" space.

The decoding of the exotic becomes much more complex if the reader happens to be a post-colonial subject who, for better or worse, was given access to the colonizers' culture for he/she found him/herself between two conflictual systems of codes: the foreign (which, in many cases, is European) and the indigenous. As a result of colonial education, the post-colonial subject inhabits unevenly[32] both the Western cultural space and his/her native one. Consequently, in his/her engagement with colonial and exotic texts that purport to describe his/her native land and people, he/she invariably finds him/herself in a position similar to the spectatorial schizophrenia Shohat and Stam analyze in their study of the fissured colonial spectators who undergo the ambivalent experience of watching themselves being "otherized" in Eurocolonial films.

On the one hand, the Western-schooled post-colonial reader is prompted by his/her education to decode descriptions of his/her own society and culture as exotic; on the other hand, what is coded as the unfamiliar, the foreign, the Other in the texts, is in fact the most quotidian and commonplace reality to him/her. Hence, when reading passages depicting Cholon, the Vietnamese chinatown, in French Indochinese literature, I realize that the text interpellates[33] the metropolitan culture-coded reader in me to interpret the evocation of the atmosphere, the sounds, the smells, and the objects as exotic. Yet as a native of Cholon, the same sounds, smells and sights constituted my once daily and most intimate habitat. Because of these conflicting codes, my reading experience of colonial and exotic literature produces in me a "turnstile" effect in which I experience my native social and cultural environment as simultaneously strange and familiar. If colonial education estranges us, the (ex)colonized, from our land and culture by a process of alienation that either exoticizes and/or denigrates our native heritage, it also produces the no less paradoxical effect of turning the metropolitan world into a *déjà vu* reality even before we ever set foot on its soil. The colonial schooling so "successfully" inculcates Western cultural codes in us that we are led to see metropolitan reality not as "foreign" or "exotic," but as "familiar."[34]

This ambiguity which I experience as a Western educated post-colonial subject vis-à-vis Orientalist texts continues to inform my engagement with

Western critical works discussing colonial and exotic literature. Like the authors they study, metropolitan critics very often presume that their readers occupy the same cultural and geographical space, a presumption increasingly untenable in a multicultural society. For example, when speaking of the exotic "elsewhere," critics rarely feel the need to justify the location of that other site, taking for granted that for their readers too the exotic is situated outside the West. A case in point is Moura's description of his use of the term "exotic" which is confined to "the representation of men and societies that do not belong to Europe" (14). Malleret likewise conceives of exoticism as an essentially Western phenomenon, an expression of Europe's angst (39), a view shared by Roger Célestin who defines exoticism "as a relation between (Western) Self and (exotic) Other" (7).

When deploying binarisms such as modernity/tradition, civilization/savagery, same/other in their discussion of the exotic, critics adopt the inevitable assumption that they and their readers occupy the same side, namely, that of the selfsame subject qua consumer of the exotic. Just as the standard definition of the exotic rests on the ethnocentric opposition of a "we" to a "not-we," critics very unselfconsciously wield the first person plural pronoun in their pronouncements on the exotic. An example is Chris Bongie's characterization of the *fin-de-siècle* exoticist project which he defines as "a discursive practice intent on recovering 'elsewhere' values 'lost' with the modernization of European society" (5). He then goes on to state that "The challenge of (post)modernity has become one of learning to live with *our* exotic memories, with the ruins of everything that came before *us* and that once upon a time, seemed to offer *us* a fullness and a 'strength' that is no longer *ours* to be had" (32; emphases added). The exotic memories in question here refer to those shared with European writers such as Conrad, Loti, and Segalen, whose exotic experience is inscribed in the non-European colonized world. Post-colonial readers hailing from those very parts of the globe that provided exotic inspiration to the *fin-de-siècle* writers may not necessarily share the latter's exotic memories in the same way as their Western counterparts.

Besides such presuppositions about their readers' cultural affiliations, critical works on colonial and exotic literature also display a gender bias since critics seem to attribute the exotic and colonial projects only to male subjects and limit their studies to works authored by men. For instance, in Moura's *Lire l'exotisme*, which traces the evolution of French exotic literature from medieval to modern times, not one woman writer is mentioned,[35] which is rather puzzling given the existence of many colonial and exotic women writers, such as Judith Gautier, Isabelle Eberhardt, Jeanne Leuba, Myriam Harry, Clotilde Chivas-Baron, Christiane Fournier, among others. The exclusion of exotic and colonial works written by women is no mere accidental oversight, but is part and parcel of a long established perception of the colonies as an exclusively male preserve. In her *Discourses of Difference*, Sara Mills explains this near total eclipse of the female presence in colonial writings in terms of the social conventions for conceptualizing imperialism which, in the British context, "seems to be much about constructing *masculine* British identity as constructing a national identity per se" (3). This prevalent male ethos in colonial and exotic writings partly explains the recurrent use of feminizing metaphors for the colonial and exotic space, which is often depicted as "virgin land," waiting to be explored and penetrated by the white male settlers.[36] A number of recent studies on colonial cultural history, however, show that the European colonial project was also built around the cult of domesticity. In her research on colonial politics in the Dutch Indies, Ann Stoler demonstrates that it is "in the domestic domain, not the public sphere, where essential dispositions of manliness, bourgeois morality, and racial attributes could be dangerously undone or securely made" (108).[37]

In *The Role of the Reader*, starting from the assertion that a reader always approaches a text from a personal ideological perspective, Eco states that "a given ideological background can help one to discover or to ignore textual ideological structures," at times leading one "to read a given text in the light of 'aberrant' codes (where 'aberrant' means only different from the ones envisaged by the sender)" (22). Eco's view certainly recalls Barthes's analysis of critical activity in "Qu'est-ce que la critique?" (What Is Criticism?), which argues that every critical language is informed by a certain ideology. Hence the "cardinal sin" in criticism is not ideology per se, but "le silence dont on la couvre" (*Essais* 254) (the silence by which it is masked) (257). The choice of a given critical language, Barthes contends, is made objectively in accordance with "un certain mûrissement historique du savoir, des idées, des passions intellectuelles" (a certain historical ripening of knowledge, ideas, intellectual passions) and subjectively in relation to "une certaine organisation existentielle," (a certain existential organization) an exercise in which the critic "met toute sa 'profondeur,' c'est-à-dire ses choix, ses plaisirs, ses résistances, ses obsessions" (*Essais* 257) (puts all his 'profundity,' that is, his choices, his pleasures, his resistances, his obsessions) (260).

My approach to the works of Segalen, Malraux, Duras, and Barthes is thus shaped by the conjunction of both objective circumstances and subjective determinations. Given my historical location as a Western-educated postcolonial subject, my relation to Orientalist writings is inevitably duplicitous, being at once the inscribed reader of the text and its Other, thereby experiencing what Fetterley describes as "an endless division of self against self" (xiii). One might characterize my reading of these texts using the notion of heteroglossia introduced by Bakhtin, by which he means the presence and co-existence of other voices and other intentions in any given utterance.[38] According to Bakhtin, instead of a unitary and monological relation between a word and its object or a word and its user, any concrete discourse "finds the object at which it was directed already as it were overlain with qualifications, open to dispute, charged with value. . . . It is entangled, shot through with shared thoughts, points of view, alien value judgements and accents" (*Dialogical* 276). While Bakhtin's concern is with the multiple voices and languages in the texts, I would add that the same heteroglossia is also to be found on the side of reception, that is, between the texts and their readers. The off-center reading I propose here is heteroglossic in the sense that it generates accents, voices, and points of view alien and at times resistant to those intended by the original senders.

In my reading, which is informed by more than one set of cultural codes, I broach the texts off-centeredly. From this off-center angle, my reading explores "what in [the] text is ideologically presupposed, untold" (Eco 22). By looking at "secondary, non-essential" textual elements such as the "setting," the "background," the "landscape," or the "figurants," my analysis brings back in focus the figures of the silenced, the unsayable, the marginal, and the exotic, in short all that which has been often considered in traditional criticism as the "minor," "incidental" and "extraneous" aspects of the works under study.

One chief strategy in off-center reading consists in re-placing the writings of metropolitan writers within colonial and exotic intertextual space. Such a re-inscription serves to foreground the "peripheral" textual features, which, I demonstrate, function as the texts' margins in relation to which the center defines itself. For example, in my reading of Malraux's and Duras's Asian novels, I focus my analysis on "background" elements such as the Cambodian jungle in *La Voie royale* or the peripheries of the colonial city in *Vice-Consul*, which are presented as the site of the Other, inhabited by subhumans like the Mois or social outcasts like the mad, the beggars, and the lepers. It is against this colonial space of the marginal(ized) used as the books' "exotic backdrop," I argue, that the drama of the European protagonists in both Malraux and Duras establishes itself as the core experience of Western humanity. While living half a century apart, Segalen and Barthes apparently seek the same solution to their disaffection with Western modernity by turning to an "elsewhere," outside the center, that still holds promise for the recovery of an ever elusive, if not illusive, exotic Other. Yet, confronted with the dearth, if not the death, of exotic space, which is perceived by Segalen and Barthes as the last outpost of their aesthetic quest, both writers have recourse to the similar strategy of resurrecting the

Other by a process of anachronization; the former reinvents the myth of the bygone Emperor and the latter re-creates an archaic feudal Japanese culture. At one level, as the space of the Other, Malraux's savage jungle and Duras's sordid colonial city seem to stand in stark contrast to the highly refined world of Segalen's Chinese Imperial Forbidden City and Barthes's Japanese empire of signs. Yet a close reading of these diverse figurations of the Other shows that they all share the common quality of being "semantic nothingness," an essence of pure alterity in whose representation, as Francis Affergan claims, "language reaches the limits of the unsayable, the ob-scene, the silence and panic" (69). While displaying important differences, Malraux's Mois, Duras's native beggar woman, Segalen's Emperor, and Barthes's Japanese signs, all converge strangely enough in the figures of absence, lack, or void.

RECONFIGURING ORIENTALISM

One of the most frequent criticisms[39] of Said's analysis of Orientalism is that it produces a monolithic, essentialist and ahistorical characterization of Orientalist discourse. In his critique of *Orientalism*, for instance, Dennis Porter attributes Said's failure to consider the possibility of alternatives to Orientalism to his static conception of hegemony, which Said uses to explain the strength and durability of Orientalism. One way to refine the Saidian notion of hegemony is to attend to Raymond Williams's analysis of the term. In *Marxism and Literature*, Williams provides an in-depth discussion of hegemony. One of the central features that explains and ensures the successful functioning of hegemony understood as "a whole body of practices and expectations" (110) is its ability to re-create, change and renew itself. According to Williams, the hegemonic as an active process is not just a simple transmission of an unchanging dominance, for "any hegemonic process must be especially alert and responsive to the alternatives and oppositions which question or threaten its dominance" (113). That is to say, it is in the very nature of a hegemony to allow for certain counter-hegemonic practices and oppositional forms. In fact, this capacity to incorporate dissidence and divergence indicates the strength of the hegemony in question.

The four writers whose Eastern texts I examine in this book certainly entertain problematic relations to their own culture. In varying degrees, they all situate themselves at the margin, if not outside of, the center that is the West, at least at the time of their writing of those texts. Yet this positioning of the self as dissenter to one's own society is quite a common topos in Orientalist literature. It needs to be read carefully and not to be taken as either a simple rejection of the West or a total acceptance of the East. In many instances, this Eastward turn is often prompted by what Spivak calls the European "consciousness crisis management" (*Post-colonial* 8). For various historical, political and personal reasons, each of the writers under consideration had an axe to grind with the society of his/her time. They developed a strong dissatisfaction with and aversion to Western civilization. By turning to an elsewhere, they sought an alternative system which might provide them with what they found amiss at home. Hence, for Segalen and Barthes, both of whom abhorred Western bourgeois materialism and philistinism, an Eastward journey was conceived as a quest for an/Other aesthetic space. What brought the young Malraux and his Western protagonists to China and French Indochina in the 1920s was the prospect of greater freedom and the opportunity to live out the dreams and ambitions that were denied them back in the metropole. Like many European children growing up in the colonies,[40] Duras had highly ambivalent feelings vis-à-vis what she calls her "fatherland," the land of the patriarchal order, which created the brutal colonial rule that victimized her mother. At one level, this turning to the East presented as the West's Other may serve to articulate, in the words of Robert Young, "an internal dislocation within Western culture" (139). Yet the outcome of any challenge to a hegemonic order remains always uncertain as the subversive act can be re-appropriated to reaffirm, if not reinforce, the dominance of that order. In my reading of the Eastern texts here, special attention is paid to the functioning of these counter-hegemonic voices, which I argue are at once critical of and complicitous with the prevalent ideology.

At one level, in presenting the East as the Other of the West, the works under consideration can be said to reproduce the Orientalist ideology that, as Said argues, turns the Orient into one of Europe's "deepest and most recurring images of the Other" (*Orientalism* 1). If we follow Barthes's argument in *S/Z* that writing is a stereographic space where different codes and voices intersect, one of the major voices that shapes the narratives of the Orient is unquestionably that of Orientalism. It is, therefore, not surprising that the texts under study abound in Orientalist topoi and references. In fact, as we shall see in the chapters that follow, the authors whose works I discuss here are all aware, albeit in varying degrees, of the weight that Orientalism exerts on their relation to the Other. Segalen and Barthes, in particular, offer a highly lucid articulation of the problem.

In *The Postcolonial Aura*, Dirlik shows how in the process of exposing himself/herself to another culture, the Orientalist becomes "Orientalized" as he/she gets closer to the Other while distancing himself/herself from his/her home culture. Hence, one of the results of inhabiting the "contact zone,"[41] a zone of domination and exchange, is the blurring of the distinctions between self and other, inside and outside, or center and periphery that are the defining features of the Orientalist formation. If the authors under study may not be appropriately called "Orientalists," a term which usually refers to scholars specializing in the study of the Orient such as William Jones or Louis Massignon, they have, nevertheless, inhabited the East physically, culturally and intellectually. Cross-cultural interventions, even if they take place under circumstances of inequality, still bring about a certain alter-ation of these writers in their perception of themselves as well as the Other. And while these changes may not bring about an eschewal of Orientalism as such, the engagements with another culture make it possible for these authors to re-figure the terms in which the relation of Self/Other has been traditionally articulated, which in turn effects a reconfiguring of Orientalist discourse itself.

CHAPTER TWO

SEGALEN'S "QUEXOTIC" QUEST

In the introduction to his collection of poems entitled *Peintures*, Segalen summarizes the nature of his entire literary enterprise: "L'exotisme entendu comme tel: une esthétique du Divers—est d'ailleurs le centre, l'essence, la raison d'être de tous les livres que Victor Segalen ait écrits et, sans doute qu'il réserve d'écrire" (Exoticism understood as such: an aesthetics of the *Divers*[1]—is, I might add, the center, the essence, the raison d'être of all the books Victor Segalen has written and will write) (*Stèles, peintures* 563). Born in Brest in 1878 and raised during the heyday of French imperialism,[2] Segalen devoted his life and work to establishing himself as one of the foremost "exotes" of his time. Besides numerous tours as a naval medical officer, Segalen himself actively sought postings overseas throughout his career. A few years after his stay in Tahiti in 1903, Segalen undertook a study of Chinese at l'Ecole des Langues Orientales. In 1909, he was posted in China where, apart from a brief break, he lived continuously for five years. In 1917, he returned to China once again for a short period of six months.

It was during these trips that Segalen's major works were conceived. One of his earliest books, *Les Immémoriaux*, which recounts the saga of the decline of Maori culture, is based on his experience with life on the island. Likewise, it is in the course of his homeward journey from the South Seas that Segalen formulates for the first time the proposal for his prolegomena to the theory of the exotic, *Essai sur l'exotisme*, a project which would remain in note form until the end of his life. Even before his departure for China, Segalen confidently expresses to his lifelong mentor, Jules de Gaultier, his hopes of reaping rich rewards from his future expedition: "In China, grappling with the most antipodal material, I expect a great deal of this unmitigated exoticism" (cf. Courtot

16). His encounter with China did indeed yield many literary projects including, among others, a book of travel notes entitled, *Briques et tuiles*; two novels, *Fils du Ciel* and *René Leys*; various collections of poems such as *Stèles*, *Peintures*, *Equipée*, *Odes* and *Thibet*; archeological writings such as *Chine. La Grande statuaire* and *Les Origines de la statuaire de Chine*.[3] Of this series of works, only *Stèles* (1912) and *Peintures* (1916) were published before their author's untimely death in 1919 while the rest awaited posthumous publication.

Given the centrality of exoticism in Segalen's work, it is useful to begin with an examination of this concept as formulated in *Essai*. My discussion focuses on two major issues underlying the Segalenian exoticist project: first, the duplicitous relationship between his exotic quest and colonial politics; second, the tension between his aspiration for a noncontaminated Other and the "always already there" character of the exotic. The latter part of the chapter focuses on how these contradictions also come to inform his novel, *René Leys*. I suggest that, while an inherent impossibility resides in the very core of the Segalenian quest, this impossibility is vital to his exoticist project which must remain unrealizable lest it be commodified. This strategic redemptive "failure" is announced at the very beginning of *René Leys* when the narrator renounces his quest of the Inside: "Je ne saurai donc rien de plus. Je n'insiste pas; je me retire.... C'est par cet aveu ... que je dois clore, avant de l'avoir mené bien loin, ce cahier dont j'espérais faire un livre. Le livre ne sera pas non plus. (Beau titre posthume à défaut d'un livre: 'Le livre qui ne fut pas'!)" (457) (I shall know no more, then. Well, I shall not insist; I shall retire from the field.... It is with this admission ... that I must close, having just opened it, this journal of which I had hoped to make a book. The book, too, will never be. (But failing the book, what a splendid posthumous title—*The Book That Never Was!*)) (17). This book, which will never be, should also not be. Should it have been actualized, it would have soon been transformed into a commodity, a fate the narrator had feared for the would-be novel: "J'avais cru le tenir d'avance, plus 'fini', plus vendable que n'importe quel roman patenté...." (457). (I thought I had it 'in the bag'—more 'consummate,' more saleable than any novel ever copyrighted....) (17).

EXOTIC QUEST AND COLONIAL CONQUEST

We have seen in chapter one that despite the many divergences that distinguish the exotic venture from the colonial entreprise, the two projects do intersect on other levels. The highly complex relationship between colonialism and exoticism,[4] a relationship at once antagonistic and complicitous, creates deep tension in the life and work of Segalen in his dual role as advocate of a pristine and purified exoticism and as medical officer of the navy, the primary military branch to ensure and enforce the French imperial presence overseas during the early part of the twentieth century.

Even if Segalen often denounces Western colonial hegemony in his writings, his "anti-colonialism" is informed primarily by aesthetic rather than political concerns. What troubles him as an *exote* is above all the corrosive effect Europeans have on native cultures. Thanks to modern technology, which had dramatically accelerated and extended the West's domination of the globe, exotic space had shrunk rapidly, like some Balzacian "peau de chagrin." On more than one occasion, he laments the dearth, if not the death, of exoticism in the modern era. He wrote to his wife, Yvonne: "the truly unexpected in exoticism no longer exists with the improvement of travel and, above all, travel narratives" (cf. Bouillier 93). Besides the disappearance of the unknown and the unexpected, another dire consequence of this penetration into the space of the Other is inevitable intercultural mixing, which in turn brings about the fatal contamination of cultures; for Segalen is convinced that "all civilization ... is deadly to other races" (cf. Bouillier 93).

His conviction of the destructiveness of cultural miscegenation deepens after he witnesses the complete breakdown of the Javanese theater resulting from its contact with Europe. In the eyes of Segalen, the latter-day Javanese theater, now combining European themes and decor, Siamese actors and mixed music, is of no further interest to amateurs of pure exoticism who are always on the lookout for the authentically autochthonous (Bouillier 88). Indeed, so perturbed was Segalen by the ravages of cultural mixing that he wrote an entire book castigating its ill effects. In *Les Immémoriaux*, originally published under the pseudonym of Max Anély, he recounts the tragic saga of Maori culture, the disintegration of which had been fatally precipitated by Western missionaries acting in consort with the colonial military forces. Nothing is immune to the corrosive effect of the European presence; even the millennial Chinese civilization soon finds itself ravaged to the core by foreign antibodies. What remains, Segalen sadly notes, is "a fruit suddenly squeezed dry, wrinkled and aged a thousand years within a few months. What is left is the sticky skin—the bitter and adulterated peel totally consumed by the European mold" ("Orange" 90).

In his critique of the erosive impact one culture has on another, Segalen's concern seems to be exclusively with the bastardization of the non-European Other all the while occulting the question of how a European culture might also be affected by such contact. Until quite recently, the premise of unilateral hybridization was widely held among colonial and post-colonial cultural critics alike. Dirlik draws our attention to this strangely uneven intercultural relation with his remark that "while we have no difficulty thinking of 'Westernized Chinese,' which is the subject of much scholarly attention, we do not often think of the 'Sinified Westerner'" (110). In fact, the eponymous character in *René Leys* is such a Sinified Westerner, yet Segalen does not consider Leys's total immersion in Chinese culture as a threat to his Europeanness.

In addition to inducing the contamination of the exotic space, modern technology and colonialism are, in Segalen's view, also responsible for the proliferation and commodification of exotic writings. The first step in rehabilitating the tarnished reputation of exoticism consists in discarding all the clichés heaped upon it by colonial writers like Bonnetain or Ajalbert and tourist agencies: "Le dépouiller de tous ses oripeaux: le palmier et le chameau; casque de colonial; peaux noires et soleil jaune ... Il ne s'agira donc ni des Bonnetain, ni des Ajalbert, ni des programmes d'agences Cook ..." (*Essai* 22) (To strip away all its tawdry trappings: the palm tree and the camel; the topee; black skins and yellow sun.... It will not be about the Bonnetains or the Ajalberts, nor the Cook's tours). In order to recover the pristine state of the exotic, one has to disengage it from the circuit of commodifying exchange by purging it of those "scories innombrables, des bavures, des taches, des ferments et des moisissures qu'un si long usage—tant de bouches, tant de mains prostitueuses et touristes—lui avaient laissés" (*Essai* 23) (numerous scoriae, smudges, spots, ferments, and molds left behind by such a long usage—through so many mouths, so many whorish and touristy hands).

What Segalen aims at in his cleansing of the exotic is to return this concept to a prelapsarian state uncoded by culture, outside and beyond that which, in Barthes's words, "a toujours été *déjà* lu, vu, fait, vécu" (*S/Z* 28) (has always been *already* read, seen, done, experienced") (20). To this end, one must steer clear of all those "notions trop positives dont [le mot 'exotique'] a été chargé jusqu'ici" (61) (too positive notions [the word 'exotic'] has been ladden with so far) and draw on terms that signify only negatively so as not to risk hypostatizing the exotic redefined in *Essai* as "qui n'est autre que la notion du différent; la perception du Divers; la connaissance que quelque chose n'est pas soi-même" (23) (that which is no other than the notion of the different; the perception of the *Divers*; the knowledge of something that is not oneself). The "Divers" is further characterized as "tout ce qui jusqu'aujourd'hui fut appelé étranger, insolite, inattendu, surprenant, mystérieux, amoureux, surhumain, héroïque et divin même, tout ce qui est *Autre*" (82) (that which until today was called stranger, unusual, unexpected, uncanny, mysterious, amorous, superhuman, heroic and even divine, all that is the *Other*). The series of attributes used here to characterize the "Divers" or "L'Autre" are terms that signify between the Oedipal pleasure described by Barthes in *Plaisir du texte* as one of denuding, of knowing, of learning the origin and the end (10) and its *interdit*, which in French means both the forbidden and the loss of words. The whole narrative challenge in *René Leys* consists, then, in suspending indefinitely the moment of disclosure that traditionally closes all exotic tales.

In the Girardian triangular structure of desire, Quixote has as his mediator Amadis while Emma finds hers among the heroines of romance novels. In the case of the narrator of *René Leys* who happens to have the same name as its author Segalen, his mediator qua initiator is the eponymous character. Yet the parallels between the narrator *Segalen* and his two predecessors stop here. Unlike the latter who, as noted earlier, are uncritical readers qua consumers of chilvary and romance books, the relation of *Segalen* to exotic literature is extremely complex, for throughout the book he incessantly constructs and deconstructs the tale of his "pénétration chinoise" through an intricate staging of a double narrative.

In the double narrative of *René Leys*, the primary narrative, which also functions as a metanarrative,[9] takes the form of a journal kept by *Segalen*. Embedded in the primary narrative is the story of the Inside, in which René Leys nominally features as narrator and *Segalen* as narratee. Peking, the locus of the double narrative, is likewise a city endowed with a double reality. In the primary narrative, the narrator *Segalen*, having recently settled in the Tartar part of the capital, finds his environs both familiar and mundane in which everything is what meets the eye. This space of the "real" or the "factual" is frequented by the likes of Master Wong, one of the narrator's Mandarin teachers, whose plain and direct speech, hiding neither secret nor mystery, deeply disappoints his student: "Toutes ces réponses sont immédiates, claires . . . un peu trop claires: il ne se dérobe pas. Il ne semble rien me cacher. Il parle comme un fonctionnaire" (470) (All his answers were straightforward and clear—almost too clear. He dodged none of my questions. He seemed to be hiding nothing from me. He spoke like a clerk) (39).

In the novel's double reality, this prosaic plane pertains to the "Dehors" (the Outside), the physical and tangible realm which the narrator fancies himself possessing and holding in both his mind and hands while perusing the map[10] of the capital: "Et, sous mes yeux, entre mes deux mains écartées de ce qu'est à peine une envergure d'homme, je vois, je déroule, j'étale, je tiens et je possède, pour un peu d'argent, la figuration plane de cette ville, de la capitale et de ce qu'elle enferme" (507) (And here, before my eyes, between my two hands spread at less than a man's full span, I see, unfurl, spread out, hold, and possess, at small financial cost, the plane representation of the city as a whole, this capital and all it contains) (101). Since the prosaic Peking is also the Peking that had fallen under Western domination during the period of the narrator's stay, the possession he refers to is no mere figure of speech, given that substantial sections of major Chinese cities were ceded as "concessions" or "legations" to Western powers. Within these areas, Europeans enjoyed unbounded privileges which are evoked more than once in the course of the novel. For example, upon hearing that Jarignoux, a fellow French compatriot, had become a Chinese citizen, the narrator's immediate concern is with the possible forfeiture of the prerogatives to which all Europeans in China were entitled:

> Sans doute, une naturalisation pleine et entière à la Chine ne va-t-elle pas sans de graves inconvénients. On voit aussitôt ce que l'on perd: ces prérogatives d'étranger auxquelles il est bon de ne pas toucher. . . . (463–464)

> (I was thinking that, in China, full and complete naturalization was very likely accompanied by serious drawbacks. The first thing that struck me is what one would lose—those prerogatives which the foreigner enjoys here and with which it is best not to interfere . . .) (28–29)

The world of the "Outside," which is accessible and open to all, serving as the diegetic space of the primary narrative, constitutes what Bouillier describes as "la part exotérique" (453) of the Chinese capital. With its well-drawn avenues and neatly arranged alleys, the "exoteric" Peking displays none of the features expected of a capital so long shrouded in mystery and secrets which have haunted the Western imagination. As Jean-Michel Coblence notes: "for centuries, Peking has been an idea, an abstract city which exists less by its walls than by what the latter enclose. An almost mythical site of absolute power, it both fascinates and frustrates the European" (98). Now that this abstraction had become an actuality under Western gunboat policy and Peking had been thrown open to all, disenchantment inevitably set in for the *exotes* for whom an unenigmatic Peking might as well not exist. As long as the imperial capital remained out of bounds to Europeans, it was loaded with meanings and mystery. After the "stone curtain" had been lifted and there was nothing to disclose, no secret to uncover, those once hermetically sealed walls instantly lost their magic and luster, for as Coblence rightly observes: "for a Westerner, nothing has greater power than that which is hidden, so that he can exert all his efforts to dis-cover and un-veil it" (98).

INSIDE STORY, STORY OF THE INSIDE

It is with this determination to make the mute stones speak once more that *Segalen* undertakes his "quexotic" quest. His quest takes him to the esoteric realm of the capital open only to the initiated. The initiator that is sent to him is none other than René Leys himself, a young Belgian, "un barbare non lettré" (a barbarian not of the literati) whom the narrator has chosen, as he himself admits, "contre toute logique" (against all logic) as his teacher of the "Kouan-houa," "le dur Mandarin du Nord" (459) (the hard northern Mandarin), the language that hopefully would provide him with the open-sesame formula. As it turns out, it does not take long for his efforts to bear fruit. A few weeks after the narrator confides to his Belgian teacher his wish to penetrate the "Dedans" (the Inside), he receives his initiation into the other world. He exultingly declares:

> Il m'initie et m'admet 'en profondeur.' Pei-King n'est pas, ainsi qu'on pouvait le croire, un échiquier dont le jeu loyal ou traître se passe à la surface du sol: il existe une Cité souterraine, avec ses redans, ses châteaux d'angles, ses détours, ses aboutissants, ses menaces, ses 'puits horizontaux' plus redoutables que les puits d'eau, potable ou non, qui bâillent en plein ciel ... Le tout, si bien décrit, qu'il parvient enfin à me faire frissonner moi-même ... (546)

> (He let me into the secret—"in depth." Pei-King is not, as one might think, a chessboard whose game, fair or foul, is played on the surface. No—there is an Underground City complete with its redans, its corner forts, its highways and byways, its approaches, its threats, its "horizontal wells" even more formidable than the wells of drinking or other water that yawn up at the open sky. . . . He describes it all so well that by the time he had finished he had got me trembling myself . . .) (171)

The "Dedans" which is associated with the Forbidden City of the Imperial Palace comes to symbolize the narrative site of the Other and the ultimate object of desire. As such, it must remain forever inaccessible. For example, at one point in the primary narrative, *Segalen* is granted official permission to enter the Palace as one of the attendants to the French Minister Plenipotentiary. After an audience with the Regent, he wants to retrace his steps in the Palace and takes out a highly detailed and accurate European plan of the Forbidden City. To his dismay, the narrator cannot find his route on the map: "Mais, pratiquement, je ne sais m'y reconnaître. Où est la route là dedans suivie? ... Où le Régent nous a-t-il reçus?" (508) (But in practice—no idea how to begin to find my way about. Where is the path we followed today? Where did the Regent receive us?) (103) The narrator who thought he had entered the Palace had, in fact, never been "Inside." The map, a traditional symbol and tool of possession and mastery of the other in colonial history, becomes totally irrelevant in the esoteric world of the "Dedans" where it no longer has any hold.

Not only is *Segalen* barred from direct access to the "Dedans," but it is moreover impossible for him to know or say anything about it. A close reading of the "Inside" story reveals that the main trope used to re-present this elusive esoteric reality is, rather appropriately, the "apophase," or "poetic formulation of negative theology" (Bouillier 303) which attempts to apprehend a reality beyond grasp via negative definitions. This apophatic technique is, in fact, widely used by Segalen to convey the presence-as-absence of the Other, its being as non-being.[11]

In *René Leys*, the world of "Dedans" is often evoked in images of void and absence. For example, when reflecting upon his audience with the Regent, the narrator recalls to himself the room of their meeting which he tried in vain to relocate on his map:

> Comment, sur un plan, retrouver mes traces? Et surtout, comment repérer *ceci* où l'on s'arrête, où l'on pénètre ... '*Ceci*' est une sorte d'*antre* civilisé, mystérieux, *caverneux et absorbant comme la bouche* à peine entrouverte du Dragon intelligent: un Palais chinois, surbaissé ... et qui serait *vide, vide,* à s'en inquiéter, si les murs, laqués de rouge, les colonnes de bois laquées de rouge, et surtout le plafond lourd et riche ... ne meublait (sic) *ce vide* et *cette absence* à l'égal d'un trésor royal attendant le souverain ... (505; emphases added)

> (How should I ever retrace my route on a map—how, above all, identify *this place* we were now entering ... ? It was a kind of *cave*, civilized yet mysterious, drawing one in like the barely open *jaws* of the Imperial Dragon—a low-slung Chinese palace.... And it would have been *empty*, disconcertingly *empty*, had not the red-lacquered walls and wooden columns and above all the massive ... ceiling furnished that *emptiness* and that *absence* with the richness of a royal treasure awaiting its sovereign lord ...) (99; emphases added)

Besides words evoking holes or hollowness such as "cave," "jaws," "empty," or "absence," another way the unnameable is suggested is through the book's use of pronouns the effect of which has not been fully conveyed in the English text, which translates the pronoun "ceci" by the noun "this place." What the translation fails to express is the narrator's *inability* to name evidenced by his use of the indefinite demonstrative pronoun "ceci." Indeed, throughout the novel, whenever it is a question of the esoteric realm, *Segalen* and René Leys, without any previous explicit agreement, tacitly refer to the inhabitants and places of the Inside with pronouns. For example, during his first visit to the Leys family, the narrator, not yet aware of René Leys's intimate relation with the "Dedans," is surprised to find two vases by the door which he believes to have come from the Inside. Noting his student's astonishment, René Leys confirms his suspicions concerning their origin by simply saying, "Oui, ils *en* viennent" (469) (Yes, they come from *there*) (36). Likewise, the Emperor is constantly referred to as "Lui" or "Le" (Him) since His name, according to the narrator, is not to be named:

> Au milieu, dans le profond du milieu du palais, un visage: un enfant-homme, et Empereur, maître du sol et Fils du Ciel (que tout le monde et les journalistes s'entêtent à nommer "Kouang-Siu," qui est la marque du temps où il régna, -c'est-à-dire, après J.-C., de 1875–1908). Il vécut vraiment, sous son nom de vivant mais indicible . . . *Lui*—et ne pouvant dire le *nom*, je donne au *pronom* européen tout l'accent incliné du geste mandchou. (457–458)
>
> (Indeed, deep in the innermost center of the Palace, a face: a child-man, and Emperor, Lord of the Sun and Son of Heaven (whom everyone, including journalists, insists on referring to as "Kuang Hsu," which actually designates the period of his reign, that is to say A.D. 1875–1908). His real name, his name during his lifetime was the unutterable. . . . *Himself*—and it not being permitted me to give the *name*, I give the European *pronoun* all the reverential emphasis of the Manchu gesture.) (18)

This "indicibilité" (the unsayable) constitutes, in fact, the essence of the "Dedans" since, as the site of the Other, the "Inside" has to be unqualifiable and unknowable in order to maintain its difference. Otherwise, once named, it would be reduced to the known, which is to say, the same. Moreover, the "Dedans," as the locus of desire, is also "indicible" in the two related senses of "inter-dicted," namely the unsayable and the forbidden. In *René Leys*, one of Segalen's most noticeable stylistic devices is precisely ellipsis. As pointed out by Christine Andreucci, in the novel "one assists truly at a mise-en-scène of an esoteric langage in which what is left unsaid is the essential and the words of which refer to an unknown code and an absent reality" (161). The means to convey this "non-dit" is the systematic use of "an elliptical writing in which the essential is unspoken" (Andreucci 163). What we find throughout the book are many unfinished sentences, half-hatched thoughts, self-addressed questions without answers, fragmented syntax with blanks and ellipses. For example, at the beginning of the novel, the narrator decides that the best method to find his way into the "Dedans" is to master the language of the Inside, "le dur Mandarin du Nord," instead of relying on mediators; yet, as to what he hopes to uncover in the process, he typically leaves the question unanswered:

> C'est tout. Abandonner la partie? Je m'accorde une chance dernière de pénétrer dans le "Dedans." C'est de me servir de son langage, le dur "Mandarin du Nord"; de me passer désormais de tout entremetteur, de tout eunuque, et d'attendre l'occasion directe qui me permette ... de dire, ou de faire ... quoi? je n'en sais rien. (459; ellipses in the text)
>
> (That has been all. Should I throw in my hand? I am giving myself one last chance to penetrate the Within—using the medium of its language, the difficult "Northern Mandarin." From now on I shall employ no intermediaries, no eunuchs; I shall wait for the opportunity that shall enable me first-hand to ... say, or do ... what? I have no idea.) (20; ellipses in the text)

The irony here is that instead of doing away with intermediaries, resorting to Northern Mandarin leads him only to language, the mediator par excellence whose function is to provide endless substitutes for our lost object of desire. According to Jacques Lacan, once past the mirror stage during which the child imagines him/herself to be one with the mother's body from which s/he has in fact been banished, the subject is thrown into the metonymic world of language in which s/he is pushed from signifier to signifier in an impossible quest for presence. In *René Leys*, the lost object which the narrator desperately attempts to recover by uncovering the secret (of the) Inside can be broached only in an aphasic fashion. Thus, every time he attempts to speak (of) his desire, his sentences invariably end in ellipses, leaving blanks to be filled in by the reader's own imagination: "Je lui communique ce que Je sais: le mystère ... toutes les suppositions ... celles que j'ai faites—en portant aux limites logiques le merveilleux éclos et contenu là, près de nous, au coeur de la Ville Violette ..." (468; ellipses in the text) (I told him all I know—the mystery of it ... all the conjectures ... those I have made myself, stretching to the limits of logic the marvels contained within those nearby walls, at the heart of the Purple City ...) (35; ellipses in the text).

The strategy of leaving gaping holes in the narrative, signifiers of the female body par excellence, testifies to the fetishistic nature of the narrator's quest. For, as Bongie, following Freud, reminds us, the original scene structuring fetishism is instigated by the (male) child's discovery of the absence of the mother's penis, an absence which generates an endless search for surrogate objects. It is perhaps revealing that the "Dedans," the object of the narrator's quest, is at one point described as "le centre ombilical de la Chine" (574) (the umbilical center of China), that is, the most fantasized, if forbidden, site of male imagination. It is likewise not surprising that the narrator constantly associates the Inside with "la Cité Violette Interdite" (the Forbidden Purple City), or we might say "viol-ette" since "viol" in French signifies "rape" and connotes the idea of "violence" or "violation": one can violate only that which is interdicted.

Though totally consumed with the "Dedans," the narrator nevertheless dares not venture in by himself. For not only is the Inside forbidden to him, it is also a most forbidding site where the specter of castration looms large, to which the presence of the eunuchs there attests. Enthroned/entombed deep within the "Dedans" is none other than the Father-Emperor, supreme Castrator, "le seul, le seul mâle, l'épuisé de plaisirs officiels, le maître d'eunuques et de femmes" (514) (the lone, sole male, spent with official pleasures, lord over eunuchs and women) (112), more powerful dead than living, more feared absent than present, ruling by his "étonnant pouvoir de l'absence" (astonishing power of absence) ("Eloges et pouvoir de l'absence," *Stèles* 113).

The threat of castration from the "Dedans" takes on many forms. For example, besides the numerous triple walls and triple gates erected to protect it from all intruders, the Inside is also heavily equipped with various self-defense devices such as treacherous hidden holes or wells which, ogress-like, suck down unsuspecting passers-by through their lipless and rimless mouths. Indeed, everything connected with the "Dedans" can suddenly take on a most menacing mien. A case in point is the famous receipt purportively proving René Leys's "first night of love in the Palace" but transformed in the course of the narrative from a simple piece of paper into something quite terrifying. The original Chinese characters which the narrator had failed to decipher earlier appear to him now either as sharp excising instruments such as knives, spears, or teeth, or as deep gaping holes ready to suck in and devour their prey:

> Et cet énigmatique reçu 'de la première nuit d'amour au palais'—qu'il croyait perdu . . . sans que je l'eusse détrompé. J'ai déjà tenté de le déchiffrer. Mais suis-je mauvais élève, ou le devoir trop dur? Ces caractères représentent des objets redoutables: des couteaux, une lance à croc, des yeux en long ou dressés en hauteur, des fleurs, des dents de rat, des femmes se cachant le ventre, des puits, des creux, des tombes, des trous lutés d'un couvercle . . . un fourneau magique . . . une bouche vide . . . un bateau. De tout cela, qu'est-ce qui exprime ce thème . . . 'Première nuit d'amour au Palais'? (570; ellipses in the text)

> (And this enigmatic receipt for his "first night of love in the Palace"—which he thought was lost . . . nor did I undeceive him. I have already attempted to decipher it. Am I a bad pupil, or is the homework too hard? The characters represent a series of the most alarming objects: knives, a barded spear, eyes placed lengthwise or vertically, flowers, rat's teeth, women hiding their bellies, wells, pits,

tombs, the stopped-up holes of some lid . . . a magic crucible . . . an empty mouth . . . a boat . . . Where in all this is the legend "First night of love in the Palace"?) (216; ellipses in the text)

This message from the "Dedans" scribbled on the receipt may not be as undecipherable as the narrator thinks after all. Wittingly or unwittingly, he may have already decoded its content in his description of those enigmatic drawings. That is to say, the mysterious pictograms may mean just what they appear to be, namely, that the price for "a night of love in the Palace" is castration. The narrative is, therefore, skillfully staged so as to evade the costly payment of the narrator's daring attempt at "la pénétration chinoise." His tactic consists of creating a "suppléant" or surrogate through whom he can vicariously live out his wildest fantasies without endangering himself. The person he sets eyes on for this task is the young Belgian, René Leys.

Starting with his highly symbolic name, "that prince of signifiers,"[12] "René" is homonymic in French with the words "re-né," or "reborn," while the Belgian family name "Leys" phonetically sounds like a Chinese surname. The very name "René Leys" suggests that the character serves as the narrator's Chinese alter ego. Born of a French mother and a Belgian father, René Leys is shown to be totally sinified. Besides acquiring a superb mastery of Mandarin which he speaks with native fluency, he demonstrates an equally impressive understanding of Chinese culture as evidenced by his exquisite appreciation of the Peking opera, which contrasts sharply with his near total ignorance of European culture. Furthermore, he appears to be thoroughly at home with his numerous Manchu and Chinese friends who treat him as one of their own. It is even suggested that the young Belgian can physically pass for a Manchu or Chinese, and, on one occasion, the narrator believes that he recognizes his language teacher in the person of a Manchu officer among the Regent's escort. At the end of the book, when examining his young friend's body, the narrator's description also draws our attention to his *métis* look[13]: "Juste assez brun pour n'être pas traîté de 'blanc' par les Jaunes . . . Et un dépoli de peau déjà froide très semblable au toucher délicat de l'épiderme chinois . . ." (569) (Just brown enough not to be dubbed "white" by the yellow Chinese. . . . And a dullness to that already-cold skin that was very like the delicate touch of the Chinese epidermis . . .) (215). Indeed, so deeply immersed is he in the Chinese way that the narrator, when taking the final tally of his friend's life, has to conclude that the latter has lived and died "à la chinoise": "Tout ce que j'ai dit, il l'a fait, à la chinoise, puisqu'il vient, à la chinoise, de m'en donner, par sa mort, la meilleure preuve—qu'il préférait perdre la vie et sauver la face . . . et ne pas se trahir ni me trahir, et ne pas démériter. . . . Tout ceci est donc vrai 'à la chinoise'?" (572;

ellipses in the text) (Everything I said, he did, Chinese fashion, for with his death he has just given me, Chinese fashion, the best proof—that he preferred to lose his life if it meant saving face ... if it was the only way of not being false either to himself or to me, of neither breaking faith nor forfeiting my esteem.... Is it all true, then—'Chinese fashion'?) (219; ellipses in the text).

Beyond this cultural *métissage*, René Leys also displays a highly ambivalent sexuality. His young Belgian friend, the narrator repeatedly claims, is endowed with great physical beauty and charms. But his seductive appeal has a powerful effect not only on members of the opposite sex, for throughout the narrative, it has been suggested that Leys's relationship with the late Emperor Kouang-Siu exceeds what the narrator perceives as the "accepted" bounds of male friendship.[14] The rather circuitous way in which the latter dissects this "amitié" leaves little doubt as to the passionate nature of the ties between the two young men:

> En effet, quand un être comme René Leys en dépeint un autre sous les couleurs et dans les contours animiques du Portrait que je viens d'écrire sous ces mots,—ces êtres ne peuvent que se détester ou s'aimer, jusqu'à la détresse ou la passion. René Leys aimait donc d'une jeune amitié cet Empereur jeune et dolent, cet abandonné ... (480)

> (And indeed, whenever a person like René Leys depicts another person in the colorful, true-to-life terms of the portrait that emerged from his words, it can only be out of the direst hatred or the deepest love. So René Leys loved with the love of youth that young and doleful Emperor, that castaway ...) (55)

His Janus-like personality enables Leys to lead a double existence which greatly intrigues *Segalen*. On the one hand, the Belgian appears quite unassuming so that even the narrator is taken in by his unsophisticated demeanor at the beginning of their acquaintanceship. Yet, unbeknownst to most, this unpretentious Leys whom the narrator at times contemptuously refers to as the "petit Belge" (461) pursues a fantastic double life in the mysterious Other world of Peking. Not only does he enjoy direct access to the "Dedans," but he is also reputedly an "intime" of first the late Emperor, and then the Regent. These contacts prove to be of no small asset to his career, since, while still in his teens, this fledging youth is promoted from being head of the "Dedans" secret police to the enviable rank of "Grand Treasurer and Paymaster of all the Princes of the Inside." To crown it all, the young Leys is granted the wearing of the much sought after "Ma-koua" or "Horse Jacket," a high honor only occasionally bestowed on a few Princes of the Blood (533).

A favorite of the Inside, Leys, the narrator's own surrogate, also comes to play the Emperor's double through a long chain of double and triple supplements. In the course of the narrative, like the Emperor or his official "Tenant-Lieu," the Regent, Leys has been surreptitiously given the use of the royal third person pronoun "Lui." In fact, there seems to be in the narrative a deliberate confusion between the Emperor/Regent and Leys through a play of pronouns as shown in a particular entry of the narrator's journal: "Après tout, j'ai promis de *l'*aider. Je joue dans son jeu. Je prends parti: le parti de nos Mandchous aux Belles Cités Interdites . . .—Que ce soir d'hiver approchant est tout d'un coup froid et désolé! Cependant c'est pour *Lui* et notre parti que je sors, vers Ts'ien-men-waï" (549; emphases added) (After all, I thought, as I went out this evening, I have promised to help *him*. I am involved in his game. I have taken sides—the side of our Manchus with their Fine Forbidden Cities. . . . Winter was in the air, and how cold and desolate everything felt all of a sudden! Yet for *Himself*'s sake and for our side I sallied forth for Chien Men Wai) (179; emphases added). While the first third person pronoun "le" evidently stands for Leys, the identity of the second capitalized "Lui" is left unclear since in this context it can refer to either or both Leys and/or the Emperor.[15]

Having enlisted such a valuable ally for his cause, the narrator can henceforth rest assured of the success of his "pénétration chinoise." In fact, it does not take long before he reaps rewards that far exceed his wildest expectations. Thanks to Leys, *Segalen* succeeds in unravelling all the "secrets d'alcôve" he so desperately wanted to decipher. Indeed, he can now safely attend the staging of the primal scene "en voyeur." Exultantly, he relishes *en connaisseur* all the little salacious details wheedled from his young unsuspecting companion who in his naiveté reconstructs for him his "night of love in the Palace" with the Empress:

> Mais René-Triomphant n'en est plus à me marchander des détails intérieurs. En peu de mots, je deviens *spectateur* de chacun des actes prévus. Je sais comment l'on s'étend sur le lit tiède ... Grâce à lui, *je pénètre véritablement le milieu le plus intime du Palais*. ... C'est ainsi que j'apprends sans détours 'qu'elle est moins grasse que ne la représentent ses portraits'—et que, même déshabillée, elle garde toujours ce 'petit triangle de soie qui pend entre les seins et le ventre, et forme une ceinture un peu haute, à la mode mandchoue.' ... Le reste, tout le reste, m'est livré en peu de mots. (537; emphases added)

(But René the Triumphant clearly did not begrudge me the domestic details. A few words made me an *eyewitness*, as it were, of each of the prescribed acts. I discovered how they lie down on the warm bed. ...Thanks to him I have really *penetrated to the most pri-*

vate center of the Palace.... He told me, for example, with perfect candor that "she is not as fat as her portraits make her look" and that even in a state of undress she retains that "little triangle of silk that hangs down between her breasts and her stomach, forming a kind of high belt in the Manchu fashion" ... And the rest, all the rest, was mine in a few words.) (155; emphases added)

With Leys, lover to both the Emperor and Empress, now working for him as his "supplement," the narrator can live by proxy the dangerous yet forever tempting scene of the Inside. In the deadly game of desire, the need for a supplement (in both senses of addition and substitute) is essential. In *Of Grammatology*, Derrida explains the double function of the supplement in connection with Rousseau:

> The supplement has not only the power of procuring an absent presence through its image, procuring it for us through the proxy (procuration) of the sign, it holds it at a distance and masters it. For the presence is at the same time desired and feared. The supplement transgresses and at the same time respects the interdict. (155)

In the staging of the bedroom scene, Leys has flagrantly transgressed the ultimate interdict in his seduction of "la personne triple et quadruplement enceinte! L'inexpugnable! la Mère de l'Empire, l'Aïeule des Dix Mille Ages!" (530) (the Triple Person quadruply enclosed, the Inexpugnable! Mother of the Empire, Ancestress of the Ten Thousand Ages!) (141), a viol-ation which inexorably calls for severe chastisement that would in turn re-establish the interdict. Leys, the surrogate, must also serve as scapegoat for the transgressive act. The narrator, though no less guilty of the viol(ence) committed, has nevertheless skillfully devised his alibi by means of multiple narrative frames.

Through this framing technique, which creates a series of intricately linked specular narratives, *Segalen* can engineer his "pénétration chinoise" while retaining his "ex(h)ote"[16] status which keeps him at a safe distance from the Inside story. In her analysis of *René Leys*, Elaine Real unravels for us the multiple layering of this elaborate specular narrative strategy:

> The secret of René Leys is nothing other than the reflection of the narrator's desire. The young man is the mirror that reflects Segalen's dreams.... The world René Leys's stories propose is the one which Segalen himself projected or desired in a previous narrative the novel has purposely erased. (144)

There are numerous examples of narrative erasures throughout the book, one significant instance occurring at the beginning of the novel when the narrator imparts to Leys the story of the Inside. In this exchange, the essential of what has been said is under erasure:

> J'ai cependant besoin de me confier. L'heure est trop lourde: et il est là. Après tout, ce garçon m'a très à propos livré le nom de la "Montagne" d'où l'on contemple.... Je me rapproche de lui. Je désigne d'un coup d'oeil le Palais, les fossés, l'eau dormante, la nuit, l'heure enfin.... Et je dis:
>
> ... Il a tout écouté sans m'interrompre; même quand il s'est agi de certains détails peu connus du noble et doux prisonnier d'Empire le Régnant de la Période Kouang-Siu. Je lui communique ce que Je sais: le mystère ... toutes les suppositions ... celles que j'ai faites. (468; ellipses and blank in the text)
>
> (Yet I felt a need to confide in someone. The hour lay heavy upon me, and he was there. After all, the young man had very pertinently given me the name of the hill from whose summit one may contemplate ... I rode up to him. Indicating with a glance the Palace, the moat, the stagnant water, the evening, the magic of the hour ... I told him all.
>
> ... He heard me through without interruption, even where I touched on certain little-known details regarding the life of that noble, gentle prisoner of Empire, the reigning sovereign of the Kuang Hsu period. I told him all I know—the mystery of it ... all the conjectures ... those I have made myself ...) (35; ellipses and blank in the text)

What has been suppressed in the blank space and ellipses is obviously the interdict which needs Leys's mediatory yet transgressive tale to be heard again. The narrator, assuming the position of the narratee, repeats the discourse of his own desire via his narcissistic Other.

As mediator, Leys comes to embody the signifier of desire in more than one way. Cast successively in a multiplicity of roles as double, Leys is transformed in the course of the narrative into a ghost character, one that is devoid of a specific identity. In the absence of any substance, he becomes a pure sign that functions both as an empty signifier (since by being everyone, he is no one) and as a signifier of the empty, represented in the text by the non-person pronoun "Lui."[17] Because of his relation to absence and lack, it is then most appropriate that Leys be designated as the bearer of the discourse of desire, which is itself an endless process of difference and absence. Thus, if desire has to speak through Leys, the latter is in turn the consummate master of the language of desire, the "Kouan-hua."

Given his character of lack as well as his lack of character, Leys is eminently Bovaryst for, according to Gaultier, what defines the Bovaryst personae is precisely the essential lack of a fixed character: "being nothing by themselves, they become something, one thing or another, through the suggestion which they obey" (cf. in Girard 63). There are in fact a number of similarities between Leys and Emma as shown in this initial portrait that the narrator makes of him:

> C'est le bon fils d'un excellent épicier du quartier des Légations. Je ne l'ai point connu près des balances paternelles. Mais il parle avec un tel respect de son père, du commerce, de la famille, des 'économies', des domestiques, des voitures, des chevaux et des principes de son père,—qu'il est manifeste qu'il croit impossible de mener à Pei-King une autre vie honorable que celle de son père ...—Littérairement, il relit Paul Féval. (459–460)

> (He is the dutiful son of an excellent grocer of the Legation Quarter. I failed to recognize him beside the paternal scales. Yet he speaks with such respect of his father, business, the family, "savings," servants, carriages, horses, and his father's principles that he clearly believes it impossible to lead, in Pei-king, a more honorable life than his father leads. . . . As regards literature, he is rereading Paul Féval) (21)

Not only do both of them belong to the petite bourgeoisie, but more importantly, they are both avid consumers of mass literature, romances in Emma's case and melodramatic adventure stories in Leys's.[18] Like the Flaubertian heroine and Quixote who identify themselves uncritically with the characters of the fiction they consume, Leys imitates the stories he reads and hears. To stage his "Quexotic quest," the narrator can find no more ideal actor than the Bovaryst Leys.

"SOUS LES TERMES REDOUTABLES DE 'LITTÉRATURES EXOTIQUES' . . ."

The story of the Inside that Leys acted out for the narrator's benefit turns out to be nothing more than one of those hackneyed plots of *les liaisons dangereuses* between European males and native females taken from the body of works known, in Segalen's words, "sous les termes redoutables de 'littératures exotiques'" (*Essai* 83) (under the dreadful name of 'exotic literature'). One paradigmatic example of the genre is, of course, *Aziyadé* by Loti, an exotic author Segalen refers to in rather unflattering terms: "pseudo-Exotes (les Loti, les touristes, ne furent pas moins désastreux. Je les nomme les Proxénètes de la Sensation du Divers)" (*Essai* 34) (pseudo-Exotes [the Lotis, the tourists, were no less disastrous. I call them Procurers of the Sensation of the *Divers*]). At the level of the plot, *René Leys* and *Aziyadé* share certain similarities, both taking the form of a journal that transcribes a story of penetration and illicit love affair ending with the death of the transgressive amorous hero. In the two stories, the penetration is carried out through the intercession of a mediator, Leys for *Segalen* and Samuel/Achmet for Loti.

Despite a lengthy list of parallels between the two books, there is, nevertheless, one crucial difference that distinguishes them. The narrative in *René Leys* is a much more self-reflexive text in comparison to *Aziyadé*. Thus, the exotic plot qua Inside story at the hypodiegetic level is repeatedly challenged in the primary narrative as the narrator frequently undermines Leys's story through parody and irony. A case in point is the narrator retelling his Belgian friend's encounter with the Regent who came to thank the "head of the Secret Police" for saving his life in an assassination attempt. The narrator's reaction to Leys's account of the meeting is highly contradictory as he appears to both believe and discredit what he is told :

> —Quand il m'a vu, en dehors de l'heure habituelle, il s'est douté.... Il a compris que j'étais intervenu, et m'a serré la main.
> —Comment, le Régent vous remerciait comme aurait fait Sadi-Carnot! Il sait donc donner une poignée de main?
> —Je veux dire qu'il m'a serré le pouce, rectifie René Leys ...
> C'est bien ça. Je sais ce qu'il me plairait de savoir. Je tiens la main du Régent dans la mienne, ou plutôt hors de la mienne. J'ai la face du Régent devant moi. Cet homme, gonflé d'importance imposée, officielle ... je n'ai rien à savoir de plus. J'ai vécu vraiment, un instant, de la vie la plus intime du Palais.
> Ce René Leys! Quel merveilleux metteur en scène! Mieux: quel homme de théâtre! Quel *acteur*! (516)

> ("When he saw me turn up at what was not my usual time he guessed what it was ... He realised that I had intervened and he shook me by the hand."
> "What—the Regent thanked you just as Sadi Carnot would have done! Do you mean he knows how to shake hands?"
> "By the thumb, I mean," René Leys corrected....
> Yes indeed, I thought. For I knew now what I had so much wanted to know, I had the Regent's hand in mine, or rather not in mine. I had the Regent's face before me ... swollen with official, borrowed importance ... I said to myself, What more need I know? I have truly, for the space of a moment, lived the most intimate life of the Palace.
> And I marveled at René Leys. What a producer—no, what an *actor*!) (117)

This passage typifies the wavering attitude of the narrator who both identifies with and distances himself from Leys's account. On the one hand, he appears not only to believe that Leys actually met with the Regent, but seems to *become* his Belgian friend so as to feel that he has "truly, for the space of a moment, lived the most intimate life of the Palace." On the other hand, the narrator also discredits Leys's account by pointing out mockingly the discrepancy between the Manchu handshake and its Western counterpart. Reference to Leys as a play producer and actor further undermines his friend's credibility suggesting that his story is pure fiction.

As the plot of the Inside thickens, the narrator's attempts at subversion intensify until at last he comes to openly doubt the veracity of Leys's stories while trying to clarify his relationship to his friend:

> Voilà moins d'une année que je connais ce garçon. Il m'a raconté toute son histoire, et ses histoires. Je n'en ai rien dit à personne. Je dégustais le développement et la saveur sans un doute sur la réalité.
>
> Or, aujourd'hui,—est-ce d'aujourd'hui seulement?—je doute de quelque chose ... c'est-à-dire, d'un seul coup,—de tout. (560)

> (I have known this lad for less than a year. He has told me all about himself, all these stories. I have not said a word to a soul about any of it. I have savored the development, the "feel" of it all without the slightest doubt to its reality.
>
> But today—only today? I come to doubt something ... that is to say, at one swoop I doubt it all.) (199)

But it is toward the very end of the narrative, at a moment that tellingly coincides with the final downfall of the Imperial Dynasty, that the finely engineered world of the Inside collapses. At one stroke, the narrator lays bare the mise-en-scène of this elaborate tale. Far from being a mere spectator/narratee of the Inside scene, he reveals himself to be its puppeteer, directing the production from behind the scenes. His revelation reverses all the roles laid out at the start, as Leys, rather than being the narrator of the hypodiegetic story, is now revealed to be its narratee, echoing back to *Segalen* the Inside story, whereas the latter, instead of being a mere narratee, turns out to be the Inside tale teller who had recruited his young friend to act out the Inside scenario.

> René Leys ne s'est pas tué. *On* ne l'a pas empoisonné ... Le poison: c'est *moi* qui le lui ai proposé ... c'est de moi qu'il l'a reçu, accepté et bu ... et cela, depuis notre première entrevue ...
>
> René Leys, fils économe d'épicier belge, ne songeait guère aux Chinois, encore moins au palais, quand, pour la première fois, je l'ai pris pour confident du mystère du Palais ... Il est vrai que sa

> réponse dépassait déjà mon attente. C'est moi le premier, qui, sur la foi de Maître Wang, l'entretins de l'existence d'une Police Secrète: huit jours après, il en faisait partie, et m'enrôlait au bout de deux mois. Les attentats à la vie du Régent ne m'appartiennent pas: on les lisait dans tous les journaux, je m'accuse de cette question répétée—Dites-moi, Leys: une Mandchoue peut-elle être aimée d'un Européen ... et ...—Et quinze jours après, il était aimé d'une Mandchoue. (571)

> (René Leys did not kill himself. *They* did not poison him. ... The poison: it was *I* that offered it to him. ... It was from me that he received it, accepted it, drank it ... and that from the very moment of our first meeting ...
>
> René Leys, the thrifty son of a Belgian grocer, hardly had a thought for the Chinese, and even less for the Palace, when for the first time I made him my confidant regarding the mysteries of the Forbidden City ... though it is true that his response exceeded my expectations right from the start. It was I who, on the strength of Master Wang, first spoke to him of the existence of a Secret Police. A few days he was a member of it, and a few months later he enlisted me. For the attempts on the Regent's life I decline responsibility—they were in all the papers for anyone to read—but I do charge myself with repeatedly asking this question: "Tell me, Leys—is it possible for a Manchu woman to be loved by a European, and ... ?" And three weeks later he was loved by a Manchu woman ...) (218–219)

This unseating of narrative roles also brings about the blurring of the categories of Inside and Outside, Self and Other that had hitherto structured the textual space. *Segalen,* who presented himself as an outsider seeking to uncover the secret (of the) Inside, turns out to have introduced Leys to the Inside while the latter, initially cast as the Insider qua initiator of the narrator, is revealed to be the outsider who had neither interest in nor knowledge of the Inside before meeting his student.

The novel ends with the narrator's refraining from "répondre moi-même à mon doute, et de prononcer enfin: *oui* ou *non*?" (572) (answer[ing] my doubt myself and finally pronounc[ing]: *yes* or *no*?) (220). By thus refusing to comment on the narrative's veracity, the narrator indefinitely suspends the moment of closure, which in turn enables him to maintain his impossible quest (a quest of the impossible) for the un-coverable Other. This ending that resists closure bespeaks the multiple paradoxes surrounding the exotic quest in the age of colonial conquest. In his crusade to salvage and restore the colonized and commodified Other, Segalen took the Western hegemonic order to task for having cannibalized alternative cultures; yet it was with the help of European military might that the doors of the Forbidden City had been forced open, so that real or pseudo *exotes* like himself or Loti[19] could undertake their "pénétration chinoise." A parallel paradox also informs Segalen's relation to colonial exotic literature since it is by the mediation of the exotic romance, a degraded genre so forcefully denounced in *Essai*, that the story of the Other can be retold as the Other story in *René Leys*. Riddled with contradictions and ambiguities, Segalen's quexotic quest can be said to inhabit a truly para-doxical discursive space that is at once parasitic and oppositional to the colonial doxa.

CHAPTER THREE

THE OTHER IN MALRAUX'S HUMANISM

In *La Jeunesse littéraire d'André Malraux*, André Vandegans contends that the young Malraux, avid reader of Orientalist authors such as Segalen, shares the latter's pursuit of "the knowledge of the self through difference by approaching the other" (344). While it is true that both writers have a lifelong involvement with the Orient, their engagements with the cultural Other diverge in salient ways due to differences in ideological perspective as well as their respective socio-historical circumstances. In the previous chapter, we noted that a major source of contradiction underlying Segalen's life and work lies in the insurmountable tension between his exoticist project and the *fin-de-siècle* colonial conquest. The period of conquest gave way to the interwar celebration of "the apotheosis of Greater France" and the inauguration of the era of colonial economic exploitation and development. Under the new politics of *mise-en-valeur*, the empire, once a remote and unknown entity, now appeared as a vast reservoir of material and human resources[1] whose potential gradually entered into the consciousness of the average French citizen. In addition to the concerted effort of the government to "educate" the public about the colonial mission,[2] mass media such as the press, the radio, and the cinema also came to play a vital role in bringing the colonial reality home.[3] The impact of these socio-political changes eventually made itself felt in the domain of literature as more and more writers turned to the empire for inspiration, some to promote the colonial cause, others to criticize it.[4] Indeed, colonial novels became so prominent that not only did a number of them receive metropolitan literary prizes, but a prize for colonial literature was also instituted in the 1920s by Albert Sarraut, the minister of the colonies and two-time governor general of Indochina (1911–1914, 1917–1919).

It was during this "golden age"[5] of the French colonial empire that Malraux made his first two trips to French Indochina which subsequently served as material for his five Asian novels, one of which, *Le Règne du malin*, remained unfinished and was published posthumously.[6] Yet, a few exceptions aside,[7] most of the studies on Malraux's fictional texts tend to elide the question of the relation of his literary work to colonial ideology. A perusal of the voluminous critical literature devoted to his novels shows that the focus of discussions is inevitably the author's metaphysical concerns. Accordingly, the problem of "humanism," be it tragic or triumphant, is said to constitute the central theme of Malraux's fiction.[8] Next to the "humanist" approach, there exists a significant body of political and Marxist analyses of Malraux's fiction.[9] In these critical works, the Asian reference is often read either in terms of Malraux's confrontation with the European postwar spiritual crisis[10] or as part of his lifelong interest in Eastern civilization.[11] Without disputing the relevance of these views (to which I will return later), I nevertheless argue that given the importance of Malraux's involvement with history, it is necessary to re-inscribe his Eastern texts within the colonial context that mediates his relation to the cultural Other. By re-articulating the Orientalist frame of his Asian novels, my reading brings out the multiple contradictions surrounding Malraux's Oriental engagement.

"POURQUOI DIABLE LA CHINE VOUS INTÉRESSE-T-ELLE?"

Malraux frequently recalls the question that Valéry asked him upon their first encounter: "why the devil are you interested in China?" (*Antimémoires* 456) but he never indicates what his answer was at the time.[12] In *Malraux*, Roger Stéphane reports that in 1967 he asked Malraux the same question about Indochina and was given two reasons: "I was attracted by Asia because, among other things, history was in the making there" and "I think that at the time, for me, China and Indochina represented the other pole of the mind" (cf. Stéphane 28, 29–30). While there is no way (and no point) of ascertaining the veracity of these answers more than forty years after his foray to the Orient,[13] the two explanations are, nevertheless, of great interest in that they succinctly summarize the two visions Malraux simultaneously held of Asia: the atemporal Asia and the historical Asia.

The East in *La Tentation de l'Occident* is, indeed, presented in every way as "the other pole" of the West. Using material derived mainly from an "exotisme livresque,"[14] Malraux constructs a highly Orientalized China for his readers. For example, in the first letter of the French correspondent A.D. to his Chinese counterpart Ling, we find a depiction of the East based on a curious mixing of different Orientalist codes. On the one hand, the text abounds in Orientalist images usually associated with the world of the *Arabian Nights*: "the harem," "caravans," "princesses," "camels," "evil magicians," "fantastic parrots." On the other hand, alongside these references which would appear exotic even to a Chinese reader, A.D. also includes in his description elements more in line with the Chinese Orientalist tradition such as "concubines," "palace," "Forbidden City," "the all-powerful Emperor" or "the China of dream and opium." What these conventional images often conjure up in the minds of Western readers is a magical fantasy land à la Marco Polo, a world frozen in immutability and immobility.[15]

Besides producing an Orientalized China that would meet the expectations of the Western public of the time, the choice of such stereotyped images of China also fulfills another specific function for, as Denis Boak remarks in his discussion of *La Tentation de l'Occident*, "Malraux's principal concern is not so much his analysis of the East, which is mainly conventional and therefore less interesting, as his attempt at dissection of the Western mentality" (23). In fact, the "Eastern turn" is a standard move in what Spivak calls the "crisis management" of the West. During the postwar years, Malraux was but one among many French intellectuals who, deeply troubled by the acute spiritual malaise of Europe, looked towards Asia for solace and inspiration, for it was believed that Asian culture, being in every way "opposite" to their own, would shed new light on the European predicament.[16] Such is the position enunciated by Malraux in his 1926 essay "André Malraux et l'Orient" in which he asserts that "the view we have of Europe when we live in Asia affects particularly men of my generation because it gives us an extreme intensity to our problems . . ." (53–54). Yet at the same time in both *La Tentation de l'Occident* and the essay, Malraux made it clear that the East could provide no real alternative to the West.

In their analysis of the European crisis which constitutes the principal theme of *La Tentation de l'Occident*, A.D. and Ling undertake a comparative study of their respective cultures which they depict as two monolithically antipodal realities. In one letter, we are told that the Oriental sensibility cultivates inaction, wholeness, detachment and submission, whereas its Western counterpart aspires to nothing less than action, fragmentation, engagement and defiance. The same dichotomy opposes Western mind to Eastern mind since, according to Ling, while the former

> veut se soumettre le monde, et trouve dans son action une fierté d'autant plus grande qu'il croit le posséder davantage. . . . L'esprit oriental, au contraire, n'accorde aucune valeur à l'homme en lui-

> même; il s'ingénie à trouver dans les mouvements du monde les pensées qui lui permettront de rompre les attaches humaines. L'une veut apporter le monde à l'homme, l'autre propose l'homme en offrande au monde. (155)

> (wants to subordinate the universe, and finds in this desire a pride that becomes greater the more the intellect seems to dominate the universe.... The Eastern mind, on the other hand, gives no value to man himself; it contrives to find, in the flow of the universe, the thoughts which permit it to break its human bond. The first wants to bring the universe to man, the second offers man up to the universe.) (85–86)

That Malraux could present Asia as a world immured in a mythical past and given to apathy, passivity and detachment is, to say the least, highly perplexing in view of the fact that not only had he spent several months in Indochina between 1923 and 1925, but he always claimed to have taken an intense interest in the activities of the Vietnamese and Chinese anticolonialist and nationalist movements during his Indochinese stay.[17] In the 1920s, China was experiencing serious political and social turmoils which eventually led to a long running civil war between the Chinese communist party and the Kuomintang. Some of these political events are, in fact, used by Malraux as narrative frames for his two Chinese novels, *Les Conquérants* and *La Condition humaine*. Hence, the paradox of the Malrucian Asian universe in which one encounters two vastly different realities co-existing anachronically side by side: the immutable archaic world of Cathay and the turbulent modern Republic of China. The sequestering of the Other in an atemporal space also informs Malraux's view of Japan. In their discussions of Malraux's relation to Japan, critics invariably note the curious contrast between his fascination with what he refers to as "le Japon éternel" and his indifference to the social and political reality of contemporary Japan.[18] "Le Japon éternel" which so captivates his imagination belongs to the realm of Japanese high art, religion, and philosophy of death (*hara-kiri*). In Malraux's eyes, these cultural practices constitute what he believes to be the Japanese essence, "son profond état d'âme" which he can secure away in his world of the "Intemporel."

THE ADVENTURERS IN THE AGE OF ENTREPRENEURIAL COLONIALISM

The East that is depicted in *La Tentation de l'Occident* as an immutable world arrested in its antiquated tradition re-emerges in the subsequent Asian novels as a place where, to use Malraux's own words, "history was in the making."

Numerous excellent studies have examined the role of history in Malraux in light of the metaphysical and/or political issues he raises; yet little attention has been paid to the ways in which the colonial context mediates the Malrucian protagonists' engagement with those issues. In this section, I will focus on the highly ambivalent relationship of the Malrucian heroes to the colonial world which, while serving their dreams and ambitions, also becomes an inhospitable place to belated adventurers like themselves.

In his *Portrait de l'aventurier*, Stéphane, drawing on Malraux's own analysis of the postwar social and spiritual crisis in *La Tentation de l'Occident*, and the 1927 essay, "D'une jeunesse européenne," reads the turn of European youth to adventure as a response to their deep disenchantment with modern European civilization: "adventure was born of the rupture between the profound demands of man and a civilization that no longer measured up to them" (86). One logical place to which these discontented souls would turn in their search for alternative lives was the colony, the land of adventure par excellence, promoted by the European imaginary as open "virgin" lands, inhabited by "savages" and untouched by the corrupting influence of civilization. To those who were critical of an overcivilized, nihilistic and decadent Europe, the colony "naturally" appeared to be the place for moral and physical regeneration. For example, in *Terres de soleil et de sommeil*, a record of his trip across the French Congo at the turn of the century, Ernest Psichari presents Africa as "one of the last refuges for national energy" (278) where "in the last unknown lattitudes . . . we recaptured life at its very source, in its bygone greatness . . . and all that remains of the male and harmonious beauty in our mediocre humanity" (287). To be sure, nineteenth-century colonial history is peopled by larger-than-life explorers and adventurers such as Cecil Rhodes, James Brooke, Francis Garnier who, by their sheer energy and courage, were said to have fought and founded kingdoms. In *The False Dawn: European Imperialism in the Nineteenth Century*, Raymond Betts sketches a portrait of those European adventurers such as Gauguin and T. E. Lawrence who fled the civilized world for faraway colonial shores: "Hardy, individualistic, or at least non-conformist, they seemed to offer proof that the colonial frontier . . . could generously accommodate and satisfy those who were socially uncomfortable at home or ambitious beyond accepted restraint" (16).

Like their real-life forebears, the Malrucian protagonists in the Asian novels are persuaded that what they want of life can never be obtained in the narrow and stifling bourgeois confines of the metropole. Garine, the main character in *Les Conquérants*, is among those who, in the words of Gérard, "n'ont jamais pu accepter la vie sociale, qui ont beaucoup demandé à l'existence" (22) (have never been able to conform in ordinary society, who have asked a great deal of life) (11). What he asks for is absolute power, "De la puissance, il ne souhaitait ni argent, ni considération, ni respect; rien qu'elle-même" (70) (He craved power for its own sake, not for the wealth, notoriety, or respect it might bring him) (41). And quite early in life, especially after his trial and conviction for financing illegal abortions, he comes to the conclusion that society is a theater of the absurd in which he wants no part. Consequently, he declares to the narrator: "Qu'on la transforme, cette société, ne m'intéresse pas. Ce n'est pas l'absence de justice en elle qui m'atteint, mais quelque chose de plus profond, l'impossibilité de donner à une forme sociale, quelle qu'elle soit, mon adhésion. Je suis a-social comme je suis athée, et de la même façon" (75) (I don't care about transforming society. It's not the general absence of justice that bothers me, but something deeper, the impossibility of pledging my allegiance to any social order, whatever it is. I'm asocial as I'm atheist, and in the same way) (44). This obsession with the unrestrained exercise of brute power and profound contempt for society are virtually the sine-qua-non of Malraux's conqueror-heroes. Thus, Perken, the chief protagonist in *La Voie royale*, is known for "la passion qu'on lui prêtait naguère pour sa domination, pour cette puissance sauvage sur laquelle il ne permettait pas le moindre contrôle" (9) (the mania he had displayed in earlier days for absolute power, a savage mastery of men, of which he would not brook the least control) (6). His craze for power is, like Garine's, accompanied by a profound disdain for his fellowmen which he expresses "par sa façon de dire 'ils' en parlant des passagers—et peut-être des hommes—comme s'il eût été séparé d'eux, par son indifférence à se définir socialement" (13) ([in] his way of saying 'They' when he spoke of the other passengers (and perhaps, mankind in general) as though by his indifference to claiming any social status he had set himself apart from them) (12). It is these very qualities in Perken which greatly impress Claude, a budding adventurer who also expresses the greatest disdain for all his former classmates who docilely subscribe to society's norms and values. For a man of his caliber, Claude proudly declares, he would "chercher ses armes où ne les cherchent pas les autres: ce que doit exiger d'abord en lui-même celui qui se sait séparé, c'est le courage" (37) (forge for himself weapons other than the weapons of the herd; and the surest arm for one who feels himself cut off from his kind is courage) (43).

For men whose sole satisfaction in life is to "compel" others and whose ambition is, in Gisors's words, "d'être plus qu'homme dans un monde d'hommes," "non pas puissant: tout puissant" (*Condition* 271) (to be more than a man, in a world of men) (not powerful: all powerful) (242), there is no place better suited to pursue this dream than the colonies, for during the heyday of Western imperialism, the mere fact of being "white" automatically conferred on one an extraordinary power over the natives. It is hardly surprising that the Malrucian protagonists, following in the footsteps of a long line of past adventurers, should choose the colonies as their privileged site of action or that their stories and actions are often deliberately associated with those of their real life predecessors. For example, in *La Voie royale*, Perken is introduced to us as descending from the lineage of great adventurers, in particular, "les blancs qui ont été mêlés à la vie des Etats indépendants d'Asie" (7) (the white man who has played a part in the affairs of independent Asiatic states) (3–4). Throughout the narrative, the daring deeds of the heroes are not infrequently juxtaposed with those of famous past explorers. In the passage of the boat trip to Indochina, the Royal Way project which Claude goes over obsessively in his mind merges (via the use of the interior monologue) with the story of Prosper Odend'hal, one of the legendary colonial figures remembered specifically for his audacious explorations and terrible death among the Indochinese highland tribes:

> Il [Claude] était fasciné par les grandes taches bleues dont il avait entouré les Villes mortes, par le pointillé de l'ancienne Voie Royale, par sa menaçante affirmation: l'abandon en pleine forêt siamoise, "Au moins une chance sur deux d'y claquer. . . ." Pistes confuses avec des carcasses de petits animaux abandonnés près de feux presque éteints, fin de la dernière mission en pays Jaraï: le chef blanc, Odend'hal, assommé à coups d'épieux, la nuit, par les hommes du Sadète du feu. . . . (11)

> (His eyes [Claude's] were fascinated by the thick blue rings with which he had encircled the Dead Cities, the dotted line that marked the ancient Royal Way, fraught with presentiments of a lingering end in the green depths of the Siamese forest. "It's an even chance I leave my bones there!" A maze of jungle tracks, strewn with the skeletons of small animals left to their fate beside the dying campfires, the tragic issue of the last expedition into the Jarai country—Odend'hal, the white chief, hammered to death with spear-hafts by the Sadete tribesmen. . . .) (9)

A few pages later, when Perken relates to his young friend his own terrifying experience among the Jarais, he prefaces his account with the story of David de Mayrena, the adventurer turned king who reigned among the savage tribesmen after defeating two tribal chiefs.

If in the narratives of their actions and goals, Perken and Claude present themselves as spiritual heirs of dashing adventurers, they nevertheless realize that the kind of adventuring undertaken by the likes of Richard Burton, René Caillié,[19] or Camille Douls[20] has become a thing of the past. With the ending of the era of conquest and pacification, the colonial policy of the postwar years focuses more and more on economic exploitation and development. As a result, the postwar colonial scene is no longer dominated by the towering romantic figure of "the intrepid explorer hacking his way across a tropical jungle ...," but rather by "the entrepreneur armed with designs for bridges and schools or figures for imports and exports" (Aldrich 115). Hence, the mercantile civilization of the metropole which Claude left behind seems to have caught up with him in the colony. Indeed, on the boat that takes him to Indochina, he meets first-hand some of the metropolitan representatives in the persons of the Homais-esque bureaucrats who, the young man realizes very soon, are highly suspicious of men like himself and Perken: "Jamais Claude n'avait vu à ce point le besoin de romanesque de ces fonctionnaires qui voulaient en nourrir leurs rêves, besoin contrarié aussitôt par la crainte d'être dupes, d'admettre l'existence d'un monde différent du leur" (15) (Claude realized so clearly how these staid government officials, his fellow-passengers, hankered after romance, their hunger for the stuff of dreams, always at odds with their horror of being "humbugged" and of admitting the existence of a world so different from theirs) (15). Later on, it is these same colonial bureaucrats who forbid the two heroes from removing the statues of the temple. But in spite of the antagonism both Claude and Perken feel vis-à-vis the colonial administration, they still need to have recourse to the latter's services. A case in point is that all the maps and the literature concerning the existence and location of the statues[21] which Claude uses to carry out his project are provided by colonial offices such as l'Ecole française d'Extrême-Orient.

Even a seasoned adventurer like Perken who could claim to have achieved the same daring feat as Mayrena—subduing the supposedly ferocious highland tribes—is unable to resist the changing tide. In the first part of the novel, the ship captain draws Claude's attention to Perken's recent curious preoccupation: "et une chose plus surprenante, c'est que maintenant, il s'intéresse à l'argent.... C'est nouveau ..." (16) (But the really odd thing is that nowadays he's keen on making money; that's something new in him) (16). Apparently, such an interest in money is unbecoming in a true adventurer who should spurn material gains. But the situation in the colony has evolved so that Perken is in need of a large amount of money to buy guns to defend his territories against the encroachment of colonial powers. His project is, as he explains to Claude, to organize a military force which he could eventually use in a struggle either between settlers and natives or between the Europeans themselves. His ultimate goal is to "Exister dans un grand nombre d'hommes, et peut-être pour longtemps. Je veux laisser une cicatrice sur cette carte" (60) (Survive for many men, and perhaps for a long time; to leave my mark upon the map of Asia) (74). Yet were he to succeed, Perken realizes, the victory would be a Pyrrhic one, for nothing can withstand the march of "civilization" as he confides to his young companion:

"La vase? Vous sentez. . . . Mon projet aussi est pourri. Je n'ai plus le temps. Avant deux ans, les prolongements des lignes du chemin de fer seront achevés. Avant cinq ans, la brousse sera traversée: routes ou trains" (61) (Can you smell the mudflats? . . . My scheme's like them: rotten and corrupted. It's gone stale on me. Before two years are out the extension of the railroad will have been completed, and within five years they'll have pushed their roads or railroads right across the jungle) (74–75). The irony is that Perken, by his rescue of Grabot from the Mois, has provided a pretext for the Siamese government to send troops to punish the tribes and impose their jurisdiction.

Perken's misgivings were indeed justified. In the last part of the novel, the narrator makes it clear that it is no longer "savages" such as the Mois that represent the real danger to adventurers like himself, but the "State" whose "civilizing mission" would spell their ultimate death: "L'Etat était au fond de cette obscurité, chassant devant lui les tribus animales avant de chasser les autres, allongeant de kilomètre en kilomètre la ligne de son chemin de fer, enterrant d'année en année, toujours un peu plus loin, les cadavres de ses aventuriers" (160) (And somewhere yonder, behind a wall of darkness, the forces of a State were on the march, scattering in flight before them the wild life of the jungle—soon to be followed by its human denizens as well—pushing on mile by mile their railhead, burying year by year a little further on the corpses of their pioneers) (219). On his return trip to his region, the dying Perken is accompanied by the advancing government troops he associates with his own imminent death: "Attentif avant tout, contre sa volonté, à la douleur qui montait et descendait comme un bateau, il retrouvait la colonne et la mort dans son soulagement; attachées l'une à l'autre, avançant toutes deux vers leur but comme les grandes fumées" (164) (Involuntarily all his attention reverted to his pain, rising and falling like a ship at sea; and only in its lulls did he regain awareness of the progress of the column and of death, working in concert, marching steadily towards their goal like the long trail of smoking fires) (224). Towards the end of the novel, in his last moment of consciousness, he sees the different symbols of destiny represented by the figure of the circle in the narrative— Grabot's turning the beam of the millstone in his hut, the circular movement of the buffaloes transporting the timber for the Siamese troops—merging with the image of the railroad encircling and imprisoning his work and world.

> Ce n'était pas seulement sur ses espoirs, mais sur son vrai cadavre, sur ses yeux pourris, sur ses oreilles mangées par la terre, que passerait cette ligne qui avançait en bélier vers les montagnes de l'horizon . . . il savait . . . que sur la grappe d'espoirs qu'il était, le monde se refermerait, bouclé par ce chemin de fer comme par une corde de prisonnier. . . . (177–178)

(For it was not only on his dead hopes the railroad, battering its way ahead towards the mountains, was to pass, but over his dead limbs as well, over his decaying eyes and ears corroded by the earth ... he knew that ... On the little nucleus of hopes that was his very life the world would set its stranglehold, clamping those iron tracks upon it, like a prisoner's chains) (243)

La Voie royale ends with the dying Perken looking at Claude as a stranger from another world: "Perken regardait ce témoin, étranger comme un être d'un autre monde" (182) (Perken gazed at him as if he were a stranger, an intruder from another world) (250). This other world is not simply that of the living he will soon depart, but also the squalid modern world in which he, the old-time adventurer, would have found no place. It is in his unfinished novel, *Le Règne du malin*, that Malraux attempts to tell the impossible tale of adventuring in this other world that Perken left behind. I shall return to this last book in the concluding section of this chapter.

A similar ambiguity vis-à-vis the social order informs the relation of Garine to the Chinese revolution in *Les Conquérants*. We have noted his asocial, if not antisocial, character, which explains that his participation in the Chinese political events is not primarily motivated by a belief in justice. In fact, according to Gérard who has been working with him in Asia, Garine is among those Europeans who "sont venus au temps de Sun, en 1921, en 1922, pour courir leur chance ou jouer leur vie, et qu'il faut bien appeler des aventuriers; pour eux, la Chine est un spectacle auquel ils sont plus ou moins liés" (22) (came along in Sun's time, 1921, 1922, to take their chances or stake their lives, who have to be called adventurers; for them China's a great pageant that they play parts in) (11). In times of turmoil, China provides opportunities for adventurers like Garine to play the chief. Yet, whatever important contributions he might have made to the revolution, he is perceived as an outsider by the party. Hence, in the last part of the novel, after the defeat of Hong Kong engineered by Garine, Nicolaïeff announces the end of the latter's role in the revolution: "Son temps est fini. Ces hommes-là ont été nécessaires, oui, mais, maintenant, l'armée rouge est prête ... il faut des gens qui sachent s'oublier mieux que lui" (260) (His day is over. Men like him were needed, but now the red army's on the march ... now we need men who don't think quite so much of themselves) (161). As I argue elsewhere,[22] adventurer-characters such as Garine, Perken and Claude entertain what can be described as a parasitic relationship to the colonial system: while refusing to be part of any social order, be it colonial or otherwise, they nevertheless live off the system.

METAPHYSICAL ERO-EXOTICISM

Different explanations have been advanced as to why Malraux chooses Asia as the theater of action for his adventurer-heroes. According to some critics such as Bourrel, this choice of places far away from Europe as the site for his protagonists' exploits is dictated, in part, by the popular demands for exotic literature in France during the post-First World War era, which witnessed a rapid proliferation of both fictional and non-fictional works by colonial writers, reporters and globe-trotters. In fact, Malraux himself is responsible during the years 1926–1928 for the re-publication of a number of exotic novels such as Paul Morand's *Rien que la terre, Boudha vivant* and Loti's *Les Pagodes d'or*. But more importantly, Bourrel argues further, Malraux's use of the exotic in his writings serves the all-important metaphysical purpose of "expressing the fundamental enigma of life" for "exoticism brings about a distancing of a metaphysical order that would allow us to see ourselves as objects—a dimension fundamental to Malraux's project which consists ... of expressing ... the 'tragic in man'" (118). An explanation in the same vein has been proposed by Vandegans, according to whom Malraux's seeking out the Orient is partly due to "his need to better understand the Westerner, to have a clearer view and a more intense feeling for his problems from the perspective of a distant continent and a civilization radically different from his" (150).

Such metaphysical readings of Malraux's novels are ubiquitous in Malrucian scholarship partly because this approach has been endorsed by the author himself according to whom the fundamental issue in *Les Conquérants* is "first of all an accusation against the human condition" ("Reply" 20–21). Taking his lead from Malraux, Joseph Hoffmann asserts that the goal of the revolution undertaken by the Malrucian characters is not to bring about the liberation of an oppressed social class as the Marxists have it, but to "promote the dignity of man by fighting against all that denies him access to it—poverty, humiliation, injustice" (210). In *La Voie royale*, the protagonists' heroic fight against the ferocious Mois and the deadly jungle is likewise interpreted as a symbolic form of man's struggle against the dark forces of destiny. It seems that, in Malraux, the metaphysical exoticism underlying the tormented world of his adventurer-heroes has superseded the aesthetic exoticism that once goaded Segalen's quest.

Like all exoticisms, Malraux's metaphysical exoticism also carries an element of the erotic. But as many scholars have noted, in the Malrucian world, eroticism is not a simple matter of seeking sexual excitement, for over and beyond the sexual encounter, it is a way for an individual (presumably male) to assert his will over another and to obtain proof of the latter's subjugation. This highly complex, if not perverse, form of sexual control and domination of the other is viewed as an expression of man's metaphysical struggle against the forces that crush him. For the Malrucian man, eroticism represents, Hoffmann rightly notes, "one of the available means for him to escape his human condition, in the same way as his adventure does; what he seeks are opportunities to dominate and to affirm his power" (172). Indeed, his characters often use a highly eroticized language to express their obsession with power as well as their metaphysical angst. For instance, in *Les Conquérants*, Garine's musings on the exercise of power are evoked in images which recall those of an animal in an orgasmic state:

> Si, repris par un besoin puéril de rêverie, il rêvait à elle (la puissance), c'était de façon presque physique. Plus "d'histoires"; une sorte de crispation, de force tendue, d'attente. L'image ridicule de l'animal ramassé, prêt à bondir, l'obsédait. Et il finissait par considérer l'exercice de la puissance comme un soulagement, comme une délivrance. (70)

> (When his young man's fancy focused on power, it was in an almost physical manner. No fantasies: a kind of tightness, tension, expectation. The ridiculous image of a coiled animal, ready to spring, haunted him. So finally he came to see the exercice of power as a sort of relief, a deliverance.) (41)

In *La Voie royale*, death and sex are likewise the two obsessions that constantly haunt the minds of its two protagonists, accompanying them at each step of their adventures. On board the ship to the Far East, Claude, in the course of his solitary rumination over the human condition, is suddenly seized by "L'austère domination dont il venait de parler à Perken, celle de la mort, [qui] se répercutait en lui avec le battement du sang à ses tempes, aussi impérieux que le besoin sexuel" (37) (the sense of death's austere dominion, [which] pervaded all his being, persistent as the throb of blood across his temples, imperious as sexual desire) (44). Later on in the narrative, when Perken tries to convey to his young companion his near-death experience, the eros-thanatos pairing is personified in the image of a woman stripped naked.

A consequence of this eroticization of the metaphysical angst in Malraux is the transformation of the Other—be it women, the Chinese revolution, the Chinese masses or the Moi tribesmen—into objects to sustain the meta/physical drive of his protagonists in their pursuit for absolute power. As Lucien Goldmann notes in his analysis of *Les Conquérants* and *La Voie royale*, Garine and Perken, in their search for some temporary "distraction" from their existential anguish, subject the Chinese revolution and the Mois to an erotic relation:

women play for them the same role as that of the group with which they associate; the revolution for Garine, the Mois for Perken. In the erotic relations between them and their partners, a community is created which they direct and in which they are the masters. And this liaison in which they treat woman as an object and which makes them feel that they exist, provides them on the limited and reduced level of eroticism, the same provisional salvation, the same precarious consciousness of their existence as the historical action on a larger level. (126–127)

One way of eroticizing the relationship between the male protagonists and the Chinese masses is to genderize China by assimilating it to the female Other. For example, in *Les Conquérants*, what the narrator refers to as the "old China" or the China without Europeans is presented as essentially a female site peopled by old women and infants. In contrast to the fast moving, brutal male world of the Western protagonists which is symbolized by the powerful modern motorboat, old China is represented by the primitive sampans that shelter the immobile domestic world of women:

> Voici la vieille Chine, la Chine sans Européens. Sur une eau jaunâtre, chargée de glaise, le canot avance comme dans un canal, entre deux rangs serrés de sampans semblables à des gondoles grossières avec leur toiture d'osier. A l'avant, des femmes, presque toutes âgées, cuisinent sur des trépieds, dans une intense odeur de graisse brûlée ... (93–94)

> (This is the old China, China without Europeans. As if in a canal, the motorboat cuts through yellowish muddy waters between two rows of jam-packed sampans like rude gondolas with wicker roofing. On their bows women, almost all of them old, are cooking over tripods that smell of pungent fat ...) (57)

A feminized China, here symbolically penetrated by the Western machine, is, like most women in Malraux's novels, to be subdued and possessed. Hence, in *La Condition humaine*, we are told apropos of the all-powerful Ferral that he "knew women" in the same way as "he knew the Chinese family relationship" or that "he knew the Chinese custom." It is his "knowledge"[23] of women and China that empowers him to possess them both.

HUMANISM'S OTHER

We have noted earlier that Malraux's main concern in *La Tentation de l'Occident* is to critically scrutinize the failed values of Western humanism. In the letters exchanged between the book's two correspondents, the East is used primarily as a sounding board to reflect and magnify the European spiritual crisis. After spending two years in China to learn more about an "alternative" worldview, A.D. makes it clear to his Chinese friend that the East can provide no solution to the problems of the West. This same conclusion is reiterated by Malraux himself in his 1926 essay, "L'Orient et Malraux," which ends with the question, "Can Asia provide us with some lesson?" (54) The answer is a negative one, and the only use the East has for the West, Malraux affirms, is to facilitate "une découverte particulière de ce que nous sommes" (54) (a certain discovery of what we are).

If, according to Malraux, the East has nothing to teach the West, the reverse is certainly not true. In spite of the total bankruptcy of its humanist value system and beliefs, which is said to leave many Europeans in the throes of the absurd, the West still has many valuable lessons to impart to the Chinese. For example, in *Les Conquérants* and *La Condition humaine* the driving force behind the Chinese revolution is fueled mainly by the heroic spirit of the Western protagonists in their capacities as both leaders and teachers of the revolutionary movement. One such great commander is Garine, the Western hero who, according to his creator, embodies the three highest European values of the time: "l'aptitude à l'action, la culture et la lucidité" ("Postface" *Les Conquérants* 286) (culture, logic and a talent for action) ("Afterwords" 179). In *La Condition humaine*, all the characters that carry the day despite their defeat are in the main Europeans[24]: Kyo, the Franco-Japanese leader of the Shanghai insurrection; Gisors, Kyo's father and spiritual director in the novel; and Katov, the Russian revolutionary who is made to die an exemplary death.

Not only are the European protagonists the true leaders of the Chinese revolution, but more importantly, they also assume the role of its ideological "accoucheurs." For example, in *Les Conquérants*, Garine proudly explains to the narrator how by his actions he has brought hope to the despairing Chinese masses: "En cet instant même, combien d'hommes sont en train de rêver à des victoires dont, il y a deux ans, ils ne soupçonnaient pas même la possibilité! J'ai créé leur espoir. Leur espoir. Je ne tiens pas à faire des phrases, mais enfin, l'espoir des hommes, c'est leur raison de vivre et de mourir ..." (196) (Right now, at this very moment, how many men are dreaming of victories that two years ago they could never even have imagined! I created their hope. Their hope. I'm not much for fancy talk, but what the hell, man's hope is his reason to live or die ...) (120). Indeed, we are told that it is due to Garine's teachings that "Toute l'Asie moderne est dans le sentiment de la vie individuelle, dans la découverte de la mort" (137) (All modern Asia is learning about individual life and discovering death) (84). This realization of the uniqueness of life which makes death irremediable, a notion central to Malraux's humanism, turns many young Chinese into terrorists or revolutionaries. One such young Chinese terrorist is Hong whose life has been profoundly transformed by the teachings of the former Genoese militant anarchist, Rebecci. From him and later from Garine, Hong learned about the unique character of life. Another Chinese character that bears a certain resemblance to Hong is Tchen of *La Condition humaine*, also presented as a pure product of Western ideas. The first person who exercises a decisive influence on him is a Lutheran missionary. Through him, Tchen is initiated into the Christian faith which is later undermined by the teachings of another white sage, Gisors, a former sociology professor at the University of Peking. A strong bond soon develops between the Chinese youth and his second mentor who "avait été des années son maître au sens chinois du mot—un peu moins que son père, plus que sa mère; depuis que tous deux étaient morts, Gisors était sans doute le seul homme dont Tchen eût besoin" (77) (for years had been his teacher in the Chinese sense of the word—a little less than his father, more than his mother; since they had both died Gisors was without doubt the only man Ch'en needed) (62). In fact, as Gisors himself puts it, Tchen is very much "son oeuvre" (77) (his work) (68).

The relationship of Malraux's protagonists to the Chinese characters reflects a colonial Western paternalism in which the Europeans, spurred by the calling of the "mission civilisatrice," descend upon the lowly natives to instruct them in the arts of true manliness. According to many of Malraux's characters, the Chinese race as a whole is unfit for any kind of manly action, given their proclivity, the two correspondents in *La Tentation de l'Occident* remind us again and again, to inaction, passivity and meditation. Consequently, the single most important condition required of any man wishing to join the revolution is, according to Garine, to distance himself "de la vie chinoise, de ses rites et de ses vagues croyances" (137) (from Chinese life, from its rituals and hazy beliefs) (84). One representative of this obsolete world of traditional Chinese values is the elderly Chinese leader of *Les Conquérants*, Tcheng-Daï, who incarnates the feeble impotence of his people. In the novel, Tcheng-Daï, portrayed as a weak, self-righteous traditional scholar,[25] is ready to sacrifice the revolutionary cause for the sake of his misplaced sense of justice, which turns out to be, in Garine's words, "la plus grande force dont puisse se parer la faiblesse profonde, irrémédiable si répandue dans sa race" (111) (the most powerful outward manifestation of the ubiquitous, deep, and irremediable frailty of his race) (68). The incompetence of Tcheng-Daï, contemptuously described as a "vieillard courtois, aux petits gestes mesurés," (polite little man of polite little gestures) who "a confiance en elle (la justice) comme *un enfant* dans une statue de la pagode" (114; emphasis added) (trusts it [justice] as a *child* trusts a statue in a pagoda) (69;

emphasis added) is made to symbolize the failure of Chinese traditional values in the "modern world," in other words, the world brought under Western hegemony. This child-like naiveté of the Chinese only confirms the reality and the urgency of the "white man's burden" of which Garine smugly reminds his Chinese rival, Tcheng-Daï, who had impudently criticized his revolutionary strategy: "Qui l'enfant doit-il préférer, de la nourrice qui l'aime et le laisse se noyer, ou de celle qui ne l'aime pas, mais sait nager et le sauve?" (168) (And whom should the infant prefer, the wet nurse who loves him and lets him drown, or the one who does not love him but knows to swim and saves him?) (103).

Next to the daring, defiant Western heroes, the Chinese do indeed appear rather pathetic in their cowardice. Not surprisingly, it has to take the exceptional mind of a Garine to put some pluck into those spineless "Chinamen," a feat which wins the admiration of the French deputy, Meunier, who proudly explains to the narrator in *Les Conquérants*: "A propos du boulot, je voulais te dire, tout à l'heure, que l'un des moments où Garine s'est montré réellement à la hauteur, c'est quand il a organisé l'école des Cadets. Là, il n'y a pas à rigoler. J'admire. Faire un soldat avec un Chinois, ça n'a jamais été facile. Avec un Chinois riche, encore moins" (52–53) (And speaking of work, I meant to tell you just now that one of the times Garine showed class was when he organized the military academy Whampoa. That was no joke. That, I admire. Make a soldier out of a Chinaman, that was never easy. Out of a rich Chinaman, even harder) (30). The Propaganda Chief achieved this seemingly impossible task by initiating the feeble Chinese into, Meunier sarcastically remarks, a "vice peu connu en Chine qui s'appelle le courage" (53) (vice not very popular in China, called courage) (31), a fact later reiterated by Garine himself who observes that "ce qui est difficile, c'est de transformer les vélléités des Chinois en résolutions" (138) (the hardest is to convert Chinese subtlety into nerve) (84).

If Malraux seems to think that the Chinese have a great deal to learn from the West, his position vis-à-vis cultural *métissage* remains nevertheless highly ambiguous. As I argue elsewhere,[26] the tragic plights of Hong and Tchen testify to their failed attempt to embrace Western ideas and ideals in the Chinese context. Like all colonial mimic-men, both Chinese protagonists can only aspire to the condition of being, in Homi Bhabha's words, "almost the same, but not quite" ("Mimicry" 86). Consequently, these "Hellenized" Asians find themselves facing the predicament of, to borrow Achebe's description, "men of the two worlds": not only do they fail to perfectly match the colonialist model, but they also sever all bonds with their own people ("Colonialist" 72). Indeed, throughout the novel, the narrator in *La Condition humaine* reiterates Tchen's total alienation from his fellow Chinese. During the critical moment of combat, when Tchen is fighting at the side of his comrades, we read that "Il n'était pas des leurs. Malgré le meurtre, malgré sa présence. S'il mourait aujourd'hui, il mourrait seul.... Pour lui ... sauf de leur douleur et de leur combat commun, il ne savait même pas leur parler" (91) (He was not one of them. In spite of the murder, in spite of his presence. If he were to die today, he would die alone.... For him ... he did not even know how to speak to them) (95). We learn likewise of the violent hatred Hong developed against his own people in *Les Conquérants*: "Sans nul doute, il hait avant tout l'homme qui se respecte, qui est sûr de lui-même; impossible d'être plus profondément révolté contre sa race" (178) (Unquestionably, he hates most the man who respects himself, is sure of himself; he couldn't be more of a rebel against his own kind) (109).[27]

Yet the fact that the Western protagonists may not have achieved complete success in transforming Chinese society is of little consequence, for, after all, their participation in the Chinese revolution is tangential to their metaphysical pursuit. We have seen that Garine, as an asocial character, did not join the revolution through any moral, social or political imperatives. What he sought in his Eastern expedition was a chance to enlist in a "great cause" which would enable him to "leave a mark on earth." In his preface to Stéphane's *Portrait de l'aventurier*, Sartre cogently argues that most Malrucian heroes, including Kyo, are too absorbed by their own singularity and their "moi" (self) to embrace a social or political cause. What they need are action scenarios in which they can play leading roles before and on behalf of a lesser race. If Garine has chosen the Chinese revolution as the stage to act out his metaphysical drama, Perken, his ideological double, is more tempted to forge the "Perken myth" among "savages" at the heart of the Cambodian jungle. His ambition is to erect his kingdom among the unpacified tribes in upper Laos.

In their grand metaphysical pursuits, a number of Malrucian heroes come to see other human groups as their underlings. If in *Les Conquérants*, the Chinese are portrayed as an emasculated and infantile race whose degeneracy results from the sheer old age of their exhausted civilization, the Mois in *La Voie royale* find themselves placed at the opposite end of the human evolutionary scale, nearer to beasts or insects than to men. Between the two infinities, Malraux's heroes, like the Pascalian man,[28] position themselves in the middle, thereby exemplifying the prototypical Homo sapiens.[29]

Before introducing the Mois, the narrator in *La Voie royale* takes great pains to create for the readers their "natural" habitat: the tropical jungle, a hostile and perilous place, totally cut off from the realm of civilization and proper "human" activities. Interestingly, this primal forest which poses such great threats to the two white adventurers, is evoked in ways which recall the maternal womb, the female site par excellence, by the recurring marine images such as the "aquarium" light of the jungle, the "ténèbres marines" (64) (sea depths) (83) of the virgin forest with a "sol semblable à l'écume des marais" (66) (soil like marsh-scum) (85). In this semi-aquatic setting, things lose their solidity and their density, that is, elements of maleness, succumbing to an amorphous chaos: tree-trunks become "porous," the soil "spongy" and forms, uterus-like, "se gonflaient, s'allongeaient, pourrissaient" (65) (grew bloated, lengthened out, decayed) (84). The only living creatures in this antediluvian world are the lowliest insects such as spiders, flies, cockroaches, ants and termites whose virulent bacterial life thrives "dans la corruption de l'air, dans l'odeur de champignon, dans la présence des minuscules sangsues agglutinées sous les feuilles comme des oeufs de mouches" (66) ([on] the corruption of the air, the stench of fungus, the swarms of tiny leeches glued together like flies' eggs beneath the leaves) (85). Nothing is more dreaded by the Western heroes who so pride themselves on their lucidity, intellect, and rational mind, hallmarks of Western humanism, than this primordial mass which insidiously wears down Claude's stamina as he "sombrait comme dans une maladie . . ." (65) (felt himself disintegrating like the world around him) (84).[30]

It is in the heart of the Cambodian jungle, "hors du monde dans lequel l'homme compte" (65) (a world where mankind has no place) (84) that the two white protagonists come face to face with the ultimate embodiment of the inhuman, namely the Mois, the jungle natives who are represented as part and parcel of the primeval forest's savagery.[31] In his depiction of the Moi tribesmen, Malraux has recourse to many of the European clichés for "savages." An example of such stereotypical representation is to be found in the two white adventurers' first encounter with the Mois. Even before they can see the tribesmen, we are told that Perken and Claude already detected the latter's presence by "une bouffée d'odeur de chair brûlée" (a smell of roasting flesh) (72). The choice of the word "chair" (flesh) rather than "viande" (meat) is intended to evoke in the Western reader's mind the practice of cannibalism, a sine-qua-non of savagery in Western adventure narratives. This olfactory clue is soon to be followed by Claude's first sighting of a "savage": "appuyé sur la hampe de sa lance miroitante, se grattant la tête et penché vers l'intérieur du bûcher, un guerrier jaune regardait, nu, le sexe dressé" (72–73) (leaning on the shaft of his flashing spear, scratching his head and bending towards the center of the pyre, a yellow warrior was gazing at the flames; he was stark naked, and in a state of erection) (93). This tribesman displays all the stock traits ascribed to all savages: his nakedness, his unbounded sexuality, his animal-like gesture (scratching) and expression (blank gazing). The sight of his first "savage" caused such an extreme reaction in the inexperienced Claude that he was suddenly seized by an overwhelming sense of revulsion as he "était fixé à ce spectacle par les yeux, par les mains, par les feuilles qu'il sentait malgré ses vêtements, par le sentiment panique qui tombait sur lui, enfant, devant les serpents et les crustacés vivants" (73) (felt himself riveted to the sight—by his eyes, by his hands, by the leaves which seemed to touch him through his clothing, and, not least, by that feeling of panic which always used to come over him, as a child, whenever he saw a live crab or lobster, or a snake) (93–94).

In each of their subsequent encounters with the Moïs, Perken and Claude never once change their perception of these people whom they regard as an inferior species. Hence, we read that one of the native guides appears to Claude as "ni tout à fait animal, ni tout à fait humain" (102) (neither wholly human nor altogether bestial) (135). The tribesmen even become less human as they appear more threatening to the two white men. For example, during the scene in which the latter find their hut besieged by the Moïs, we see Claude suddenly reliving the horrendous sensations he previously experienced in the jungle:

> Et une fois de plus, comme si rien n'eût pu vaincre les formes de la forêt refoulée, Claude entra dans le monde des insectes: des cases plantées au hasard, silencieuses et apparemment abandonnées tout à l'heure, *les Moïs sortaient sans qu'il vît où, se coulaient dans le sentier avec leurs gestes précis de guêpes, avec leurs armes de mantes.* Arbalètes et lances se détachaient sur le ciel, parfois, avec une précision d'*antennes* ... (122; emphases added)

> (And once again, as if nothing could subdue the onset of the forest and its form of life, Claude felt himself transported into an insect-world. From the scattered huts which, only a moment before, were silent and seemingly unoccupied, now, through invisible exits, a *swarm* of Moïs was emerging; with nimble, *wasp-like* movements they streamed along the path, brandishing their *mantis-like* weapons. Now and again the spears and cross-bows stood out against the sky clean-cut as waving *antennae)* (163–164; emphases added)

What Claude sees in front of him are no longer human beings, but man-size insects scurrying around him, engaged in activities quite alien to his "human" understanding. And as the danger intensifies, the Moïs undergo yet another metamorphosis. This time, instead of being perceived as insects, the tribesmen appear to the two besieged heroes as "fauves à l'affût" (a herd of beast of prey) with "ces regards de brutes avides ... en face de ces paupières plissées, de ces cous tendus de chiens" (127) (their look of feral hunger ... of staring eyes slotted between puckered lids, of craning, dog-like necks) (171).

The ultimate "coup de grâce" to whatever is left of the tribesmen's humanity is delivered by Perken in one of his metaphysical rhetorical addresses occasioned here by the sight of his "savage" interpreter during his bargaining for Grabot's release:

> Sa destinée, à lui, Perken, se jouait sur cette *masse vivante*. Sa vie aboutissait comme à un passage à ces jambes couvertes d'eczéma, à ce pagne ignoble et sanglant, à cette *humanité capable seulement de pièges et de ruse, ainsi que les bêtes de la forêt*. Il dépendait totalement de cet être, de ses pensées de larves. Quelque chose en cet instant vivait sourdement dans cette tête, comme s'ouvrent les oeufs de mouches pondus dans le cerveau. (137; emphases added)
>
> (His fate, his future, were staked on that *lump of squalid flesh*. All the years of his life had served but to bring him to this pass, to confront him with that *sub-human creature, versed like the wild beasts of the jungle only in ruse and treachery*, that body scabbed with eczema and girdled with a filthy, blood-stained loin-cloth. On this creature and on its rudimentary mind he depended utterly; on the embryonic thoughts which in the dark recesses of its skull were squirming into life, like flies' eggs hatching in a dead man's brain.) (184–185; emphases added)

It is clear that the unspeakably repulsive Mois are made to incarnate the diabolic forces of destiny incessantly abating the dignity of "Man." Yet, and here lies the paradox of the Malrucian humanist narrative, does not this portrayal of the tribesmen as sub-human creatures diminish, if not altogether deny their humanity? How does one account for such a dehumanization of another human group, albeit a non-Western one, in a work that claims to promote human dignity?

UNFINISHED BUSINESS: THE OTHER'S HUMANISM

In our earlier discussion of *La Voie royale*, we noted that David de Mayrena, the would-be king of Sedangs, is one of the legendary adventurers who the novel's two main protagonists consider to be one of their own. From Malraux's own account, we know that the story of Perken is to some extent inspired by that of Mayrena.[32] Interestingly enough, the same Mayrena makes his appearance again in Malraux's incomplete Asian novel, *Le Règne du malin*, in which he features as the main protagonist. Who is Mayrena? His real name was Marie-Charles David, born in Toulon in 1842. He went to Cochinchina for the first time in 1863 as a Spahi and returned there again in 1885 after a series of failed attempts to establish himself in France. It was during his second sejourn in Indochina that he sought out the Sedangs in the Annamite highlands; after organizing the tribes into a confederation, he proclaimed himself king with the title of Marie I in 1888. Without the support and recognition of the colonial government, however, his kingdom rapidly disintegrated, and he died on the island of Tioman in the South China Sea in 1890.[33]

In their discussions of the genesis of this work, many Malrucian exegetes are of the opinion that this novel might very well have been book two of the trilogy *Puissances du désert* of which *La Voie royale* constitutes the initial volume. According to Larrat who edited the Pléiade version of *Le Règne du malin*, the groundwork for both projects was laid by their author during the same period, but the research for the unfinished novel continued well into the 1930s, and the actual writing was carried out around 1939–1940. For whatever reasons, Malraux abandoned this project,[34] but even in its unfinished form, *Le Règne du malin* constitutes a turning point in Malraux's thinking of the Other, which explains my interest in the work.

Conceived at the same time as *La Voie royale* and based on certain common sources, the Mayrena novel shares with it a number of structural similarities. Both books recount the tribulations of two European adventurers among "savage" tribesmen in the Indochinese highlands. Like Perken who teams up with the younger Claude, Mayrena has also an assistant in the person of Mercurol. Both men harbor the same ambition of establishing a stronghold among the Mois. Both narratives follow the same sequences of events: the boat trip, the crossing of the jungle, and the arrival among the highland tribes.

Yet these structural similitudes aside, *Le Règne du malin* is, curiously enough, in almost every way a photographic negative of *La Voie royale*. Starting with the chief protagonist, the Mayrena in the unfinished novel is not only a far cry from the Mayrena in *La Voie royale*, where he appears as the quintessential romantic adventurer going alone into the jungle to fight savages, but, more importantly, he is presented as the very foil of Perken. Both adventurers share the Quixotic predicament of aspiring to a heroic life in an unheroic world, but, unlike Perken, who clings to a superannuated image of the adventurer-hero, Mayrena realizes that the only role left for him is to be a parody of the Cervantesque knight.[35] Indeed, the two Malrucian protagonists are portrayed as opposites: the willful isolation of the one stands in marked contrast to the gregariousness of the other. For example, during the boat scene in *La Voie royale*, Claude understands very quickly that his new acquaintance is a self-styled loner who, by his silence, makes clear to the other passengers of his "volonté de solitude" (15) (obvious determination to keep aloof from them) (15). In contrast to the self-absorbed Perken, Mayrena, in a parallel boat trip scene, spends the whole night entertaining his fellow travelers with fantastic tales of adventures in the hope of hoaxing them into financing his gold expedition project. Far from being an angst-ridden tragic figure à la Perken, the hero, or rather anti-hero, of *Le Règne* is a "gaillard aux belles dents, ancien directeur du Théâtre municipal, un tantinet escroc, bon journaliste" (a strapper with beautiful teeth, former director of the municipal Theater, a tiny bit of a crook, good journalist) (983), known for engaging in a number of petty transactions of a dubious nature.

Narrating the story of such an anti-hero, it is of no surprise then that *Le Règne* reads more like a parody of the high adventure narrative, adopting a tone that deflates the epic mode we find in *La Voie*. The narration of the Perken saga is done in a consistently high linguistic register to carry the sublime weight of the protagonist's existential drama; the elliptical and terse style of the book is intended to convey the intensity of the heroes' feelings as well as the sense of tragic fate and imminent doom. In *Le Règne*, the lofty language is quite absent; some sections of the book are presented as "notes de mission" that are written in a telegraphic style. At other times, the narrative even takes on a "vaudeville" character as seen in the highly amusing scene of the soirée at the home of Resident Chaminade. In the course of the evening, Mayrena plays the gallant with his hostess Mrs. Chaminade—a "poetess" with great literary ambition unmatched by her talent—by pretending to be deeply moved by her mawkish verses. More noticeable still are the numerous conscious attempts throughout the work to subvert the epic mode of the high adventure genre. One such instance is the narrative of the surrender of the "pirate" Dé-Tham. Given the historical notoriety of Dé-Tham, one of the most feared leaders of the anti-French resistance, the story of his defeat would have been perfect material for a colonial epic. In the novel, not only has the engineering of the surrender been attributed to the totally *unheroic* Mercurol, Mayrena's side-kick, but the narrative of Dé-Tham's capitulation is given three versions, each more farcical than the previous one. The first version, narrated in the form of an interior monologue by Mayrena, is already quite deflated. The second version is provided by Mercurol himself while under the influence of hashish, which makes his story hardly coherent. The last version, which Mayrena calls "mercuroles épiques" (993), is in the form of the tale of Red Riding Hood told by Mercurol to his child, with Dé-Tham playing the big bad wolf. The ultimate irony is that it is among the tribesmen that the epic song can survive as a living cultural practice as seen in chapter twelve of the novel in which a native bard declaims the tribal *chanson de geste* in front of an attentive public.

In his commentary on the novel, Larrat lists a number of contradictions in the text that might explain the difficulties Malraux had in finishing the book. One such contradiction pervades the colonial politics of the Third Republic: the colonizing act could be justified only if it took on "the dimension of an heroic myth, of an epic worthy of Alexander or the crusades," yet the rationalist Third Republic, incapable of providing the inspiration and enthusiasm necessary for the "noble" kind of colonization, had to be content with the economic exploitation of the colonies. This contradiction in turn explains the ambiguity of the Mayrena character who, like a conquistador lost in the Third Republic, would have failed even if his energy and determination had matched his dreams. All these impasses, Larrat concludes, account for the unsteady character of the work, "hesitating between epic, burlesque epic and ethnographic novel" (1336–1337).

While it may be true, that in the staid and pragmatic bourgeois world of the Third Republic, the epic inscription of heroic adventuring had become a thing of the past, the demise of the monoglossic epic, as Bakhtin argues in *The Dialogical Imagination*, in fact marks the advent of the heteroglossic novel. Malraux's "failed" book, it seems to me, reflects the shifting of generic modes. It is precisely the eroding of the epic monoglossia in Mayrena's narrative that opens up a space for other voices as well as the voices of the Other. Indeed, there is no greater contrast than that between the representations of the Mois in the two adventure novels. We have seen how, in *La Voie royale*, the tribesmen are portrayed as reprehensible sub-humans submerged in savagery. Nameless, faceless and voiceless, they seem more akin to the insects and wild beasts of the jungle than to human beings. In *Le Règne du malin*, on the contrary, the same Mois are now endowed with a full humanity. Like any other human community, they are seen to function with dignity in their own society and culture.[36]

With their humanity restored to them, the Mois can engage in full dialogue with the European protagonists. In the course of the novel, we read of Mayrena's debates with the natives on subjects such as the merits of supernatural versus scientific explanations of natural phenomena. Rather than imposing on the natives the superiority of Western ways, these discussions not infrequently force Mayrena to rethink his own cultural biases. Besides the question of cultural relativism, the book also explores the notion of "l'homme fondamental," a theme Malraux would take up again in his two subsequent works, *L'Espoir* and *Les Noyers de l'Altenburg*. Two scenes in particular illustrate in a poignant way Mayrena's discovery of a common humanity. In one of these scenes, after Mayrena tries unsuccessfully to give a scientific explanation of drought to his Bahnar guide, his Annamite interpreter remarks that the latter is not "un homme sage. . . . Il est très animal" (a wise man. . . . He is very animal-like). The comment prompts Mayrena to turn around and look at his guide with the following reflection: "Animal . . . sa nudité, son odeur de fauve, son rapport obscur avec la forêt n'affaiblissaient pas, renforçaient, au contraire, son humanité. . . . Le guide avait l'odeur du fauve, mais il en avait aussi l'équilibre solennel; pour la première fois, Mayrena comprenait qu'être un homme, c'est se tenir debout" (1028) (Animal-like . . . his nudity, his beastly smell, his obscure link with the forest, did not weaken, but on the contrary, reinforced his humanity.... The guide had the smell of a wild beast, but he also had its dignified balance; for the first time, Mayrena understood that being a man means to stand on one's two feet). This observation takes us a long way from the vision of Claude and Perken to whom, as we have seen, the Mois' nakedness was a sign of their sub-human nature. A few pages later, Mayrena is confronted with the grief of a Bahnar whose little nephew had been carried away by a tiger in the jungle. His own helplessness in face of the man's distress allows him to see how men become brothers in sufferings: "Il [Mayrena] regardait, le coeur serré, cette face paysanne qui ne le regardait même pas. Ce n'était pas la première fois qu'il constatait entre tous les paysans du monde une mystérieuse ressemblance. Il ne comprenait pas un mot de ce que disait maintenant le Bahnar; mais cette voix simple et lasse ... c'était la voix des paysans français après l'inondation ou l'incendie" (1032) (He [Mayrena] looked sadly at this face of a peasant who was not even looking at him. It was not the first time that he noticed a mysterious resemblance among all the peasants of the world. He did not understand a word of what the Bahnar was now saying; but his simple and weary voice ... was also the voice of the French peasants after a flood or a fire).

The demise of the epic mode as exemplified by this novel certainly bears some comparison with the dissolution of the "aura" around the works of art of which Walter Benjamin speaks in "The Work of Art in the Age of Mechanical Reproduction." Both instances are marked by a sense of loss, loss of the absolute in one case and the authentic in the other. Yet these losses are also compensated by a certain form of emancipation. For Benjamin, mechanical reproduction liberates the work of art from its parasitical dependence on ritual. In Malraux, the passing of the epic moment in colonial narrative marks the beginning of the end of Western hegemony whose disintegration has always already been inscribed in the very logic of the civilizing mission. While we may never know why Malraux did not complete his novel, even in its unfinished form, *Le Règne du malin* is an amazingly complex and powerful book that would have been ahead of its time had it been published during the period of its composition. Last in the order of publication but certainly not the least of his works, this novel opens an altogether new vista onto the view of the Other in Malraux's humanism.

CHAPTER FOUR

DURAS ON THE MARGINS

Born and raised in Indochina during the 1910s and 1920s, Marguerite Duras was living in the colonies at the time of Malraux's visits. The Asian experience which was so central to the author of *La Condition humaine* plays an equally determinant role in the work of Duras, a fact that she herself acknowledges in many interviews. In *Les Lieux de Marguerite Duras*, she speaks at length to Michelle Porte of her Indochinese childhood and the story of her mother's victimization by the colonial administration. In a later interview with Suzanne Lamy, she reiterates the strong presence of the Indochinese years in *India Song*: "Yes, it is a very clear part of the least forgotten memory. Everything in *India Song*, the whole of *India Song*, the fluvial decor, the river, the railings, the tennis courts, the woman, they all come from a childhood year. I must have been between eight and nine when I knew all this and it stays absolutely intact" ("Interview" 59). Commenting on Duras's work, her biographer Alain Vircondelet states succinctly: "Her entire oeuvre feeds on sources in white Indochina" (13).

While both set their fiction in the Asia of the 1920s, the colonial world Duras evokes in her Asian novels cannot be more different than that of Malraux, at least on the surface. We have seen that the Malrucian universe is an all-male space inhabited by virile and angst-ridden adventurers who left the metropole in search of power in the heart of colonized Asia. The Durassian world is, in contrast, a gynaeceum peopled with impoverished widows and dolorous mothers wrestling with the squalid problems of living. These differences notwithstanding, partly because of her position as a "white Indochinese,"[1] Duras's relation to the colonized Other is in many ways even more problematic than that of Malraux. The task in this chapter is to examine this complex relation through a reading of the different forms of Self/Other marginalization that structure her Asian texts. But before engaging her fictional work, I will first examine a little discussed non-fictional piece[2] that Duras co-authored with Philippe Roques. The book, *L'Empire français*, was published in 1940 under her patronymic Donnadieu, but has never been reprinted, which accounts in part for its critical neglect. Moreover, the subject matter of the book does not easily fit into the psychoanalytical and/or feminist readings that many critics apply to Duras.[3] Since my concern here is with the colonial relation in Duras, this work, which addresses the subject of the empire, is particularly relevant to my discussion.

"L'EMPIRE EST FAIT"

"The Empire is made." Such is the central message *L'Empire français* meant to convey to its metropolitan readers who may not have fully realized the extent to which France had become a great imperial power. The authors take upon themselves the task of "apprendre aux Français qu'ils possèdent outre-mer un immense domaine" (informing the French people that they own an immense domain overseas) (9). And so they do. After a brief history of colonial expansion, the book provides a short introduction to the physical and ethnographic geography of the empire, which is then followed by three chapters on the military, economic, and spiritual might of the dominion.

In their narrative of empire building, besides extolling the great deeds of the founding fathers such as Bugeaud, Lyautey or Gallieni, the authors recount the numerous success stories of the civilizing mission carried out by the brave sons of the nation who brought law and order to the primitive and unruly tribes. We read, for example, of the splendid work the French settlers did to shake the African sub-continent out of its millenial slumber: "cette grande Afrique se secoue de sa torpeur sous l'impulsion des colons français. Cinquante ans à peine après la conquête, elle connaît la prospérité. N'est-ce-pas la meilleure preuve de la vitalité de la France qui a su faire ces terres incultes un véritable Empire . . . ?" (94–95) (vast Africa rises from her torpor under the impetus of the French settlers. Hardly fifty years after the conquest, she now enjoys prosperity. Is this not the best proof of the vitality of France which managed to transform these uncultivated lands into a true empire . . . ?). While praising the rapid changes the colonies were experiencing under the benevolent leadership of France, the authors, nevertheless, sound a note of caution on the subject of granting political rights to the natives. Whatever important changes Africa had achieved, the Africans were still in a state of civilizational infancy, and not yet to be trusted with political power: "Est-ce à dire que la France doive accorder sans contrôle des droits politiques à des indigènes qui en useraient mal? . . . L'éducation de l'indigène n'est pas arrivée au terme de son évolution; notre immense Afrique est encore en tutelle. La race noire est en enfance, habituée au régime de la tribu et du village" (230–231) (Should France grant unconditionally political rights to the natives who would put them to bad use? . . . The education of the native has not yet reached the end of his evolution; our vast Africa is still under our guardianship. The black race remains in infancy, used to the system of tribes and villages). As these citations show, the predominant tone of the book is one of benevolent paternalism vis-à-vis the subjects of the empire who are constantly perceived as children living off the "trésors de bonté et d'intelligence" (231) (bounties of kindness and intelligence) of the "Mère-Patrie."

L'Empire français is not as anomalous within the Durassian corpus as it might initially appear if we re-contextualize it within the author's biography. Five years after her return to France, Duras applied to work for the Ministry of Colonies in 1937 and was given an administrative post in the Intercolonial Information and Documentation Service. A year later, she was appointed to the Propoganda Committee for the French banana trade.[4] The book was probably written while she was working in the colonial office. In hindsight, one may wonder why she offered her service to the colonial branch of the government which had caused so much pain to her mother. Vircondelet argues that this colonial engagement is indicative of a contradiction in Duras who "participates in the maintenance of the colonial system and at the same time viscerally repudiates it" (64).

But is it really a contradiction that Duras, who grew up as a white Indochinese during the "golden age" of French imperialism, should sing the praises of "Mère-Patrie" and "douce France" (*Empire* 10)? The answer, it seems to me, is both "yes" and "no." If we re-situate her within the colonial context, her pro-empire position is, in fact, quite consistent with the milieu of colonial settlers from which she came. Let us also not forget that both her parents were teachers nurtured by the Third Republic of Jules Ferry. The young Marguerite must have been subjected throughout her childhood at home and at school to the rhetoric of France's civilizing mission. Vircondelet writes in his biography that, in Indochina, Duras "had never read anything but adventure stories, prize books, all that morally uplifting literature found in colonial libraries—Pierre Benoit, Pierre Loti, Claude Farrère, Roland Dorgelès" (59). At one level, given her background, it is not at all inconsistent that Duras should have pledged her support to the imperial mission since many former colonial settlers had written similar books upon their return to the metropole.⁵ This being said, there are, nevertheless, reasons why *L'Empire français* might perplex readers who are familiar with Duras's other works, especially *Un Barrage contre le Pacifique*. In this fictionalized autobiography, we find not only a virulent denunciation of the corrupt colonial bureaucracy which had ruined the life of the mother, but also a pathetic account of the horrendous plight of the Vietnamese peasants who were robbed of their lands by the Chinese pepper planters with the complicity of the colonial administration. The appalling condition of the peasantry is completely passed over in silence in *L'Empire français*, which gives us instead a most reassuring picture of their situation: "le paysan annamite . . . mène une vie des plus patriarcales. Respecté et entouré d'une vaste famille . . . il mène l'existence du paysan de toujours, économe, dur à la tâche" (111) (the Annamite peasant . . . leads a most patriarchal life. Respected and surrounded by a large family . . . his existence is like that of the immemorial peasant, thrifty and hard-working).

A COLONIAL MISADVENTURE

If *L'Empire français* is a hymn to the grandeur of the imperial adventure, *Un Barrage contre le Pacifique* is, in contrast, the tragic tale of a colonial misadventure. On more than one occasion, Duras speaks of the autobiographical nature of this 1950 novel, which is based on her Indochinese childhood, in particular the horrid experience of her own mother victimized by a corrupt colonial administration. In the history of colonial migration, Marie Legrand (Duras's mother)⁶ must have been one among only a handful of French women willing to move to Indochina in the 1900s, since, at that time, emigration to such a distant outpost was still considered a "risky" affair. In the predominantly male world of the colony, this widow of limited means, not surprisingly, stood little chance in her fight against the colonial bureaucracy, which robbed her of her life savings by leasing out to her uncultivable land.

Un Barrage contre le Pacifique recounts the saga of "Ma," a widow with two adolescent children, who, like the author's own mother, was driven to despair by the corrupt colonial administration under similar circumstances. In fact, even before leaving for the colony, Ma, then a young woman, was already an easy prey to the lure of the exotic à la Loti, as well as to the empty promises of great fortune awaiting her in the colonies. What ultimately wins her over is a propoganda poster depicting an idyllic scene with "à l'ombre d'un bananier croulant sous les fruits, le couple colonial, tout de blanc vêtu, [qui] se balançait dans des rocking-chairs tandis que des indigènes s'affairaient en souriant autour d'eux" (23) (a Colonial couple, dressed in white, sitting in rocking-chairs under banana trees while smiling natives busied themselves around them) (17). This stereotype of a colonial fantasy-land materialized later in Ma's life, but only in a caricatured form. After suffering numerous setbacks in her fruitless attempts to fence off the Pacific waves which annually inundate and destroy all the crops in her concessions, Ma resigns herself to growing bananas, the exotic fruit par excellence[7]: "La mère taillait ses bananiers. . . ." (Ma was pruning the banana trees), for in her stubbornness, she "feignait de croire que ses bananiers exceptionnellement soignés, donneraient des fruits exceptionnellement beaux et qu'elle pourrait les vendre" (114–115) (pretended to believe that her banana trees, exceptionally well cared for, would bear exceptionally fine fruit which she would be able to sell) (90).

The drama at the center of the family saga of the heroine Suzanne is her mother's hopeless fight against the unscrupulous cadastral agents who make their fortune by embezzling half of the revenues coming from the leasing of the over-priced and uncultivable lands to unsuspecting settlers. In the process of unfolding the epic of this one-woman struggle, the narrator relentlessly exposes the abject ignominy of colonial society. For example, at the beginning of the second part of *Un Barrage*, we find a highly critical account of the lifestyle and mentality of the white colonialists[8] who enclose themselves in their zoo-like "white town," in which the locals are tolerated only as domestics or café waiters. Their pretentious obsession with "cleanliness" as a way to enhance their "whiteness," "couleur d'immunité et d'innocence" (168) (color of immunity and innocence) (135), is ridiculed. Their affluence is made into an object of scandal as the narrator explains how the fantastic wealth enjoyed by the whites in the upper district, this "bordel magique" (magic brothel), grows out of the sweat and blood of the native workers:

> C'était la grande époque. Des centaines de milliers de travailleurs indigènes saignaient les arbres des cent mille hectares de terres rouges, se saignaient à ouvrir les arbres des cent mille hectares des terres qui par hasard s'appelaient déjà rouges avant d'être la possession de quelques centaines de planteurs blancs aux colossales fortunes. Le latex coulait. Le sang aussi. Mais le latex seul était précieux, receuilli, et, receuilli, payait. Le sang se perdait. (169)

> (It was the glittering age, the *grande époque*. Hundreds of thousands of native workers bled the trees of hundreds of thousands of hectares of red earth, bled themselves to open the trees that grew in an earth which, by chance, had been called red before being possessed by a few hundred white planters of colossal fortune. Latex flowed. Blood, too. But only the latex was collected as precious, only the latex paid a profit. Blood was wasted.) (137)[9]

This excessive opulence of the whites appears all the more odious as it stands in stark contrast to the dire poverty of the natives whose children die of starvation by the thousands each year. In fact, we are told that "Il en (enfants) mourait tellement qu'on ne les pleurait plus" (118) (They died in such a number that they were no longer mourned) (93). The most pathetic embodiment of this extreme misery is the Corporal, the mother's only servant whom she could never discharge on account of his legs, for he "avait été en effet tellement battu que la peau de ses jambes était bleue et mince comme de l'étamine" (248) (had, indeed, been so beaten that the skin of his legs was blue and thin as cheesecloth) (197). During his endless wanderings in search for food, the Corporal went to join the chaingang used in the building of roads for the colonial government. In exchange for the hard work, the constant flogging and the prostitution of his wife to the militia, he was given food everyday. Indeed so great was his destitution that "il n'arrivait pas à trouver une commune mesure entre la sienne et celle-ci [la mère]. Chez la mère on mangeait quand même chaque jour et on dormait sous un toit" (248) (he could never manage to find a common denominator for his and her [Ma's] poverty. At Ma's they ate everyday, no matter what happened, and they slept under a roof) (197).

The staunch criticism of the colonial system here may seem at first sight to curiously contradict the lauditory tone of *L'Empire français*; however, a close analysis shows that the two texts do not really stand in opposition to each other. What has been condemned in *Un Barrage* is not the principle of colonialism, but rather the *abuses* of the system which generate so much injustice. This position was also that of Malraux in the editorials of *L'Indochine* and *L'Indochine enchaînée*[10] where he denounced the corrupt practices of the colonial government which, he warned, would be detrimental to the metropole since France has a great deal at stake in her colonies. This view that the "Mère-Patrie" has certain common interests with her dominion is fully endorsed by the authors of *L'Empire*, who explain to their readers that "Il serait erroné de croire que notre action . . . tende à élever l'indigène à un meilleur sort pour son seul bien, aux dépens des intérêts mêmes de la métropole. L'oeuvre indigène de la France est conforme à ses intérêts" (205–206) (It would be wrong to think that our work . . . improves the condition of the native only at the expense of the interests of the metropole. The work France does for the native is in keeping with her own interests). Since the interests of the two parties are so closely linked, a brutally corrupt system would in the end kill the colonial goose that lays the golden eggs; hence it is imperative to correct the abuses of the colonial machinery.

It is also interesting to note that, like Malraux, who became involved in Indochinese politics after he himself suffered from colonial injustice, Duras's critical relation to the colonial establishment is also the result of her mother's victimization by the system. The reason why the mother is targeted as an object of persecution is due to her being both a woman and a poor white. The class issue does, in fact, play a crucial role in *Un Barrage* as well as the subsequent fictionalized autobiographies. Socially, Suzanne's family belongs to the class described by the narrator as "la pègre blanche" (poor white trash), that is, those whites "qui n'avaient pas fait fortune, les coloniaux indigènes" (171) (who had made no fortune—the Colonial natives) (138). As such, they are sandwiched between the rich whites and the natives. Their position is reflected in the limbo zone reserved for them in the Colonial city, a district "situé entre le haut quartier et les faubourgs indigènes" (171) (situated between the Haut Quartier and the native suburbs) (138). Trespassing into the upper district is to be paid for dearly, a lesson which Suzanne painfully learns the first time she ventures alone into the white sanctuary. No sooner does she step into the "Haut Quartier" than the young heroine comes to the awful realization that "Il n'était pas donné à tout le monde de marcher dans ces rues, sur ces trottoirs, parmi ces seigneurs et ces enfants de rois" (186) (Not everyone could walk in these streets, on these sidewalks, among these lordlings and these children of kings) (150). She is not only out of place in the midst of so much beauty, elegance and wealth, but her very presence there appears to her to be plainly ridiculous. Burning with shame, Suzanne "se persuadait qu'elle était scandaleuse, un objet de laideur et de bêtise intégrales" (186) (was convinced that she was something scandalous, an object of complete ugliness and stupidity) (150).

Within the white community, Suzanne and her family find themselves living at the margins of the wealthy settlers' world, good enough to socialize only with other "petits blancs" such as Pa Bart, owner of a squalid bar, and Carmen, daughter of a prostitute and a prostitute herself. The same issue of social segregation resurfaces in the two autobiographies, *L'Amant* and *L'Amant de la Chine du Nord*, where the narrator reiterates the fact that she had never been admitted in the Cercle français, a club reserved for rich whites such as Anne-Marie Stretter.[11] Yet, however lowly Suzanne and her family may be in the world of the *grands colons*, as whites they enjoy a position of superiority which places them above all non-whites, whether rich or poor. As a result, the white protagonists in *Un Barrage* merely reproduce the same kind of segregation in their own relationship to the natives so that, for example, Suzanne and her brother Joseph develop no friendships with the Vietnamese. In fact, the two young heroes invariably turn to their own kind for any social intercourse at all, even if this means that they have to drive all the way to Ram where the company available to them is of the most doubtful kind such as Pa Bart, whose reason for living is his glass of Pernod. Throughout the novel, the natives feature mostly as silent and docile extras who blend inconspicuously into the narrative background.

The one interracial relationship that is developed at some length in the book is that between the Corporal and the Mother, but it is one of mistress to servant. Ma, to be sure, has been a good mistress to the Corporal whom she refuses to discharge despite his deafness. This generosity is not without reciprocation, for where could one find such a faithful and devoted servant as the Corporal who demands nothing as long as he is fed and sheltered? This passivity is partly due to the fact that the Corporal displays little awareness of his own victimization by the oppressive colonial system, attributing the cause of his bottomless misery solely to his own deafness: "il était misérable, disait-il, parce qu'il était sourd et fils de sourd, et il n'en voulait à personne, sauf aux agents de Kam, mais à cause du tort qu'ils avaient fait à la mère" (249) (he was poverty-stricken, he said, because he was a deaf man and the son of a deaf man, and he held nothing against anyone, except the Kam agents, and that only because of the wrongs they had inflicted upon Ma) (197–198).

Apparently, the Corporal is not the only native who has no understanding of his own exploitation, as the peasants of the plain are said to be equally unaware of the unjustice they endure. Faceless and nameless masses, they are defined by poverty, ignorance and passivity. It is due to the leadership of Ma, an old woman without means, that the peasants are able to organize to work for their future and participate in the building of the dikes which, if successful, would reclaim cultivable lands for them. It is also from her, a member of the oppressor group, that they learn about their own oppression.[12] This relationship between Ma and the peasants typifies the contradictions lived by the colonizer. For on the one hand, there is a strong element of colonial paternalism (or rather maternalism) in this relationship. Ma, being more "civilized" and "enlightened," acts as the protector of the ignorant and uneducated peasants.[13] With her help, it is believed, life on the plain would improve. Everyone would grow rich; the children would no longer die of starvation. But above all, Ma is the one to enlighten those benighted minds to the true cause of their misery: if they have been so often deprived of their lands for the benefit of the Chinese pepper planters, it is thanks to those swine, the cadastral agents in Kam. Yet what Ma fails to realize is that the same authority which empowers her persecutors also legitimizes her own presence in the colony. If that power were to go, then she, too, would have neither right nor reason to stay. In his analysis of the dilemma of the leftist colonizer, Memmi points out that a colonizer who genuinely supports the liberation movement of the colonized soon realizes that, out of the struggle, a new social order will be born where there will be no room for her/him. Such a historical reality is dramatized in Ma's failure to convert the

Pacific plain into productive lands. Her vain attempt to contain the force of the Ocean by erecting a seawall against its waves, which annually destroy all her crops and hence her chance for permanence, mirrors the equally hopeless efforts of the colonizers to hold back the tide of history by maintaining their colonial domination through force.

The race/class contradiction also finds its way in the later autobiography, *L'Amant*. At the beginning of the book, the first-person narrator points out with no small irony the discrepancy between the racial and economic realities that underlie the existence of her family:

> Les enfants-vieillards de la faim endémique, oui, mais nous, non, nous n'avions pas faim, nous étions des enfants blancs, nous avions honte, nous vendions nos meubles, mais nous n'avions pas faim, nous avions un boy et nous mangions, parfois, il est vrai, des saloperies, des échassiers, des petits caïmans, mais ces saloperies étaient cuites par un boy et servies par lui. (13)

> (Children like little old men because of chronic hunger, yes. But us, no, we weren't hungry. We were white children, we were ashamed, we sold our furniture, but we weren't hungry, we had a houseboy and we ate. Sometimes, admittedly, we ate garbage—storks, baby crocodiles—but the garbage was cooked and served by a houseboy.) (6–7)

Yet in *L'Amant*, the race/class issue is further complicated by the gender factor as exemplified in the scene of the narrator's first encounter with her Chinese lover on the ferry boat:

> L'homme élégant est descendu de la limousine.... Il regarde la jeune fille au feutre d'homme et aux chaussures d'or. Il vient vers elle lentement. C'est visible, il est intimidé. Il ne sourit pas d'abord. Tout d'abord il lui offre une cigarette. Sa main tremble. Il y a cette différence de race, il n'est pas blanc, il doit la surmonter, c'est pourquoi il tremble. (42–43)

> (The elegant man has got out of the limousine.... He looks at the girl in the man's fedora and the gold shoes. He slowly comes over to her. He's obviously nervous. He doesn't smile to begin with. To begin with he offers her a cigarette. His hand is trembling. There's the difference of race, he's not white, he has to get the better of it, that's why he is trembling.) (32)

It is noteworthy that, even before any significant exchange occurs between them, the narrator immediately interprets the Chinese man's trembling in terms of racial hierarchy: he, an older and wealthy man, trembles in front of the young girl, because she is white and he is not. It is, indeed, most intriguing that the narrator should choose race as the only explanation of the Chinese lover's reaction. Couldn't he tremble under the violence of his desire for the young girl? Or couldn't his nervousness be explained by the fact that he was trying to seduce an under-age girl? Furthermore, since the Chinese lover had already known other white women when he was in France, "whiteness" may not exert this sacred aura on him as the narrator seems to imply.[14] The race factor is also evident in the reception of the Chinese by the narrator's family. It is as racial superiors that her brothers situate themselves vis-à-vis the Chinese lover whom they treat with utmost contempt, for they find it unthinkable that one of their own should have any kind of feelings for a non-white.

READING THE DETAIL

In a discussion with Porte on *India Song*, Duras remarks that "Le colonialisme, ici, c'est un détail, le colonialisme, la lèpre et la faim aussi" (*Lieux* 77) (Colonialism is here a detail, colonialism, leprosy and hunger too). Indeed, in *India Song* and its matrix-text, *Le Vice-consul*, the colonial theme which figures so prominently in *Un Barrage* seems to have receded, even though the colonies continue to serve as a narrative backdrop to the two texts. How are we to interpret the author's statement that colonialism has become a detail in her work? One way is to take it in a literal sense as meaning that colonies are just details. Scattered throughout *Le Vice-consul* and *India Song*, one finds occasional references to anodyne details such as "tropical park," "oleanders," "palm trees," "colonial decor," "incense-burners," "Hindoustani," "cithars," "Savannakhet," "buffaloes," "rice-fields," and so on. To the Western or Western-educated readers for whom Duras's work is intended, all these details "naturally" point to a specific "seme,"[15] namely, the seme of the exotic. As its root "ex-" indicates, the very notion of the exotic carries within itself the connotation of an outside, of margins and of deviation in relation to a subject posited as the center, the norm, the inside. In this sense, then, the colonies represented as and through these details would invariably appear to the denizens of the metropole as somewhat exotic, strange, mysterious, unsettling, in short as displaying the characteristics expected of all things marginal.

At one level, colonial society in Duras is a rigidly compartmentalized world, one strictly defined as inside/outside, center/margin. We have seen earlier how the colonial city in *Un Barrage* is divided into two self-contained parts: the white town or the *Haut Quartier* and the other city at the periphery in which no white people reside. A similar segregation marks the textual space in

Le Vice-consul and *India Song*: the French embassy—the inner sanctum of white Calcutta—occupies a strategically central position from which one commands a bird's eye view of the rest of the city with its two concentric rings of lepers, beggars, starving people and stray dogs. The topological marginalization of the natives on their own soil is further compounded by their social and economic degradation. This underlies the paradox of a colonial society in which the indigenous people are demoted to the rank of pariahs and outcasts in their own land while the outsiders settle there as masters and hosts. The Indians in *Le Vice-consul* are either docile domestics or beggars and lepers who can survive only by feeding themselves on the scraps of the French embassy. This polarization of colonial society is further dramatized throughout the book by the antipodal juxtaposition of the two communities. On the one hand, we read for page after page about the utter squalor in which hordes of lepers and beggars live, wallowing all day alongside stray dogs in the filth and stench of the Calcutta dumps. Standing in marked contrast to this subhuman, alienating subsistence, is the life of the glamorous embassy society where ladies change their dresses at least twice a day and men shave and shower just as often—cleanliness being, after all, the enhancer of whiteness—and where grapes, champagne and foie gras are flown from the metropole to grace the table of the European hosts.

Besides their topological and social centrality, the European protagonists in *Le Vice-consul* and *India Song* also serve as the main source for textual focus. In fact, throughout the narrative, the reader's perception of India and her people is filtered through the prism of colonial prejudice and obsessions. For example, we first encounter the eponymous character in *Le Vice-consul* while he gazes upon a street scene in Calcutta which he surveys from the balcony of his apartment:

> Le vice-consul à Lahore regarde Calcutta, les fumées, le Gange, les arroseuses, celle qui dort. Il quitte son balcon, rentre dans sa chambre.... Il s'est rasé, c'est chose faite, il retourne une nouvelle fois sur le balcon de sa résidence, regarde une nouvelle fois la pierre et les palmes, les arroseuses, la femme qui dort, les agglomérats de lépreux sur la rive, les pèlerins, ceci qui est Calcutta ou Lahore, palmes, lèpre.... (32)
>
> (The Vice-Consul of Lahore surveys Calcutta, the smoking chimneys, the Ganges, the water-sprinklers, the sleeping woman.... He goes indoors.... He has shaved. Well, that's done. He goes out on to the balcony again, and, once more, surveys the buildings and the palm trees, the water-sprinklers, the sleeping woman, the hordes of lepers on the river banks, the pilgrims. Such is the stuff of Calcutta, or Lahore, palm trees, lepers....) (20–21)

The Vice-Consul is not merely occupying a position which elevates him above the native crowd. This vantage point also bestows upon him an added sense of control and power (as suggested by the verb "regarde") over the miserable natives beneath him. The hierarchical topology is here reinforced by the further contrast between the character's sense of his own distinctiveness as an individual and the anonymity of the faceless masses. In view of all these differences that separate him from the object of his scopic drive, the Vice-Consul can dismiss the reality of Calcutta or Lahore as some lifeless stuff that can be easily accounted for by a simple process of repetitive enumeration.

Further along in the narrative, we encounter another instance of this panoptical surveillance, this time by Charles Rossett, the new attaché to the French embassy:[16]

> C'est la première fois qu'il voit se lever le jour ici. Au loin, des palmes bleues. Le bord du Gange, les lépreux et des chiens emmêlés font l'enceinte première, large, la première de la ville. Les morts de faim sont plus loin, dans le grouillement dense du Nord, ils font la dernière enceinte. La lumière est crépusculaire, elle ne ressemble à aucune autre. Dans une peine infinie, unité par unité, la ville se réveille. (164–165)[17]

> (This is the first time he has seen day break in Calcutta. In the distance, blue palm trees. On the banks of the Ganges, lepers and dogs interspersed encircle the city. They form the wide outer ring of the city. The thousands dying of hunger are farther off to the north, in the seething bowels of the city. They form the inner ring of the city. The murky light is unlike any other. The people of the city, each after his kind, wake to endless travail.) (131)

While commanding a wider panoramic perspective of the place than the Vice-Consul, the content of Rossett's vision is in some respect strikingly similar. Both see the same palm trees, the same hordes of lepers milling around the banks of the Ganges. Both descriptions, cast in the style of a tableau vivant, evoke the same timeless and endless misery. The attaché visually assimilates the natives so closely to the dogs that they appear to him as inseparable as suggested by the word "emmêlés." Likewise, the starving people are compared to a swarm of insects or worms as connoted by the noun "grouillement," an image strongly reminiscent of Claude's vision of the Mois in *La Voie royale*. While the humans here are reduced to the level of beasts or invertebrates, the city is ironically personified as it is said to awaken in the murky morning light, an effect unfortunately not conveyed in the translation. Such a contrast, as Bal has pointed out, further reinforces the dehumanizing of the Indians (66).

One consequence of making the European characters the only focalizing agents is to further enhance their status as the center, subject and master of the colonial order, and of the text at the expense of the natives who, condemned to silence, are left without a voice, consciousness or even a recognizable human face. It is intriguing that the natives represented from the whites' perspective are in the main limited to two specific groups, lepers and mad beggars, the two most marginal figures of society. According to Foucault,[18] madness in the history of the West is a re-incarnation of leprosy after the latter's extinction in Europe towards the end of the Middle Ages. Victims of both illnesses shared very similar fates and treatments in Western society, which denied them "le droit de la cité." As a result, lepers were traditionally confined to the margins of the community at the city's gates whereas madmen, before their massive confinement in the mid-seventeenth century, were sent off on the *Narenschiff*, the ship of fools. In the Western imaginary, Foucault contends, madness and leprosy were once believed to partake of the non-human realm and therefore necessitated severe measures of containment in the form of rites of purification and banishment.

Such is likewise the lot that befalls the native world, a site/sight of horror[19] which the colonial power carefully fences off from the white community through the implementation of a vast array of intricate protective devices. In her study, Bal examines the multiple forms of these self-defence mechanisms, the most prominent of which is the iron railings motif which, according to her count, occurs no less than twenty times in *Le Vice-consul*. Yet, these stringent safeguard measures, which were intended to create a sense of security in the white world, ironically produce the opposite effect. Instead of feeling protected, its inhabitants find themselves in a permanent state of besiegement and surveillance as they are, like Anne-Marie Stretter, at all times surrounded by "grilles au loin, sentinelles en uniforme kaki..." (166) (wrought-iron gates in the distance, sentries in khakhi uniform) (132). Or, if they are newcomers to the colony, like Charles Rossett, not yet accustomed to the system, they may feel trapped like an animal, an experience that overwhelms the new attaché during his wanderings in the fenced property of the Prince of Wales Hotel, a haven marked "for whites only":

> Il cherche à quitter le boulevard, prend des chemins de traverse, tombe sur le grillage élevé contre la mendicité, revient, cherche encore et trouve finalement une porte dans ce grillage, sort, s'aperçoit qu'il vient d'avoir eu peur, peur absurdement de ne pas pouvoir sortir de cette zone de l'île qui lui est assignée pour sa plus grande paix. (202)

> (He leaves the drive, turning into a side-path, and runs up against the wire fencing erected to keep marauders out. He turns, and gropes

along the fence, until at last he comes to a gate. After he has gone through it, the realization comes to him that he was frightened, absurdly frightened, of not being able to escape from this area of the island, which is fenced in for his greater protection.) (160–161)

BORDERS CROSSING

This paradox brings us to the second moment in our reading of the colonial detail in Duras, a moment of reversal and displacement. In the forever shifting and fluid Durassian land of swamps and marshes, there can be no fixing or fixed borders to separate the self from the Other. One sign of the fissuring of the seemingly watertight, comparmentalized colonial society is the deep malaise gnawing its white hosts and guests. The Europeans find their presence in the colony unbearable, in spite of the paraphernalia of protective artifices, ranging from devices such as iron railings and closed shutters to advice such as "Hygiène pendant la mousson. Il faut boire du thé vert brûlant pour couper la soif" (*Vice-consul* 130) (Health precautions during the monsoon. Having to drink scalding green tea to quench one's thirst) (102). Everything there seems to conspire to make life impossible for them, whether it is due to the dampness of the monsoon season which would put the piano—symbol of Western culture—out of tune overnight, the suffocating heat and the blinding glare of the sun that can cause nausea, or the sheer monotony of colonial life. Such a discomfort seems to sap the vitality of the European hosts, who notice with alarm a rapid deterioration in their health as shown when the young Charles Rosset claims that "il est arrivé ici comme un étudiant en voyage mais que de jour en jour il vieillit à vue d'oeil" (*Vice-consul* 102) (he arrived here feeling like a student on vacation, but that he seems to be aging visibly with every day that passes) (78–79).

In fact, no part of the white establishment seems to be immune from the impact of the native presence. Even the hermetic world of the embassy, the heart of white India, has been pried open and violated. Despite its many iron gates, guards, shutters, and huge park which form a formidable buffer zone of protection, the indigenous element still manages to make its way into the fortified preserves. Discordant noises, alien and (to Western ears) incomprehensible shouts from the outside penetrate as far as the reception hall, clashing harshly with the "civilized" sounds of cocktail conversation. Similarly, strange and unpleasant smells such as the funeral scent of the poisonous orleanders mingled with the odor of leprosy and the stench of the river mud infuse the whites' living space. The native presence actually infiltrates the innermost sanctum of Anne-Marie Stretter's boudoir, reminding its beautiful host and her distinguished guests of death and decay while they immerse themselves, à la Proust, in the immortal music of Schubert (*Vice-consul* 162/129).

Death and decay, hitherto the sole province of the native world, now find their way into the European community as we are told of the strange happenings during the times of famine in the colony:

>—Vous avez remarqué? Les Blancs ici ne parlent que d'eux-mêmes. Le reste . . . Et pourtant . . . les suicides d'Européens augmentent avec les famines
>
>—. . . dont ils ne souffrent pas . . . (*India Song* 90–91)
>
>(—Have you noticed? Out here the white people talk about nothing but themselves . . . The rest . . . And yet the time when most Europeans commit suicide is during famines . . .
>
>—. . . which don't cause them any suffering . . .) (87)

Yet, more bizarre than the occasional suicide is the whites' obsession with leprosy, a native curse, which provokes in them both revulsion and fascination. Terrified as they are by the mere idea of the contagiousness of the disease, they nevertheless cannot stop talking about it, making leprosy a favorite topic of conversation in social gatherings. For some of them, the interest is more than platonic, since they seem to be actually drawn to the lepers as in the case of the Vice-Consul of Lahore who claims to welcome the disease: "La lèpre, je la désire au lieu d'en avoir peur " (*Vice-Consul* 131) (Far from dreading leprosy, I would welcome it) (102). The irony, of course, is that the Vice-Consul is in his own way some sort of a social leper. Treated like an outcast in his own community after the Lahore scandal, he provokes in the other whites as much repulsion and attraction as the lepers. With the exception of the Club Director who is himself an outcast, no one is willing to approach him. He is shunned and ignored by most people. Yet, reluctant as they may be to socialize with the Vice-Consul of Lahore, the embassy guests are nevertheless drawn to him by a malicious curiosity. They constantly watch his every move, making him the focus of their attention, as happens during his dance with the Ambassador's wife in the course of which "toute l'Inde blanche les regarde" (*Vice-Consul* 121) (The eyes of the whole of white India are now upon them) (94).

If the Vice-Consul of Lahore, the man from the outside (La-hors),[20] is "understandably" ostracized by his peers as a pariah, the supreme irony is that leprosy has also struck the very heart and soul of the white world in the person of Anne-Marie Stretter, who is said to suffer "une lèpre, du coeur" (*India Song* 34) (a leper of the heart) (29). Leprosy may have, indeed, eaten deep into the European community, which seems to suffer its own kind of moral and spiritual decay. Thus, if the lepers appear to Charles Rossett as men made of "une matière friable, et une lymphe claire circule dans leur corps. Armées d'hommes en son sans plus de forces, hommes de son à cervelle de son, indolores" (*Vice-Consul* 165) (crumbling flesh and thin, watery blood. An army of men of straw, with no more strength than a bundle of straw, men whose heads are stuffed with straw, insensate) (131), aren't the whites themselves in an important sense such hollow men of straw? In their indifference and insensitivity towards the natives' misery, they are no more capable of any moral feeling than the lepers are of physical sensation. Despite appearances, the Europeans are, in fact, as parasitic as the native beggars and lepers, since, like the latter, they are unproductive and inactive, spending their time in idle and malicious gossip. The juxtaposition of the whites and the native lepers and beggars at the symbolic level completely unsettles the margins that the colonial order has drawn to contain the colonized Other.

The permeability of borders is likewise a central motif in *L'Amant* and *L'Amant de la Chine du Nord*, which recount the narrator's liaison with a Chinese man. By having an affair with a non-white person, the young girl breaks the taboo of the colonial society which regulates stringently all interracial sexual relationships, but in particular those between white women and non-white men.[21] Hence, when rumours of her story with the Chinese lover reach her schoolmates and their parents, the narrator finds herself immediately ostracized by the white community. By crossing the racial border, the young white girl also transgresses the topological boundaries in her *errances* across the chinatown of Cholon during her outings with the lover.[22]

While the interracial love affair in *L'Amant* has no doubt succeeded in undermining the strictures of colonial society, the subversive act nevertheless remains problematic in at least two respects. First, given the nature of an amorous liaison, the relationship is private and short-lived just as it brings about little, if any, change to the social and political inequality between colonizers and colonized. In fact, the memory of the lover which apparently remains vivid with the author does not move her to any political action during the long years of the Vietnamese struggle for independence. The transgressive effect of the story derives mainly from the fact that it is presented as a tale of forbidden desire. My second caveat concerns the way that some feminist critics read the crossing of the gender border in the narrator's relationship with the Chinese lover. It is often argued[23] that, by presenting the Chinese man as a meek male, totally submissive to the will and desire of the young white girl, Duras deconstructs the traditionally defined gender roles. What has not been taken into consideration in this kind of argument is the racialism that defines the relationship. Indeed, as we have noted earlier, the issue of the racial difference between the young girl and the Chinese was raised upon their very first encounter by the narrator herself. One wonders whether this domination of the non-white male by a white female, despite age and economic differences, is not in a certain way made possible by colonial racial politics.

THE OTHER WRITING/WRITING THE OTHER

In 1974, in a series of conversations with Xavière Gauthier in *Les Parleuses*, Duras describes herself as a marginal(ized) writer, "clandestine" and "prohibited" in France. She attributes this critical ostracization to being a woman writer and to her style of writing. It is no doubt true that, with the exception of her earlier novels, Duras's works were long considered "difficult," "obscure," or even "unreadable." It was not until the advent of what Elaine Showalter calls "gynocriticism" and the popularization of literary psychoanalytical theory that a critical language was found to broach the Durassian text. Indeed, aside from a handful of studies such as Marini's *Territoires du féminin avec Marguerite Duras* (1977), most of the book-length critical works did not appear until the 1980s.

In their discussions of the Durassian aesthetic, critics often draw our attention to the opacity and obscurity of her work, which is said to resist rational meanings. Her writing is often characterized as "fragmentary," "lacunary," and "porous."[24] Rather than telling a story or expressing ideas, the Durassian texts engage in a continuous "travail de perte" (practice of loss) producing stylistic effects such as "dépouillement" (stripping)[25] and "évidement" (voiding).[26] Characters, plots, and decors undergo a process of continual erasure from one text to the next. In her study of "madness" in Duras, Udris reads the practice of loss as a "textualization of the disintegration of reason and logos," (26) which permeates different aspects of her texts: her female characters empty themselves through the loss of their ego and their memories, or the text loses itself in its "blancs" and "mot-trou." For many Durassian commentators, this kind of anti-logos writing exemplifies "l'écriture féminine" or the Other writing, that is, a writing that turns its back on the Law of the Father.

This *écriture féminine*, often equated with the writing (of) the body,[27] is personified by a number of Durassian female protagonists;[28] but the most problematic among them is the character of the "mendiante," the beggar woman, who appears to many critics as the emblematic figure of another feminine (and) writing. In her brilliant analysis of *Le Vice-consul* in *Les Territoires du féminin*, Marini reads the beggar woman's story as a narrative of "un autre devenir féminin" (another becoming of the feminine): "the story of the young girl from Battambang is exemplary in different ways. It traces the trajectory of another becoming of the feminine" (198). In "L'Histoire de la mendiante indienne," Borgomano writes that the story of the beggar woman constitutes "the most original 'form-meaning' of the Durassian writing" (485). Following Marini, Mireille Rosello likewise sees in the story of the "mendiante" the emergence of another language and another form of text, that of "bavardage" (chattering): "Like the beggar woman, the chatter-writing wanders off" (522).

The beggar woman, indeed, shares many of the attributes of Durassian writing as we can see in this description by Borgomano: "the beggar woman, 'site of writing' . . . thus becomes this void, this hollow space towards which writing rushes . . . she figures this 'absent word'. . . . The beggar woman, the written figure of the impossibility of writing" ("Histoire" 484). Like the Durassian writing which engages in a continuous "travail de perte," the beggar woman's story is also one of progressive loss from the time of her adolescence. Banished from the maternal site/sight for her illegitimate pregnancy, the young girl embarks on a long peregrination which eventually brings her to Calcutta. While adopting the form of the *Bildungsroman*, her narrative also completely de-forms the genre. Instead of being the formative journey of initiation and gain (gain of knowledge and social recognition), her ten-year long march brings about a total loss of the self, which is, in fact, what she had set out to do as we read at the beginning of *Vice-consul*: "Il faut se perdre" "Je voudrais une indication pour me perdre," (p. 9) (Get lost) (I need some signpost to lead me astray) (1); "si elle la rejoignait, commencerait-elle à se perdre?" (11) (Might not that be the place where she could begin to lose herself?) (2). In the course of her wandering, the young girl undergoes a process of gradual self-dispossession, losing her family, her children, her memory, her language and ultimately her reason. By the time she reaches Calcutta, the end point of her journey, she has been stripped of everything that would have linked her to a past or given her a semblance of identity. What remains is but a song and the word "Battambang," which nobody understands. In Calcutta, she has become an empty shell, hairless, weightless, without thoughts and feelings: "Sous le lampadaire, grattant sa tête chauve, elle, maigreur de Calcutta pendant cette nuit grasse, elle est assise entre les fous, elle est là, la tête vide, le coeur mort, elle attend toujours la nourriture. Elle parle, raconte quelque chose que personne ne comprendrait" (*Vice-consul* 149) (Throughout this night of plenty, she, symbol of emaciated Calcutta, squats under the lamp-post amongst the mad beggars, scratching her bald head. With vacant mind and withered heart, she waits, as always, for food. She chatters, telling some tale that no one understands) (118). In her utter destitution, the beggar woman becomes so dehumanized that she returns to the elemental state:

> Elle est sale comme la nature même, ce n'est pas croyable ... ah, je ne voudrais pas quitter ce niveau-là, de sa crasse faite de tout ... je voudrais analyser cette crasse, dire de quoi elle est faite, de sueur, de vase, des restes de sandwiches au foie gras de tes réceptions de l'ambassade, vous dégoûter, foie gras, poussière, bitume, mangues, écailles de poisson, sang, tout ... (*Vice-consul* 182).
>
> (She is as dirty as nature itself, it's incredible.... Oh! I want to dwell on that, her filth compounded of everything.... I want to analyse her filth, describe what is in it: sweat, river-mud, scraps of stale foie-gras sandwiches from your Embassy receptions, dust, tar, mangoes, fish-scales, blood, everything ...) (145–146)

It is this beggar woman who is "hors communication" (outside communication) that, Duras asserts, figures "le lieu de l'écrit" (cf. Borgomano "Histoire" 482). How, then, is one to understand this apparent paradox of having a languageless, illiterate, insane and almost bodiless non-European pariah embody the site of writing for one of the most critically acclaimed Western practitioners of "écriture féminine"? This figuration of the native Other as the site of the Other writing needs to be recontextualized in the French feminist movement of the 1960s and 70s. One of the major strategies of the French feminists of that time was to recover "une écriture féminine," distinct from male "logocentric" writing. According to Cixous, the history of phallocentric writing in the West is underwritten by the hegemony of reason. Hence, the emergence of women's authentic voice can come about only through their liberation from the shackles of reason, which then would result in an "other" writing. As Gauthier suggests: "if 'full' words belong to men, how then to speak 'in another way' (autrement), unless maybe by *making us hear* that which agitates and suffers, mute, in the *blanks of speech* (*trous du discours*), in the un-said or the non-sense" (96).

Yet, this quest for the "other" is wrought with numerous perils and snares of which Cixous herself speaks in *Newly Born Woman*: "in History ... what is called 'other' is an alterity that does settle down, that falls into the dialectical circle. It is the other in a hierarchically organized relationship in which the same rules, names, defines, and assigns 'its' other." For if the "Other" is truly "other," and not just an invention of the Same, Cixous argues, "there is nothing to say; it cannot be theorized. The 'Other' escapes me. It is elsewhere, outside: absolute other" (71). In other words, for Western readers, the absolute Other, being the unsayable and the unrepresentable, cannot be derived from within their culture, but has to come from the outside. Hence Duras's choice of a non-European female pariah to figure the absolute Other, which in turn engenders one of today's most canonical forms of *écriture féminine* in the West.

Indeed, for many Western feminist critics, the narrative of the native beggar woman exemplifies an/Other space that resists and subverts the Western patriarchal system. The opposition between the beggar woman, figure of the Other, and the selfsame male is dramatized in Peter Morgan's narrating the story of the "mendiante" in *Le Vice-consul*. In *Territoires du féminin*, Marini draws our attention to the contrast between these two characters: one is white, male, articulate, rich and powerful while the other is non-white, female, illiterate, inarticulate, destitute and powerless. The very first line of the novel is built on the antithesis between the two protagonists: "Elle marche, écrit Peter Morgan" (9) (She walks on, writes Peter Morgan) (1). These two clauses are constructed around several contrastive features. Syntactically, they are presented as each other's mirror images: the subject predicate order of the first clause ("She walks") is reversed in the second whose predicate precedes the subject ("writes Peter Morgan"). The subject of one is the feminine third person pronoun "she," which, Benveniste tells us,[29] stands for the non-person while the subject of the other "Peter Morgan" is a fully identified person with name and surname that indicate both his gender and national origin. Semantically, the two clauses portray two opposed situations. The man is featured in a static pause, engaged in the mental act of writing which is carried out by the hand, whereas the woman is undertaking the physical action of walking with her legs.

Ordered in a hierarchical way, the contrastive features in the novel's inaugural sentence seem at first sight to reproduce traditional gender roles and relations where the man uses his intellectual prerogative to speak about and for the woman. The domination of the former over the latter is also reflected in the syntactical structure of the line "Elle marche, écrit Peter Morgan" in which the second part functions as the main clause that encloses and directs the first part, its subordinate. Yet, as the novel moves on, we see that, not only does Peter Morgan experience the greatest difficulty in writing the beggar woman's story, but his narrative of the Other slowly disintegrates into an/Other narrative that dislocates the rational and chronological linearity of traditional story telling. The beggar woman's text bears all the traces of the "dis-order" implicit in her directionless wanderings across the "vaste étendue de marécages que mille talus traversent en tous sens on ne voit pas pourquoi" (9) (the vast marshlands, bewilderingly criss-crossed by a thousand causeways) (1). The structure of her narrative reproduces the circularity and the numerous deviations of her march: "elle piétine, elle tourne. Elle contourne une ville. On lui dit que c'est Pursat. Elle dépasse un peu l'endroit où se trouve Pursat, continue en zigzaguant, à peu près droit, en fin de compte, vers les montagnes" (14) (She wavers. She goes round in circles. She comes to a town which, she is told, is Pursat. She makes a circuit of it, keeping to the outskirts. Pursat is behind her. She follows a zig-zag course which, in the long run, takes her nearer to the mountains) (5).

If as "le lieu de l'écrit," the beggar woman does engender an/Other scriptural space, this effect of Otherness is made possible precisely by Duras's casting her as the cultural Other. As such, the begger woman is both someone coming from a non-Western culture and the Other of culture, that is, the uncultured, the savage. In fact, it is not so much her madness alone that generates the effect of absolute Otherness; in truth, there are many "mad" characters in Duras's work such as Lol V. Stein, the mother or the Vice-Consul. Yet none of them is nearly as dispossessed and lost as the beggar woman. It is both the latter's madness and her non-Europeanness that produce the full import of non-representability in the eyes of Western readers to whose "incompréhension," Duras claims in *L'Homme Atlantique*, "je m'adresse toujours" (I always speak to) (18). Perhaps her non-Europeanness is part of her madness, since most of the Indians in *Le Vice-consul* appear as demented in the eyes of the Europeans. In fact, the beggar woman's non-representability is symbolised by a non-European word: "Battambang," her word-talisman: "Battambang la protégera, elle ne dira rien d'autre que ce mot dans lequel elle est enfermée, sa maison fermée" (62) (Battambang will keep her safe. She will never utter any word but that. It is her shelter, her home) (46). Even at the phonological level, the word "Battambang" must sound completely alien to French ears and produces an effect of alterity, strangeness and incomprehensibility to Western readers. In the West, the incomprehensible adheres to that which locates outside reason. The beggar woman is said to be afflicted with dementia, but, as an Oriental, she is also doubly incomprehensible to European readers for whom the East is conventionally the site of mysticism and unreason.

The Western readers who journey through the "Durasian"[30] topography may experience the same reactions as those of Christopher Columbus upon his first encounter with the ultimate Other, the native Americans. Commenting on the Genoese's travel diary, Affergan notes that "in the reading of these excerpts language touches the confines of the unsayable, of the filthy, of silence, and of panic.... Their significance lies in their untranscribability, sign that one is entering into absolute alterity ... (which) indicates an absence. Who is then at the place of the Indian? Nudity precisely.... The 'Naked' symbolises the place of lack of the Other" (69–70). Indeed, the beggar woman's narrative, which is in every sense a narrative of dispossession and loss, embodies the most radical form of "dénuement" (destitution) and "mise à nu" (stripping/ baring). At the end of her journey, stripped of everything and turned barren, she comes to occupy the place of lack, that is, "le lieu de l'écrit au féminin" since, according to Duras, women can only write "dans le lieu du désir."

However powerful and effective the narrative of the beggar woman may be from the Western feminist perspective, writing the Other into an Other writing is problematic in more than one way. In order for her to embody the site of feminine writing, the character of the "mendiante" is cast as the "prehistoric woman" Rita Felski speaks of in her analysis of the myth of the feminine. Like Felski's writers of the last fin-de-siècle, Duras displays a fascination with the archaic and the elemental that precedes and precludes the process of symbolic differentiation. In the course of her evolution (or rather devolution), the "mendiante" gradually regresses to a state of biological and cultural indifferentiation. What Marini calls "un autre devenir féminin" apropos the beggar woman really belongs to the utopian vision of the feminine which, as Felski argues, "exists outside categories, distinctions, and patriarchal structures of individuation and socialization" (53). In this space of non-differentiation, the feminine body is "idealized as the exemplum of nonalienated plenitude or interpreted as an emblem of horror and abjection" (Felski 53). Horror and abjection are exactly the feelings the beggar woman arouses in Rossett when he finally comes face to face with her on the island. Emerging from the muddy water of the lagoon, the "mendiante" appears before the petrified attaché as a dark laughing Medusa with eyes shining like nests of sun wrinkles ("les yeux sont au fond des nids de rides de soleil") and a skull covered with a brown crust of slimy grime:

> Elle cherche dans sa robe, entre ses seins, elle sort quelque chose qu'elle lui tend: un poisson vivant. Il ne bouge pas. Elle reprend le poisson et, lui montrant, elle croque la tête en riant davantage encore. Le poisson guillotiné remue dans sa main. Elle doit s'amuser de faire peur, de donner la nausée. (*Vice-consul* 205)
>
> (She fumbles inside her dress, between her breasts. There is something in her hand. She holds it out to him: a fish, a live fish. He does not move. She withdraws her hand, lifts the fish up so that he can see it, and bites its head off. Laughing more than ever, she chews the fish head. The decapitated fish jerks in her hand. He is terrified, nauseated.) (163)

Such re-turning of women to the inchaote pre-symbolic order which troubles some feminist critics[31] is, interestingly enough, tied to another kind of return in the Durassian texts, that of nostalgia, whose Greek root "nostos" means return home. The "home" for Duras is the land of her childhood of which she remains, as she declares in *L'Amant de la Chine du Nord*, "inconsolable" (36). Not only does the beggar woman, the "site of feminine writing," originate from Duras's homeland as stated in *L'Amant*,[32] the homeland itself has also returned in her text as its scriptural space. A number of critics draw our attention to the similarities between the shifting swampy Asian plain and the writing à la dérive of Duras.[33] In the process of re-writing the Motherland into the site of an Other writing, Duras "alters" a land and a people she once called her own. In *Les Lieux*, she speaks of her total identification with the Vietnamese as a child: "we were more Vietnamese ... than French ... we were from over there" (22). This same claim is reiterated in *L'Amant de la Chine du Nord* where we read: "Elle (la mère) dit qu'elle est devenue une indigène à la longue, comme nous, Paulo et moi" (106–107) (She [the mother) says that she's become a native finally—like us, Paulo and me) (93).

As in many Orientalist writers, the othering of the indigenous people in Duras, be they Vietnamese or Indian, is achieved through a process of dehistoricization. For example, in *Le Vice-consul* there is not one reference to the socio-historical conjuncture that gave rise to the predicament of the native young girl who is reduced to homelessness and starvation. Why is her hunger so intense that she is driven to eat dirt? Why does she have to sell her body until the near term of her pregnancy? Why could she not keep her child? Raising these questions may probably be deemed as a sign of a "naive" misreading of the novel, since, according to one critic, "Hunger of the beggar-woman. Hunger-pain of India. *Le Vice-consul* is not for all that a work that represents a scandalous situation in the world and thereby pertains to History. Anne-Marie Stretter's feeding the lepers should not be interpreted as the paternalistic gesture of the colonizer to the colonized in a context of class oppression" (Besnard 79). Naive or not, the fact remains that the horrendous plight of the native young girl is unfortunately the dramatization of a historical reality. During the years of French colonization, many Vietnamese women from the countryside endured terrible hardship because of French economic policy, which not only destroyed many farming communities, but also ruined traditional crafts such as spinning, weaving and silk worm raising that formerly secured women a livelihood.[34] The fact that Duras is able to induce or seduce her readers into seeing the colonial drama of the Indians and the beggar woman as part of an expression of the European protagonists' "expérience limite" (Besnard 81) is deeply disquieting to me. That the sufferings of large masses of human beings should serve as backdrop to enhance the aesthetic experience of a "happy few" brings to mind the indignant response of Achebe to the image of Africa in Joseph Conrad's *Heart of Darkness*: "Africa as a metaphysical battlefield devoid of all recognizable humanity, into which the wandering European enters at his peril. Can nobody see the preposterous and perverse arrogance in thus reducing Africa to the role of props for the break-up of one petty European mind?" ("An Image of Africa" 12).

There are no doubt moments in Duras's texts in which the lines drawn to define and confine the native Other become blurred as when the white young girl in *L'Amant* crosses over to the chinatown to see her lover or when the beggar woman passes through the guarded gates to sneak into the embassy park. Yet within the panoptical structure of the colonial machinery, these occasional transgressions only serve to confirm the power of its surveillance. As Foucault argues, transgression seeks neither to oppose nor to transform an order, but "incessantly crosses and recrosses a line which closes up behind it . . . and thus is made to return once more right to the horizon of the uncrossable" (*Language* 34). Hence, the transgressive moves of the Durassian characters, rather than creating a counter-hegemonic space, ultimately restore the borders they seek to trespass. The colonial status-quo is in fact reaffirmed by the autobiographical narrator who, in *L'Amant de la Chine du Nord*, declares herself to be an "indigène," a category instituted by the colonial judiciary system to survey and discipline the colonized. What does it mean for a (former) member of the empire to assume the disenfranchised position of a "native" instead of contesting its existence?

CHAPTER FIVE

ANOTHER BARTHES

One of the important insights that Barthes puts forward in *S/Z* is that the "I" who approaches the text is not an innocent subject, but is already a plurality of other texts and codes. He illustrates his point by analysing the codes that create the network (le réseau) through which Balzac's novella *Sarrasine* becomes text. Defined as a perspective of quotations, a code pertains to that "quelque chose qui a toujours été *déjà* lu, vu, fait, vécu: le code est le sillon de ce *déjà*" (28) (something that has always been *already* read, seen, done, experienced; the code is the wake of that *already*) (20). In *L'Empire des signes*, Barthes claims for himself the status of reader rather than visitor ("je suis là-bas lecteur, non visiteur") (105/79) of the text of Japan. If we apply the view on reading and text that Barthes develops in *S/Z* to his own reading and writing of Japan-as-text, we can ask the following question: what are some of the texts that make up Barthes as reader-of-Japan? To answer this question, we need to examine the intertextual relationship between *L'Empire des signes* and Orientalism, which, in turn, will help us to determine whether and to what extent the book on Japan has met the challenge that Barthes formulates in *Plaisir du texte*: "Comment un texte, qui est du langage, peut-il être hors des languages?" (50) (How can a text, which consists of language, be outside languages?) (30).

IN-DIFFERENT VOICES OF THE ORIENT

In *S/Z*, to illustrate the working of the codes, Barthes gives us the following example: "l'*Enlèvement* renvoie à tous les enlèvements déjà écrits" (27–28) (The *Kidnapping* refers to every kidnapping ever written) (20). Does the Orient in *L'Empire* also refer to every Orient ever written? In the very first fragment of the book, Barthes takes care to distance himself from a certain Orient (or Orients) in his criticism of the ideological re-appropriations which "consistent à toujours acclimater notre inconnaissance de l'Asie grâce à des langages connus (l'Orient de Voltaire, de la *Revue Asiatique*, de Loti ou d'*Air France*)" (8) (consist in always acclimating our incognizance of Asia by means of certain known languages (the Orient of Voltaire, of the *Revue Asiatique*, of Loti, or of *Air France*)) (4). In 1958, Barthes wrote an essay entitled "Le Dernier des écrivains heureux" in which he criticizes Voltaire's representation of the Oriental who, instead of being "l'object, le terme d'un regard véritable" (the object, the term of a genuine consideration) serves merely as "un chiffre usuel, un signe commode de communication" (*Essais* 98) (a cipher, a convenient sign of communication) (87). In Voltaire, Barthes further argues, the journey is not a way to acquire knowledge about the Other, but an affirmation of the "human essence." As a result, "ces pays d'Orient . . . sont pour Voltaire des sortes de cases vides, des signes mobiles sans contenu propre, des degrés zéros de l'humanité, dont on se saisit prestement pour se signifier soi-même" (*Essais* 98–99) (these Oriental countries . . . are for Voltaire so many forms, mobile signs without actual content, humanity at zero degree [Centigrade], which one nimbly grasps in order to signify . . . oneself) (88). As I will later demonstrate, Barthes's own engagement with Japan displays some of the same features, albeit under different guises, that he condemns in the Voltarian tales. More surprising yet is Barthes's marking his difference from Loti here, since in 1971, a year after the publication of the book on Japan, he wrote an essay on *Aziyadé* in which he seems to show a positive appreciation of Loti's Turkish novel. (I will return to the Loti article in the last section of this chapter.) Even his distancing from the Orient of the tourist guide as exemplified by the *Air France* magazine is not as unproblematic as it appears, since some critics do argue that by providing practical advice on eating out, shopping and getting around the city, the author of *L'Empire* "stays firmly within the genre" of tourist guide (Knight, *Barthes and Utopia* 153).

Barthes's anxiety to separate his Orient from that of others is reminiscent of Segalen's effort to reinvent a new form of the exotic that is cleared of all the tawdry trappings heaped upon it by other colonial writers and the tourist industry exemplified by *agences* Cook. Such a quest to get outside the "already read, seen, done, experienced" is, as we have seen in the case of the author of *Essai sur l'exotisme*, easier said than done. In fact, more than most, Barthes fully appreciates the power of language or language as power as shown in his perceptive analyses of modern social myths. In his inaugural lecture in Collège de France in 1977, he again reminds his audience of the ubiquity of power that is inscribed in language and present not only in the State or classes, but also "in the most delicate mechanisms of social exchange . . . in fashion, public opinion, entertainment, sports, news, family and private relations" (*Barthes Reader* 459).

At one level, one can easily identify in *L'Empire des signes* a number of Orientalist topoi. "Là-bas" (Faraway) which features as the title of the introductory fragment is one of the most coded expressions in French to refer to the exotic elsewhere. It immediately brings to mind, for example, Baudelaire's poem, "Invitation au voyage," which starts with an exhortation to the beloved "aller là-bas vivre ensemble," and this "là-bas," which is never named in the text, is the place said to be adorned with "la splendeur orientale." In fact, this first fragment is replete with textual strategies commonly deployed in Orientalist writings. A case in point is Barthes's renouncing of any pretention to represent the Orient as a "reality." Such a gesture is a standard move of Western writers to defend themselves against charges of "misrepresentation" of the Other. Hence, when questioned about the relevance of India in the film version of *India Song*, Duras likewise claims that the India in her writings belongs to her "fantasme" and that "in this film . . . I never wanted to show India" ("Rencontres" 6). The unreality of the place called "India" is prominently advertized in the text, *India Song*, as the readers are notified from the start of the "falsity" of all the geographical, political and human references to India which have only "un sens musical" (a musical sense).

After announcing his disengagement with the "real" Orient, Barthes goes on to state that "l'Orient m'est indifférent, il me fournit simplement une réserve de traits dont la mise en batterie, le jeu inventé, me permettent de 'flatter' l'idée d'un système symbolique inouï, entièrement dépris du nôtre" (7) (to me the Orient is a matter of indifference, merely providing a reserve of features whose manipulation—whose invented interplay—allows me to 'entertain' the idea of an unheard-of symbolic system, one altogether detached from our own) (3). This statement of purpose seems to strangely corroborate Said's critique of Orientalist discourse in which the Orient, constructed out of Europe's ideological suppositions and fantasies, serves as the latter's "deepest and most recurrent images of the Other" (*Orientalism* 1). Since the book is not concerned with the "real" Japan, Barthes explains, one will not find in it any reference to capitalist Japan, American acculturation and technological development (8/4), in short, all that pertains to the economic, political and social life of modern Japan. We have noted this same occultation of the contemporary face of the cultural Other in Segalen's relation to China. Like the author of *René Leys* who seeks in China new literary forms, what interests Barthes in Japan is a certain aesthetic experience which will provide him with other possibilities of writing: "le Japon l'a mis en situation d'écriture" (10) (Japan has afforded him a situation of writing) (4). If Segalen has discovered the Chinese "stèles" to serve as inspiration for a collection of poems with the same name, Barthes derives from his exposure to the Japanese haiku the art of writing in fragments.

More surprising still, Barthes's Japan displays striking parallels to Malraux's "Japon éternel," while their views on many other issues are so often diametrically opposed.[1] As I mentioned in chapter three, Malraux nourished a lifelong fascination for Japanese culture which is confined, as in Barthes's case, to what is perceived as its "feudal" past. This shared interest in "ancient" Japan in turn leads them both to focus on similar aspects of Japanese culture such as painting, calligraphy, music, theater, Zen gardens and religion though their specific readings of these cultural phenomena may differ. Like the author of *L'Empire*, Malraux declares his indifference to the "Americanized" side of Japan. In *Antimémoires*, Malraux stages a dialogue between himself and a Japanese he refers to as "le Bonze" (the Monk) in the Zen garden of Ryonji. The Japanese interlocutor he introduces in the text is a professor of art, which explains why their exchange is centered on the differences between Western and Eastern arts and philosophies. Like Malraux himself, we are told that the "Bonze," whose son died fighting the Americans during the war, strongly disapproves of the "démocratisation-et-américanisation" of modern Japan (*Oeuvres complètes* 3 428). These similarities in Barthes and Malraux's approaches to Nipponese culture cogently testify to the power of Orientalism as a discursive formation. Despite the ideological differences that separate the two writers, their relations to Japan are nevertheless coded by the same language, the "culturalist"[2] language of Western intellectuals.

THE TEMPTATION OF THE EAST

A prominent strategy in Barthes's reading of the empire of signs is one that has been exploited and perfected by a long line of real or imaginary traveller-narrators within the tradition of "exotisme philosophique." As Moura points out, philosophical exoticism has been widely practiced by thinkers such as Voltaire and Montesquieu who use "the exotic theme as a means to distance themselves from their society" (62). Like his eighteenth-century predecessors,[3] Barthes challenges some of the most deeply held premises and beliefs of contemporary Western culture by scrutinizing them in the light of an outside system so as to expose their "naturalized" arbitrariness. One tactic Barthes adopts here is what Jacques Ehrmann describes as "la critique du sens par dis-location" (the critique of meaning by dis-location) in which "he foregrounds the gap between the sign and its signified and thereby seeks to bring about the rupture between the two terms" (53).

"La critique du sens" was indeed a lifelong battle Barthes waged against bourgeois hegemony. The term "sens" (meaning), whose name is legion, assumes myriad guises in the Barthesian universe. Some of its most recurrent manifestations take the form of the "Doxa," which he defines as "l'opinion courante, le sens répété, *comme si de rien n'était*" (*Roland Barthes* 126) (current opinion, meaning repeated *as if nothing had happened*) (122). What characterizes the doxa or "Le mauvais objet" (*Roland Barthes* 75) (The wrong object) (70) is its pretense to be "natural" and to speak in the name of "common sense" whose only one and ultimate answer to every argument is "cela-va-de-soi" (it goes without saying). This war against "naturalness" dates back to the very beginning of his career. In a period of two years, from 1954 to 1956, Barthes wrote for *Les Lettres nouvelles* short articles whose main thrust is to dismantle what he calls "les mythes de la vie quotidienne française" (the myths of French everyday life). One way to expose the ideological message hidden behind the naturalized surface of mythic objects is to submit them to a semiological reading by treating the myth itself as a semiological system, that is, as a system of signs. In "Le Mythe, aujourd'hui," armed with the analytical tools of Saussurian linguistics, Barthes unravels for us the intricate and insidious working of the mythic sign.

Indeed, nothing provokes in Barthes a more visceral aversion than the Western petit-bourgeois order. It is in reaction against his own culture that he turns toward Japan, which is seen as embodying a totally different system. In an interview with Raymond Bellour on *L'Empire des signes*, Barthes explains his interest in Japanese culture: "I profoundly refuse my civilization to the point of nausea. This book expresses the absolute claim of a total alterity which has become necessary to me" (230). In marked contrast to what he calls "la sémiocratie occidentale," the Japanese signs in the Barthesian world, from the most insignificant to the most notable, are endowed with qualities that bring them closest to his own vision of the ideal semiological system. As he writes on the cover of *L'Empire des signes*, Japan is:

> le pays de l'écriture: de tous les pays que l'auteur a pu connaître, le Japon est celui où il a rencontré le travail du signe le plus proche de ses convictions et de ses fantasmes, ou, si l'on préfère, le plus éloigné des dégoûts, des irritations et des refus que suscite en lui la sémiocratie occidentale. Le signe japonais est fort: admirablement réglé, agencé, affiché, jamais naturalisé ou rationalisé. Le signe japonais est vide: son signifié fuit, point de dieu, de vérité, de morale *au fond* de ces signifiants qui régnent *sans contrepartie*.

> (the country of writing: of all the countries the author has known, Japan is the one where he found a working of the sign that is near-

est to his convictions and his fantasies, or, if one likes, the furthest away from the revulsions, irritations and rejections that the Western semiocracy arouses in him. The Japanse sign is strong: wonderfully regulated, constructed, and displayed, never naturalized or rationalized. The Japanese sign is empty: its signified flees, no god, no truth, no morality *at the bottom* of these signifiers which reign *without opposition*.)

In order to bring out the "mauvaise foi" and the authoritarian character of Western signs, Barthes puts them in juxtaposition to Japanese ones. In so doing, the author of *L'Empire* engages in the rather conventional practice of cultural critique, which uses other cultural patterns to reflect self-critically on one's own. In spite of Barthes's initial disclaimer that his intention is not to oppose East and West, throughout the book the two cultures are constantly being measured against each other, a textual strategy that is not without resemblance to the East/West dialogue in Malraux's *La Tentation de l'Occident*. Needless to say, in every bout, it is the home culture that takes a beating. When comparing the workings of the two languages, we are told that in Japanese (which Barthes does not speak at all), due to the proliferation of functional suffixes and the complexity of enclitics, the speaking subject functions like "une grande enveloppe vide de la parole" (12) (a great envelope empty of speech) (7), whereas his/her less fortunate French counterpart, shackled by the tyrannical rule of the signified, sees him/herself turned into "ce noyau plein qui est censé diriger [ses] phrases, de l'extérieur et du haut" (12) (a dense kernel which is supposed to direct [his/her] sentences, from outside and from above) (7). In the Barthesian axiology, "plein"[4] is one of those attributes consistently associated with the insufferable realm of immanence, an exclusive domain of the petite bourgeoisie as typified by the Poujades in whose world, Barthes tells us, "tout est ramené dans un ordre court, mais plein, sans fuite, celui du paiement" (*Mythologies* 96) (everything is restored to a brief but complete and airtight order, the order of payment) (*Eiffel Tower* 51).

In *L'Empire des signes*, this opposition "plein-vide" forms the basis of a series of binary pairs which structure Barthes's perception of the two cultures. Hence, when commenting on the relative merits or demerits of the two national eating habits, Barthes berates French food as being "accumulée, dignifiée, gonflée jusqu'au majestueux, liée à quelque opération de prestige, [elle] s'en va toujours vers le gros, le grand, l'abondant, le plantureux" (24) (heaped up, dignified, swollen to the majestic, linked to a certain operation of prestige, [it] always tends toward the heavy, the grand, the abundant, the copious) (15).[5] In contrast to this inordinately pretentious prodigality, Japanese culinary art, according to Barthes, "s'épanouit vers l'infinitésimal" (24) (tends towards the infinitesimal) (15). There, one no longer has to endure the thick and viscous "nappage"[6] so indispensable to Gallic cooking, as every item in the Japanese diet pertains to the realm "du léger, de l'aérien, de l'instantané, du fragile, du transparent, du frais, du rien" (36) (of the light, the aerial, of the instantaneous, the fragile, the transparent, the crisp, the trifling) (26). Indeed, in this empire where nothing is left to non-sign, even food consumption is to be experienced in semiological terms as Barthes observes at the end of the fragment on the Japanese meal:

> Ainsi la nourriture japonaise s'établit-elle dans un système réduit de la matière (du clair au divisible), dans un tremblement du signifiant: ce sont là les caractères élémentaires de l'écriture, établie sur une sorte de vacillation du langage, et telle apparaît bien la nourriture japonaise: une nourriture écrite.... (22)

> (Hence Japanese food establishes itself within a reduced system of substance (from the clear to the divisible), in a shimmer of the signifier: these are the elementary characters of the writing, established upon a kind of vacillation of language, and indeed this is what Japanese food appears to be: a written food....) (14)

If French cuisine fares so unfavorably in the empire of signs, Western theater seems to make an even worse impression there. In a series of articles originally written for the review *Théâtre populaire*,[7] Barthes diagnoses the numerous "maladies" in French dramaturgy which constantly succumbs to "les ravages épidémiques du mal vériste dans l'art bourgeois" (*Essais* 54) (the epidemic ravages of the veristic malady in bourgeois art) (42). With very rare exceptions such as the work of Bertolt Brecht or that of Adamov, Western dramatic art still finds itself ensnared in the trappings of its own dualist metaphysics of body and soul, cause and effect, agent and action, Destiny and man, God and creature. As a result, what we find in the West is, according to Barthes, a theater informed by "l'art psychologique [qui] est d'abord un art du secret" (*Essais* 75) (a psychological art [which] is above all an art of secrecy) (63). The situation is altogether different in the empire of signs, where the art of theater has reached a form that answers most closely to Barthes's own vision of the ideal "healthy" stagecraft. There, alibis and hysteria, the common ills of Western theater, are simply non-existent. What one finds instead, as illustrated by the Japanese puppet theater, the *Bunraku*, is a superb demonstration of the art of "distancing" as elaborated by Brecht:

> cette distance, le *Bunraku* fait comprendre comment elle peut fonctionner: par le discontinu des codes, par cette césure imposée aux différents traits de la représentation, en sorte que la copie élaborée

> sur la scène soit, non point détruite, mais comme brisée, striée, soustraite à la contagion métonymique de la voix et du geste, de l'âme et du corps, qui englue notre comédien. (70–71)
>
> (that distance is made explicit by *Bunraku*, which allows us to see how it can function: by the discontinuity of the codes, by this caesura imposed on the various features of representation, so that the copy elaborated on stage is not destroyed but somehow broken, striated, withdrawn from that metonymic contagion of voice and gesture, body and soul, which entraps our actors.) (54–55)

One of the reasons why Barthes is attracted to Japanese theater is that he finds its form very close to the Brechtian dramatic art that he so admires. Yet, Brecht, as we know, draws his inspiration for his notion of distancing from the Peking opera, in particular from the Chinese actor, Mei Lan-Fang, known for his repertory of female roles. Interestingly, Barthes, an aficionado of the dramatic art in its different forms, seems to have written little on Chinese theater. In 1955, he wrote an editorial[8] in the review *Théâtre populaire* for a special issue on the Peking Opera, which was touring Europe at the time. The text is relatively short and says very little about Chinese dramaturgy besides making the general point that it could serve as a lesson to Western theater. The issue includes a translation of an act from the famous play *Farewell My Concubine* and four articles, one of which was by Brecht on Chinese acting.

THE (M)OTHER WORLD

At one level, it is evident that *L'Empire des signes* continues the critical task of demystification started in *Les Mythologies* by presenting to the readers their mirror image in the form of "les mythologies heureuses." Yet, the use of an alien culture as a reflector to de-naturalize and demystify one's own, a practice which dates back to Montaigne, has itself become a mythic enterprise that, as Barthes is only too well aware, has already been re-appropriated by the doxa. What is then the new strategy? The alternative, Barthes suggests, is to engage in what he calls "une science du signifiant" which aims no longer at the analysis of the sign, but works at its "dislocation." *L'Empire des signes* can be said to be situated at the cusp of these two moments. While still retaining some of the early tactics of demystification, the text on Japan also marks the advent of the new "science du signifiant" as Barthes himself confirms in a discussion of his book with Bellour: "Lastly I must say that this essay is situated at a moment in my life during which I felt the need to enter completely into the signifier" (223). This swichting of tactics is elaborated in the article, "Changer l'objet lui-même," written a year after *L'Empire*:

> la science du signifiant ne peut que se déplacer et s'arrêter (provisoirement) plus loin: non plus à la dissociation (analytique) du signe, mais à la vacillation même: ce ne sont plus les mythes qu'il faut démasquer (la *doxa* s'en charge), c'est le signe lui-même qu'il faut ébranler: non pas révéler le sens (latent) d'un énoncé, d'un trait, d'un récit, mais fissurer la représentation même du sens, non pas changer ou purifier les symboles, mais contester le symbolique lui-même. (614–615)
>
> (the science of the signifier can only shift its place and stop (provisionally) further on—no longer at the (analytic) dissociation of the sign but at its very hesitation: it is no longer the myths which need to be unmasked (the doxa now takes care of that), it is the sign itself that must be shaken; the problem is not to reveal the (latent) meaning of an utterance, of a trait, of a narrative, but to fissure the very representation of meaning, is not to change or purify the symbols but to challenge the symbolic itself.) (166–167)

When confronting an opponent as formidable and impregnable as the bourgeois order itself, Barthes realized as far back as the 1950s that direct frontal attacks in the form of traditional contestations are of no avail. In fact, a few occasional oppositional outbursts here and there are not only tolerated, but encouraged by the system. A case in point is the avant-garde, which always enjoys the blessings of the very power it defies for the simple reason that "l'avant-garde, ce n'est au fond qu'un phénomène cathartique de plus, une sorte de vaccine destinée à inoculer un peu de subjectivité, un peu de liberté sous la croûte des valeurs bourgeoises" (*Essais* 81) (the avant-garde is in fact another cathartic phenomenon, a kind of vaccine intended to inject a little subjectivity, a little freedom under the crust of bourgeois values) (68). In order to effectively take on the bourgeois order, Barthes proposes the recourse to ruse, which aims not at destruction, but at confounding and beguiling the enemy, a strategy whose goal is "de déjouer le signifié, de déjouer la loi, de déjouer le père" (*Grain* 137) (to foil the signified, thwart the law, baffle the father) (145). The tactics used would include acts such as "tricher, dérober, subtiliser (dans les deux acceptions du mot: raffiner et faire disparaître une propriété), c'est-à-dire: à la rigueur parodier, mais encore mieux simuler" (*Grain* 114) (cheat, steal, refine—parody, if you must, but, better yet, counterfeit) (119).

These tactics frowned upon by the code of the Law of the Father as being "unmanly" and "dishonest" are highly prized in the empire of signs. One of the most important art forms in Japan, the haiku, functions precisely by parody and simulation. By its extreme simplicity, clarity and commonness of language, the haiku simulates to perfection the "readerly" as it seems to be totally accessible to our comprehension. Yet, what invariably baffles the Western readers is that, or so Barthes contends, "tout en étant intelligible, le haïku ne veut rien dire" (89) (while being quite intelligible, the haiku means nothing) (69). What attracts the author of *L'Empire* to this form of Japanese writing is that it achieves the exemption from meaning within a perfectly readerly discourse and without falling into the worst of meanings, that is, non-meaning:

> c'est une forme pour laquelle j'ai une admiration profonde; c'est-à-dire un désir profond. Si je m'imagine écrivant d'autres choses, maintenant, certaines seraient de l'ordre du haïku. Le haïku . . . se caractérise par sa matité. Il n'engendre pas de sens, mais, en même temps, il n'est pas dans le non-sens. (*Grain* 199–200)
>
> (I have a profound admiration, that is, a profound desire, for this form. If I imagine myself writing other things, some of them would be on the order of the haiku. The haiku . . . is characterized by its matteness. It engenders no sense, but at the same time it is not nonsense.) (211)

The discovery of the haiku had a lasting impact on Barthes's own writing, which increasingly favors the form of the fragment.[9] Not only is the fragment an essential part of Japanese culture as presented in *L'Empire des signes*, but the text itself is written in the form of fragments. From fragment to fragment, Barthes goes from one subject to the next without following any specific direction or development, thereby letting the text drift—or to use one of Barthes's own favorite expressions—"aller à la dérive." "La dérive" in Barthes, as Serge Doubrovsky points out, is a move that allows him to "form a habitation which would protect him against the constant threats of fixity (Norm, Ideology, and Stupidity)" (333).

Fixity[10] or, in Barthes's own word, the "figé" ou "fiché," is one of, if not the most, dreaded states of being that forever threatens him with castration. For fixity in the Barthesian axiology constitutes the quintessential character of the bourgeois monocentric and monotheistic ideology, a world completely "à huis clos" dominated by the Law, the Father posited as the Center, the ultimate Signified that puts a halt to all significance. The readers are by now familiar with the multifarious allomorphs of the Castrator: they are the *Doxa*, the stereotypes, the Same, the Universal Discourse, the Dissertation, the Natural, the *nappé*, the Last Word and so forth. All through his career, one of Barthes's major obsessions is to elude the grips of what he calls "le monstre de la Totalité" (*Roland Barthes* 182) (the monster of totality) (179). The fear that his ideas would, like the "nappage," thicken, set and take, prompts him to constantly distance himself from his former positions, especially if they are at risk of becoming fixities or fixations in the dominant discourse. Hence, the importance of constantly disengaging himself from his past associations and to embark on an endless displacement.

Against the threat of being "fixé," the best antidote, Barthes says, is the embracing of the "atopique" which he defines as "l'habitacle en dérive" (*Roland Barthes* 53) (of a drifting habitation) (49). In Barthes's writings, the "atopique" takes up myriad forms. It can be "le texte [qui], lui, est atopique, sinon dans sa consommation, du moins dans sa production" (*Plaisir du texte* 46) (the text [which] itself is atopic, if not in its consumption, at least in its production) (29). Or it can be "le *Neutre*, catégorie éthique qui vous est nécessaire pour lever la marque intolérable du sens affiché, du sens oppressif" (*Roland Barthes* 128) (the *Neutral*, an ethical category which is necessary to you in order to erase the intolerable scar of the paraded meaning, of the oppressive meaning) (124). Whatever guises it assumes, the important thing is that nobody and no language should have a permanent hold or power over others. Hence, Barthes's great fondness of the gaming metaphors (his favorite ones being "le jeu aux barres" [playing prisoner's base], "le jeu de la main chaude" [playing hand over hand] or "le jeu de la pierre, de la feuille et des ciseaux" [scissors, paper, stone]) or the metaphor of the onion which he describes as "feuilleté de peaux sans noyau" (*Roland Barthes* 54) (layers of skin without a core) (50). The common denominator in these images is the absence of a core, or a center conceived of as a position of mastery or Truth, which represents for Barthes the ideal situation where the last word is ajourned indefinitely.

In the empire of signs, the vying for control and mastery is conspicuously absent, since nowhere in the system can we locate a true center which, in the West, symbolises the site of primacy and power. Every aspect of Japanese life is characterized by a certain decenteredness. An example is the Japanese meal which is presented in such a way that: "Entièrement visuelle ... la nourriture dit par là qu'elle n'est pas profonde: la substance comestible est sans coeur précieux, sans force enfouie, sans secret vital: aucun plat japonais n'est pourvu d'un *centre*. (32) (Entirely visual ... food thereby says that it is not *deep*: the edible substance is without a precious heart, without a buried power, without a vital secret: no Japanese dish is endowed with a *center*) (22). Or again, one of the most interesting paradoxes encountered in the empire of the signs is the empty center. One of Barthes's often quoted examples is the city of Tokyo, which "possède bien un centre, mais ce centre est vide" (43–46) (does possess a center, but this center is empty) (30).

This decenteredness also comes to inform the writing as/of fragment in *L'Empire des signes*, which presents neither a fixed structure nor a central core. In fact, the order of the fragments can be easily inverted without thereby affecting the reading of the text, which displays the same reversibility as the Shikidai Gallery evoked by Barthes at the end of his book:

> dans le corridor, comme dans l'idéale maison japonaise, privé de meubles (ou aux meubles raréfiés), il n'y a aucun lieu qui désigne la moindre propriété: ni siège, ni lit, ni table d'où le corps puisse se constituer en sujet (ou maître) d'un espace: le centre est refusé.... Incentré, l'espace est aussi réversible: vous pouvez retourner le corridor de Shikidai et rien ne se passera, sinon une inversion sans conséquence du haut et du bas, de la droite et de la gauche: le contenu est congédié sans retour ... il n'y a rien à *saisir*. (146)
>
> (in the Shikidai gallery, as in the ideal Japanese house, stripped of furniture (or scantly furnished), there is no site which designates the slightest propriety in the strict sense of the word—ownership: neither seat nor bed nor table out of which the body might constitute itself as the subject (or master) of a space: the center is refused.... Uncentered, space is also reversible: you can turn the Shikidai gallery upside down and nothing would happen, except an inconsequential inversion of top and bottom, of right and left: the content is irretrievably dismissed ... there is nothing to *grasp*.) (108–110)

The decentered empire in Barthes's imaginary Japan from which the Master is vacated is permeated by the feminine, in particular the maternal. In *Reading in Detail*, Naomi Schor notes that, in the Japan of *L'Empire des signes*, "the detail reigns supreme" (88). And the detail which is traditionally associated with the ornamental and the everyday, pertains to, Schor reminds us, the realm of the feminine in the Western paradigm. A close reading of *L'Empire* shows that the maternal, indeed, infuses every aspect of Barthes's Japan. Confronted with a language which is totally incomprehensible to him, Barthes, instead of feeling alienated, derives the greatest pleasure from being thus wrapped in the "pellicule sonore" (17) (auditory film) (9) of the foreign tongue. The traveler not only finds himself "deliciously" protected like a child "contre la bêtise, la vulgarité, la vanité, la mondanité, la nationalité, la normalité" (17) (against stupidity, vulgarity, vanity, worldliness, nationality, normality) (9), but he is given a rare chance by his very incomprehension of the language to relive the pre-Oedipal semiotic[11] experience, which connects the infant directly to the mother without the intermediary of the Symbolic through the grasping of "la respiration, l'aération émotive, en un mot la pure signifiance" (17) (the respiration, the emotive aeration, in a word the pure significance) (9) of the unknown tongue.

Given the preeminence of the maternal in the empire of signs, it is then of little surprise that one finds in the text a dominance of fragments devoted to food (four out of twenty-six, equaling the number of fragments reserved for the haiku). For Barthes, food is closely linked to the mother: "En tant que fait culturel, la nourriture signifie au moins trois choses pour moi. D'abord, le prestige ou le goût du modèle maternel, la nourriture de la mère telle que celle-ci la fait et la conçoit: ça, c'est la nourriture que j'aime" (*Grain* 250) (As a cultural object, food means at least three things to me. First, the aura of the maternal model, nourishment as it is considered and prepared by the mother: that is the food I like) (265). In the food fragments, the maternal element figures prominently. Its presence is to be felt, we read, in the movement of the Japanese chopsticks in which Barthes notes "quelque chose de maternel, la retenue même, exactement mesurée, que l'on met à déplacer un enfant" (26) (something maternal, the same precisely measured care taken in moving a child) (16). These same chopsticks can also "[transformer] la matière préalablement divisée en nourriture d'oiseau et le riz en flot de lait; maternelle, elle conduit inlassablement le geste de la becquée" (27–28) (transform the previously divided substance into bird food and rice into a flow of milk; maternal, they tirelessly perform the gesture which creates the mouthful) (18). A few pages later, the maternal milk returns again in the creation of this most delicate dish: the *tempura,* which is prepared, we are told, in flour "délayée si légèrement qu'elle forme un lait, et non une pâte" (34) (diluted so lightly that it forms a milk and not a paste) (24).

The assimilation of the Mother to the Other continues to inform Barthes's later work. In his discussion of *La Chambre claire,* Richard Stamelman makes the same point when he states that, in his last book, Barthes "again deals with the relationship of self to other, but this time the other is a unique and significant being whose relationship to the self has determined its amorous relationship to all other human beings. This primal, originary other is the mother. She is the Other of others, the alpha and omega of alterity" (260). The motif of the Other as the site of the mother resurfaces again in the very last article Barthes wrote before his fatal accident, "On échoue toujours à parler de ce qu'on aime," in which he talks about Stendhal's love for Italy. That Barthes uses Stendhal's Italy as a mediating instance to speak of his Japan is quite obvious, since Barthes himself declares that "J'ai connu quelqu'un qui aimait le Japon comme Stendhal aimait l'Italie" (I knew someone who loved Japan just as Stendhal loved Italy) (33).[12] In his description of the Beylian passion for Italy, Barthes makes the following observation:

> Il y a dans l'amour d'un pays étranger une sorte de racisme à l'envers . . . pour Stendhal du mauvais côté, la France, c'est-à-dire la *patrie*—car c'est le lieu du Père—et du bon côté, l'Italie, c'est-à-dire la *matrie,* l'espace où sont réunies 'les Femmes.' (33)

> (There is in the love for a foreign country a kind of reversed racism . . . for Stendhal, the bad side is France, that is, the *fatherland*— for it is the place of the father—and the good side is Italy, that is, the *motherland,* the site where 'Women' gathered.)

This remark can aptly be applied to Barthes's own position vis-à-vis France, which he, too, perceives as the father-land, the realm of the Law, God, the Last Word where "the freeing of the signifier has been hampered for more than two thousand years by the development of a monotheistic theology" (Bellour 231). As opposed to France, "la patrie," Japan for Barthes, like Italy for Stendhal, is "la matrie," the space of the maternal and the feminine. And it is from the site of the (M)other that Barthes inaugurates the strategy of fissuring the Symbolic, the Order of the Father.

RETURNING (TO) ORIENTALISM

When commenting on Barthes's Oriental writings, critics often note the marked contrast between these texts and his early works such as *Les Mythologies*.[13] In her detailed discussion of Barthes's critique of colonial mythologies in *Barthes and Utopia*, Knight shows that in his readings of the exhibition "The Family of Man," the *Blue Guide* or the film *The Lost Continent*, Barthes is highly critical of the denial of history in these narratives. Yet, the same dehistoricization, critics argue, also informs Barthes's own relation to and image of the Orient which is, moreover, highly eroticized. In "Barthes and Orientalism," Knight contends that the sexual politics in his text on Morocco, *Incidents*, "tie Barthes to an Orientalism which he seeks, in other ways, to go beyond" (624). A critique along the same line has been formulated by Ross Chambers in "Pointless Stories, Storyless Points. Roland Barthes Between 'Soirées de Paris' and 'Incidents'." What appears most problematic to Chambers in his reading of the Moroccan text is the author's erasure of the colonial context as a condition for the emergence of his gayness.[14] In her discussion of *Alors la Chine?*, a short text Barthes wrote after his visit to China with the Tel Quel group, Lisa Lowe likewise discusses at great length what she sees as Barthes's change from being a critic to a practitioner of Orientalism: "The shift in Barthes's writing—from the targeting of orientalism as an object of criticism in the late 1950s to the dramatic practice of orientalism as a writing strategy in the mid-1970s—marks the changes of emphasis in his larger critical project during this period" (153).

It is no doubt true that, in his Oriental texts, Barthes seems to espouse positions he once denounced in other authors. One of the more obvious instances of such a reversal is that his text on Japan reproduces some of the problems he sees in Voltaire's Orient. As mentioned earlier, in "Le Dernier des écrivains heureux," Barthes faults the philosopher for transforming the historically dynamic Oriental countries into so many forms and mobile signs without actual content, humanity at degree zero. Yet, cannot the same be said of

Barthes when he presents Japan as the empire of empty signs? How are we to account for these contradictions? First, one should remember that Barthes is known to cultivate the art of paradoxa, which is a way for him to free himself of all doxa.[15] More profitably, one can also read Barthes's contradictions in the same way as he himself reads the contradictions in Gide to whom he feels a strong affiliation. Indeed, Barthes's earliest writings are devoted to Gide, and, in "Das Schaudern," he speaks at great length of the Gidian contradictions. In one section, Barthes describes how some people never change their positions while others do, but Gide chose a third way, which is the crossroad:

> Gide, lui, s'est tenu à un carrefour ... au carrefour ... par où passent les deux plus grandes routes d'Occident, la grecque et la chrétienne; il a préféré cette situation *totale* ... protégé par rien, mais aussi enfermé par rien, il a prêté à toutes les attaques, il s'est offert à tous les amours. (*Oeuvres complètes* 1: 27–28)

> (Gide stayed at a crossroad ... at the crossroad ... where pass the two greatest roads of the West, the Greek and the Christian; he preferred this *total* situation ... protected by nothing, but also enclosed by nothing, he lent himself to all sorts of attacks, he opened himself to all sorts of love.)

In his Orient, Barthes, too, is open to all sorts of attacks and all sorts of love: homosexual love, love of writing, love of the mother. Love today, Barthes says in his autobiographic text, is "transgression of transgression": "réintroduire dans le champ politico-sexuel ... *un brin de sentimentalité*: ne serait-ce pas *la dernière des transgressions*? ... Car enfin de compte ce serait l'*amour*: qui reviendrait: *mais à une autre place*" (*Roland Barthes* 70) (reintroducing into the politico-sexual field ... *a touch of sentimentality*: would that not be the *ultimate* transgression? ... For, after all, that would be *love*: which would return: *but in another place*) (65–66). Like his return to love, Barthes's return to Orientalism is one that comes back, but in another place. This return (or "retour" in French meaning both going back and turning over) is exemplified by the emergence of another writing of the Orient that renounces some of the time-honored Orientalist textual strategies.

In the decentered and reversible universe of the empire of signs where meaning is constantly prevented from melting, running, internalizing and deepening, "profundity," one of the most valued attributes of the signified in bourgeois ideology, is unceremoniously edged out to make place for the play of surfaces. In contrast to Western rhetoric, whose goal is to "disproportionner le signifiant et le signifié, soit en 'délayant' le second sous les flots bavards du premier, soit en 'approfondissant' la forme vers les régions implicites du contenu"

(99) (make signifier and signified disproportionate, either by 'diluting' the latter beneath the garrulous waves of the former, or by 'deepening' form toward the implicit regions of content) (75), the working of Zen thinking aims precisely at obtaining "un langage plat" (96) (a *flat* language) (74), a state of "*a-langage*" (97/75), characterized by a certain "matité" (matteness), "vacance d'adjectifs" (absence of adjectives). This flatness also characterizes the fabric of Japanese life, where everything is pure surface, pure appearance in the same manner as the Japanese eye which, Barthes recalls, is "plat . . . ni exorbité, ni renfoncé . . . il est la fente lisse d'une surface lisse . . . inscrit à même la peau" (134–35) (flat . . . neither exorbital nor shrunken . . . it is the smooth slit in a smooth surface . . . inscribed at the very level of the skin) (101–102).

In the absence of any hidden secret to be pierced, the Western ways of interpretation, whose ultimate goal lies in penetrating as deeply as possible beneath the surface in order to retrieve the Truth or decipher an enigma, are deemed here as simply impertinent in both senses of the term. Indeed, what is remarkable in *L'Empire des signes*, whose subject is the Orient, is the total absence in the text of the metaphor of penetration, the sina-qua-non of Orientalist literature as typified by Segalen's *René Leys*, whose narrator's all-consuming passion is to penetrate inside the Violet Forbidden City. On more than one occasion, Barthes openly criticizes such a gesture of domination by penetration as an atavistic trait of Western ideology. In *Alors la Chine?*, Barthes vehemently denounces this will to meaning so deeply ingrained in the intellectual tradition of the West:

> On part pour la Chine, muni de mille questions pressantes et, semble-t-il, naturelles: qu'en est-il, là-bas, de la sexualité, de la femme, de la famille, de la moralité . . . ? nous agitons l'arbre du savoir pour que la réponse tombe et que nous puissions revenir pourvus de ce qu'est notre principale nourriture intellectuelle: un secret déchiffré. (7)

> (We leave for China, armed with thousands of urgent and, it seems, natural questions: what about sexuality, woman, family, morality over there . . . ? We shake the tree of knowledge so that the answer will fall and that we could come back in possession of that which is our main intellectual sustenance: a deciphered secret.)

And should it turn out that there is no secret to be unveiled, one would have to be invented, for, Barthes continues, "Nous voulons qu'il y ait des choses impénétrables pour que nous puissions les pénétrer: par atavisme idéologique, nous sommes des êtres du déchiffrement, des sujets herméneutiques; nous croyons que notre tâche intellectuelle est toujours de découvrir un sens" (8) (We want impenetrable things so that we can penetrate them: by ideological atavism, we are creatures of decipherment, hermeneutic subjects: we consider it our intellectual task to always discover a meaning). Countering the hegemonic practice of domination through knowledge, *L'Empire des signes* reveals neither secret nor truth about the Other. As Ehrmann keenly observes, all the metaphors of the hidden secrets inviting penetration and denudation so prevalent in Western Orientalist literature are here replaced by the vertiginous play of surfaces:

> the eroticism of the signs is thus here, (contrary to a certain form of Westerm erotism of depth and penetration, which is supposed to bring out meaning and reach the remotest recesses of the conscience . . .) in Barthes's Japan, an eroticism of surfaces, that of the ink sowing the white page: scratch or caress . . . of the epiderm. (60)

Barthes's valorization of appearances and surfaces can be said to partake of the practice of seduction,[16] a strategy traditionally excluded from the realm of the Father as being "feminine," therefore "unmanly." The art of seduction, Jean Baudrillard contends, can most effectively challenge the Symbolic order dominated by the discourse of interpretation and meaning. Working with empty, arbitrary and non-discursive signs, the game of seduction (or seduction as game) privileges, Baudrillard writes, the "superficial," the "manifest," rather than the hidden meaning. As such, seduction, instead of seeking the truth which is the object of interpretation, plays with appearances: "Appearances not at all frivolous, but the site of a play and a stake, of a passion for diversion—seducing the signs themselves is more important than the emergence of any kind of truth" (78).

In the seductive space of the Barthesian text (or text as seductive space), one assists at an unending and euphoric dance of signifiers of "jeu-texte-écriture." In this universe of the "writerly," every trait or event functions according to Zen practice which, in its constant war against the prevarication of meaning (95), aims at creating "un *vide de parole*" (10) (*an emptiness of language*) (4). It is paradoxically from this emptiness of language that every aspect of Japanese culture is to be written: its gardens, its gestures, its houses, its flower arrangements, its faces, its violence (10/4).

Not only is "emptiness" the one trait that constitutes the foundation (or rather the absence of foundation) of the Barthesian Japan, where every event, from the trivial to the elevated, takes part in this "exercice du vide," but the text of *L'Empire des signes* is itself such an exercise of the empty. Indeed, there is no more apt description of our experience of reading this book than the one Barthes gives of the Japanese art of packaging, which is characterized by a considerable disproportion between the insignificance of the thing inside and the luxury of the envelope:

c'est dans l'enveloppe que semble s'investir le travail de la *confection* (du faire), mais par là même l'objet perd de son existence, il devient mirage: d'enveloppe en enveloppe, le signifié fuit, et lorsque enfin on le tient (il y a toujours un petit *quelque chose* dans le paquet), il apparaît insignifiant, dérisoire, vil: le plaisir, champ du signifiant, a été pris: le paquet n'est pas vide, mais vidé: trouver l'objet qui est dans le paquet ou le signifié qui est dans le signe, c'est le jeter. (61)

(it is in the envelope that the labor of the confection (of the making) seems to be invested, but thereby the object loses its existence, becomes a mirage: from envelope to envelope, the signified flees, and when you finally have it (there is always a little *something* in the package), it appears insignificant, laughable, vile: the pleasure, field of the signifier, has been taken: the package is not empty, but emptied: to find the object which is in the package or the signified which is in the sign is to discard it.) (46)

Likewise, the content or signified of *L'Empire des signes*, if one may call it so, is rather trite as opposed to the sumptuous writing displayed in the seemingly endless layers of fragments which, in the manner of intricate Japanese boxes, ensconce a pure "nothing" while creating a veritable "feuilleté de peaux sans noyau." Similar to the haiku Barthes so admires, some of his fragments offer the same quality of being "lisible" while resisting any commentary or interpretation that aims at uncovering a truth or assigning a meaning. To cite only one of the numerous examples in the text, the minute evocation of the Japanese cooked rice in the fragment, "L'Eau et le flocon" [Water and Flake], with its many fanciful details illustrates superbly the sort of graphic gesture written, to use Barthes's own expression, "*juste pour écrire*" (110) (*just to write*) (82), as it expresses neither the essence nor the meaning of the thing. What is left for us to appreciate is pure writing itself:

Le riz cuit ... ne peut se définir que par une contradiction de la matière; il est à la fois cohésif et détachable ... il est ce qui tombe, par opposition à ce qui flotte; il dispose dans le tableau une blancheur compacte, granuleuse ... et cependant friable: ce qui arrive sur la table, serré, collé, se défait, d'un coup de baguette, sans cependant jamais s'éparpiller, comme si la division n'opérait que pour produire encore une cohésion irréductible. (21)

(Cooked rice ... can be defined only by a contradiction of substance; it is at once cohesive and detachable ... it is what sinks, in opposition to what floats; it constitutes in the picture a compact whiteness, granular ... and yet friable: what comes to the table, dense and stuck together, comes undone at a touch of the chopsticks, though without ever scattering, as if division occurred only to produce still another irreducible cohesion.) (12–14)

As the example so convincingly shows, our inability to comment on Barthes's writing does not mean that it is uninteresting. Quite the contrary, like those "choses" in Francis Ponge, the Barthesian objects, which would hardly attract our attention in their normal setting, take on a most alluring appearance in the empire of signs. There, we see them as they have never been seen before. Yet the writing is such that it invites, if not a "no comment," then at most an admission of its "justesse," another trait of the haiku.

In several interviews, Barthes repeatedly states that his turn to Japanese culture is prompted by his deep dissatisfaction with his own society. To a certain extent, his Eastern quest is not unlike Segalen's, since both rest on the common theme of lack: we do not have what the cultural Other has. Yet the paradox here is that what Barthes desires in Japan, that which is lacking in the West, is precisely the "lack" itself, the figure of the Other par excellence in the empire of signs, where everything can be brought to "rien" (nothing) and "vide" (empty). In the history of Orientalism, the narrative of the Other as lack, as well as the lack of narrative of the Other, constitutes one of its central themes. For in the nineteenth-century Eurocentric conceptualization of the world, Dirlik reminds us, Europe used herself as the yardstick to measure other cultures which were assessed "not by what they had, but by what they lacked" (108). By promoting the figure of the Other as lack, Barthes does return (to) the Orientalist discourse in both senses of going back and reversing. In the Western narrative of development, what non-European countries lack has to be remedied by the politics of *mise-en-valeur*, which would eventually bring "prosperity and plenitude" to the underdeveloped peoples, a dream, we have seen, that Ma in Duras's *Un Barrage contre le Pacifique* tried to realize in Indochina among the impoverished peasants. In Barthes, on the contrary, absence and void is what he cherishes the most, absence of the ultimate Signified which he associates with the bourgeois order, the order that also founded the colonial empire. What we witness in *L'Empire des signes* is effectively a return to Orientalism, but at another place.

ANOTHER PLACE, ANOTHER BARTHES

In his reading of *Incidents*, Chambers explains what he sees as Barthes's inconsistencies in terms of a momentary slack in the latter's critical attention: "That there's an R. B. forgetful of Barthes's lesson doesn't mean, though, that critical intellectuals are hypocritical or lacking in self-knowledge. What it does mean is that vigilance has to be their stock-in-trade, and that such vigilance never needs to be exercised more carefully than when they are on vacation or taking time off" (29). Given his long-standing practice as critic of Western cultural productions, it is quite unlikely in my opinion that Barthes was not aware of the "controversial" nature of his Oriental texts when read within certain political parameters. In fact, Barthes broaches his own relation to the Orient "de biais" via his reading of Loti's *Aziyadé* in the preface he wrote for the Italian translation of the novel in 1971.

We have noted earlier that, in the first fragment of *L'Empire des signes*, Barthes takes care to distance his writing from a number of "langages connus" (known languages) of the Orient, one of which is precisely Loti. Yet, interestingly enough, the essay on Loti's Turkish novel, "Pierre Loti 'Aziyadé'," abounds in Barthes's own figures of the Orient: "rien" (nothing), "fuyant" (fugitive), "degré zéro de la notation" (notation degree zero), "creux" (absence), vide (empty) (173/108), "in-signifiant" (174) (in-significant) (109), "le sens rompu ... exempté" (175) (the meaning broken ... exempted) (110), "la dérive" (184) (drift) (118), and so forth. This rejection/attraction of Loti is, in fact, not unique to Barthes, but also informs the works of other French writers writing about the Other. In chapter two, we have seen the same ambiguity vis-à-vis Loti in Segalen. On the one hand, the author of *Essai sur l'exotisme* expresses his abhorrence for exotic literature à la Loti; on the other hand, he uses a parodied form of the Loti plot in his novel, *René Leys*. Duras has a similar duplicitous relation to the Loti exoticism. In *Un Barrage contre le Pacifique*, the narrator explains Ma's presence in Indochina as a result of her succumbing to the exotic lure, victim of the "ténébreuses lectures de Pierre Loti" (23). Yet, the love story between the young white girl and a native man in *L'Amant* is not without certain intertextual links with the exotic romance à la Loti. For example, the autobiographical narrator's foray into the chinatown to meet her lover certainly recalls lieutenant Loti's venturing into the Muslim district of Eyoub, where he can receive in secret his native mistress, Aziyadé.

While my concern here is not to explore the complex relationship these writers entertain with Loti, an amateur of the exotic they love to hate, I believe that Barthes's own rapport to Orientalism is mediated through his reading of Loti's *Aziyadé*. In the essay, he starts by situating the novel within French Orientalist literature, showing how the name of the eponymous character refers to other such Oriental names found in the works of a long line of Orientalist writers, starting with Hugo in *Orientales*, and, after him, other philhellene romantic poets. However, the intertextual positioning of the novel is immediately followed by the suggestion that one can broach Loti's work from another perspective: "Cependant, d'une autre région de la littérature, quelqu'un se lève et nous dit qu'il faut toujours *retourner* la déception d'un nom propre et faire ce retour le trajet d'un apprentissage" (170; emphasis in the text) (Yet, from another region of literature, someone comes and tells us that we must always *reverse* the disappointment of a proper name, making the reversal into the trajectory of an apprenticeship) (105; emphasis in the text). This "retournement" (which in French means among other things going back to, reversal and turning around) consists precisely of turning "l'image triste d'un roman démodé" (the pathetic image of an outdated novel) into a "*texte*: fragment du langage infini qui ne raconte rien mais où passe '*quelque chose d'inouï et de ténébreux*'" (171) (*text*: fragment of the infinite language which tells nothing but in which occurs '*something unheard-of and shadowy*') (106). In his ensuing discussion, Barthes shows that, under its old-fashioned looking crust, Loti's novel is in fact a very modern text.

Barthes's reading of *Aziyadé*[17] has been criticized by Bongie for its ahistoricism and a partiality that privileges only the journal aspect of the novel while leaving out the journal's ambivalent relation to "its uneasy complicity with the historical process of colonialism" and "its ideological (but increasingly untenable) identification of, and with, the realm of the exotic as a real alternative to the modern world" (86). According to Bongie, the journal occupies an inter-mediate space that is constituted by the state of tension it seeks to elude. While it is true that, in his essay, Barthes makes no explicit reference to the colonial history underlying the story of *Aziyadé*, he nevertheless is aware of the ternary situation Bongie mentions. For him, the tripartite elements are reflected in the triple identity of Loti he discusses in section two of the essay: lieutenant Loti (also known as Arif), a young man totally disillusioned with life who hopes to find an alternative to the modern world in an archaic Turkey; Julien Viaud, captain of the French navy, representative of France's imperial presence overseas; and Pierre Loti who occupies an inter-mediate position, between Loti/Arif and Viaud: "celui qui est et n'est pas son personnage, celui qui est et n'est pas l'auteur du livre" (171) (the one who is and is not his character, the one who is and is not the book's author) (106).

A more interesting point to be made here is that, through the rereading of *Aziyadé*, a novel reputed to be "démodé" precisely because of its trite Orientalist exotic plot, Barthes seeks to "retourner" (turn around) the equally old-fashioned Orientalist discourse that informs not only Loti's Turkish novel, but also any other texts about the Orient, including his own. He does so by exploring another kind of relation to the Other that would sidestep the dichotomy of the exotic Other and the colonial Same that Bongie elaborates in his reading of Loti's Turkish novel. Instead of the two-term dialectic, Barthes seeks another dialectic by discovering a third term, which is not a synthesis but a "*déport*: toute chose revient, mais elle revient comme Fiction, c'est-à-dire à un autre tour de la spirale" (*Roland Barthes* 73) (*translation*: everything comes back, but it comes back as Fiction, that is, at another turn of the spiral) (69). It is the search for a third term that prompts Barthes into privileging the inter-mediate text in the novel, that of the journal which is made up of in-significant incidents, given to drift (la dérive), unanchored from history. Barthes's practice of "désanchrage historique" in his reading of *Aziyadé* aims at skirting the traditional Orientalist paradigm, in which the Orient is posited as the contrastive term to the Occident, so as to arrive at something else: "Turc ou maghrébin, l'Orient n'est que la case d'un jeu, le terme marqué d'une alternative: l'Occident ou *autre chose*" (182) (Whether Turkish or Maghrebi, the Orient is merely a square on the board, the emphatic term of an alternative: the Occident or *something else*) (116).

My reading of Barthes through Barthes's own reading of Loti leads me back to Chambers's comment on the Moroccan text. Chambers's linking of Barthes's forgetfulness of history in *Incidents* to his being "on vacation" may turn out after all to be right on the mark in a sense perhaps slightly different from what was intended. The Orient for Barthes no longer represents the place of the Other, but rather *another* space, namely, the "vacational" space, the site of vacancy, a state closest to what he conceives perfection of relationship to be: "Il considère que la perfection d'un rapport humain tient à cette *vacance* de l'image" (*Roland Barthes* 47; emphasis added) (He finds the perfection of a human relationship in this *vacancy* of the image) (43; emphasis added). In this same fragment from his autobiographical text, Barthes cites precisely Morocco as the place where there is an absence of his image (or himself as image): "(Au Maroc, ils n'avaient visiblement de moi aucune image; l'effort que je faisais, en bon Occidental, pour être *ceci* ou *cela*, restait sans réponse: ni *ceci* ni *cela* m'était renvoyé sous la forme d'un bel adjectif)" (47) ((In Morocco, they evidently had no image of me; my efforts, as a good European, to be *this* or *that* received no reply: neither *this* nor *that* was returned in the form of a fine adjective)) (43). And it is from this (an)other space which is not the Other of the West that another Barthes emerges, a Barthes that is neither this nor that. This (an)other space bears, indeed, a certain resemblance to the "third space" that Bhabha describes as an "interstitial" space that "is sceptical of cultural totalization" and contains forms "of cultural identification, which subverted authority, not by claiming their total difference from it, but [because they] were able to actually use authorized images, and turn them against themselves to reveal a different history" ("Between Identities" 190).

To return to the question that was asked at the beginning of the chapter: is the text of Japan or Japan-as-text outside languages? The answer is yes, but a qualified one. We have noted that Barthes still has recourse to different Orientalist strategies and topoi ranging from dehistoricization to eroticization, yet these languages find themselves in the empire of signs "tournés" (gone bad or gone off as they say in British English) and "retournés." Rather than being outside, it may be more accurate to say that the text of Japan is beside or off the side of those "langages connus." Or, to use Barthes's own phraseology, the text of Japan is a text "avec son ombre" (with its shadow): "cette ombre, c'est *un peu* d'idéologie, *un peu* de représentation, *un peu* de sujet: fantômes, poches, traînées, nuages nécessaires: la subversion doit produire son propre *clair-obscur*" (*Plaisir* 53) (this shadow is *a bit* of ideology, *a bit* of representation, *a bit* of subject: ghosts, pockets, traces, necessary clouds: subversion must produce its own chiaroscuro) (32).

Conclusion

The rearticulation of the intertextual relations between metropolitan and colonial cultural productions that I have undertaken here not only challenges the center/margin, high/low hierarchy, but, more importantly, it also problematizes the facile dichotomy between the colonial Self and the exotic Other that colonial discourse critics frequently deploy in their discussions of the Western representation of non-European cultures. As my readings show, the Eastern works under study are still very much informed by Orientalist motifs, themes, and references as their authors continue to reproduce certain received Western ideas and images of the East, which has been successively aestheticized, dehistoricized, genderized and eroticized. Yet, in their engagements with the Other, these texts are also variously fissured with doubts and contradictions as other voices and the voices of the Other weave into their scriptural textures. The self that emerges from these works undergoes constant shifts and finds itself not infrequently "altered." As a result, the constructions of Self and Other, far from being fixed and unchanging, are beset with ambiguities and dissonances.

The work of Segalen unquestionably exemplifies in a most vivid manner the Babelic complexity of "Othering." We have seen how in *René Leys*, the distinction of inside/outside which is traditionally used to anchor the Self/Other divide falters as the two spaces are constantly shifting and switching places in such a way that, by the end of the novel, readers are at a loss to decide who is the insider and who the outsider. On one level, *Segalen* the narrator, as a non-Chinese living in China, is the outsider. Indeed, all through the story, he often positions himself as an external observer of Chinese culture. In the course of the narrative, the site he occupies most frequently is by the outer wall of the Forbidden City, the "In-site" into which he seeks entrance. Yet, as the narrative develops, the narrator reveals himself to be the inventor of René Leys's narrative of the inside.

In his Asian novels, Malraux seems initially to reproduce in a rather noncritical fashion the stereotypical views of the Chinese and the Mois as his representation of the Chinese culture relies heavily on Orientalist clichés and his portrayal of the Cambodian tribesmen in *La Voie royale* draws on the *images d'Epinal* Europeans have of "savages" or "primitives." Yet, the culturally monoglossic universe of the early works is shattered in his unfinished novel, *Le Règne du malin,* whose textual and generic dissonances not only pose a challenge to Western hegemony, but also open the text to the voices of the Other. More intricate still is the Self/Other relation in the Durassian universe. As a white Indochinese, Duras develops highly ambiguous relationships to both the colonial power and the colonized, a situation which is further complicated by class and gender factors. Her works also ceaselessly undermine the center/margins division as the different characters in her stories criss-cross the many social and racial barriers instituted by the colonial power to segregate and contain the native world. But it is in the decentered world of *L'Empire des signes* that we find the most innovative rethinking of the discourse of the Other. In the text on Japan, not only does Barthes reverse the hierarchical difference between Self and Other, but, more importantly, he deconstructs the hierarchical structure itself. In the empire of signs, binary pairs such as center/margin, high/low, top/bottom, right/left that usually frame our perception of Self and Other prove to be both ineffective and inconsequential.

The foregrounding of the voices of the Other in these Eastern texts helps to debunk a certain narrative of the "civilizing mission" according to which the colonized, being "backward" and "subservient," could only submit themselves to the influence and the will of the colonizers, whereas the colonizing culture is presented as an impregnable fortress totally impervious to other ways and values. What my readings show is that all cultures, be they dominating or dominated, have always already undergone mutual contamination upon contact. Notwithstanding the imbalance of power between colonized and colonizers, or East and West, when two peoples are brought into the presence of one another, they inevitably influence each other and bring about changes in their respective lives and cultures. In fact, a number of recent works in the field of colonial history re-establish important mutual affiliations and influences in many cultural formations in both the colonies and the metropole. For example, in *Masks of Conquest. Literary Study and British rule in India,* Gauri Viswanathan documents how nineteenth-century India served as "an experimental laboratory" for testing new educational ideas that could not be carried out in England. It was in India that English literature was instituted as a subject of curriculum before its re-importation back to the mother country. Likewise, the works of Stoler and McClintock, whose research has been conducted in the Dutch and British colonial fields respectively, demonstrate how European middle-class identity during the nineteenth century was constituted through the colonial experience. They further argue that colonies have served as "laboratories" for European modernity, and that the very notion of "Europeanness" finds its formulation and self-definition in Europe's rapport to its dominions. One last (but not the least, in scope and significance) example of the impact of the colonized culture on the metropole is the foundation of the sociology of Bourdieu which, as explicited in his *Outline of a Theory of Practice*, was grounded in his fieldwork in Algeria among the Kabyles.

This cross-cultural exchange, which no doubt took place (and continues to take place) under unequal terms, leads us to rethink notions such as "hybridity" or "*métissage*." In a great many post-colonial studies, there seems to be a presumption that hybridity is, for better or worse, solely the predicament of colonized and post-colonial subjects. Indeed, hybridity is presented as a sine-qua-non of postcoloniality that has been celebrated in the writings of Bhabha, Said, Maryse Condé, and Salman Rushdie among others. Yet my reading of four French authors shows that cultural mixing is a two-way street. As Dirlik argues, if there are "Westernized Chinese," there exist also "Orientalized Westerners" as well as "Orientalized Orientals." Hybridization has also affected the Western Other, albeit differently than the colonized and the post-colonial subjects. In Malraux's *La Condition humaine*, old Gisors is one such "Orientalized Westerner," not just because he married a Japanese woman and lived in China for the greater part of his life, but mainly because he was very much immersed in the local culture, even if the latter was perceived in Orientalist terms. As a "native" of Indochina, Duras claims openly for herself the status of *métisse*. In her autobiographical fiction, *L'Amant de la Chine du Nord*, the young protagonist is said to have "cette gracilité du corps [qui] la donnerait comme une métisse" (39) (her slenderness [which] suggests a half-caste) (29). In the case of Barthes, it is after his exposure to Japanese haiku that he seriously explores and adopts writing in fragments. Even Segalen, while condemning cultural mixing, not only creates the highly sinified character of René Leys, but incorporates a great many Chinese elements in his most important writings known as "le cycle chinois."

If language, as Bakhtin has it, is by its very nature heteroglossic, lying on the "bordeline between oneself and the other" (293), one would then want to question the politics of "Othering" as practiced in literary studies that institute as separate categories metropolitan, colonial, and post-colonial texts. In the field of French and Francophone studies, while the first and, increasingly, the last of the three groups occupy a great deal of critical attention, colonial literary and cultural productions remain "untoucheable." Post-colonial scholars occasionally point out the influence of metropolitan writers on their Francophone counterparts such as the impact of Lautréamont, Baudelaire, Mallarmé, Rimbaud, Claudel, Breton or Saint-John Perse on Léopold Senghor, Aimé Césaire and Edouard Glissant. Yet, there is very little discussion on the relation between colonial and post-colonial Francophone literatures.[1] Such a neglect is all the more perplexing given the fact that for historians the links between colonial and post-colonial histories are so evidently crucial. In Anglophone literatures, we also find post-colonial Anglophone writers refuting, reworking and re-accentuating British colonial literary texts. A case in point is Achebe whose *Things Fall Apart* is written as a counter-narrative to the colonial novels about Africa and Africans (in particular Joyce Cary's *Mister Johnson*).[2] In David Dabydeen's *The Intended*, there is a marvellous re-telling of the Conradian tale, *Heart of Darkness*.

In addition to the question of cultural mixing, colonial and post-colonial writings also share other common issues such as exile, migration, loss of identity, and alienation. To a large extent, while occurring at different historical moments, the Europeans who migrated to the colonies encountered problems similar to, albeit from a different perspective and position, those faced by those post-colonial subjects who undertook the reverse migratory movement to the metropole. And a great number of Europhonic post-colonial writers are, to use Rushdie's term, "migrants." More importantly still, both colonizers and post-colonials went through the one common experience of colonial rule from opposite sides. While it may not be to everyone's liking, cultural contamination is at the core of the colonial legacy to both colonizers and colonized. It is by practicing a heteroglossic reading of the cultural productions of these three overlapping spaces—metropolitan, colonial, and post-colonial—that one might begin to hear the voices of the Other in the hybridized selves of both (former) colonized and colonizers.

NOTES

Whenever available, standard translations are used; otherwise, all translations are mine.

INTRODUCTION

1. For a discussion of the question of the subaltern, see Gayatri Spivak, "Can the Subaltern Speak?" and Benita Parry, "Problems in Current Theories of Colonial Discourse."

2. For a discussion of the issue of languages in post-colonial studies, see Ngugi wa Thiong'o', *Decolonising the Mind: The Politics of Language in African Literature* and Aijaz Ahmad, *In Theory: Classes, Nations, Literatures*.

CHAPTER 1. READING OF THE ASIAN OTHER

1. The critical literature on the Western representation of non-Western regions produced in the Anglophone world is massive. Some of more recent titles are: on the Middle East and North Africa, Edward Said, *Culture and Imperialism*; Ali Behdad, *Belated Travelers: Orientalism in the Age of Colonial Dissolution*; Lisa Lowe, *Critical Terrains: French and British Orientalisms*. On sub-Saharan Africa, Abdul JanMohamed, *Manichean Aesthetics: The Politics of Literature in Colonial Africa*; Christopher Miller, *Blank Darkness: Africanist Discourse in French*; Patrick Brantlinger, *Rule of Darkness: British Literature and Imperialism, 1830–1914*. On India, Brantlinger's book; Jenny Sharpe, *Allegories of Empire: The Figure of Women in the Colonial Text*. On the Caribbeans, Peter Hulme, *Colonial Encounters: Europe and the Native Caribbean 1492–1797*.

2. One relatively recent study of Francophone Vietnamese writers is Jack Yeager, *The Vietnamese Novel in French*.

3. For a study of the importance of "chinoiseries" in European decorative arts, see Madeleine Jarry, *Chinoiserie: Chinese Influence on European Decorative Art 17th and 18th Centuries*; Oliver R. Impey, *Chinoiserie: the Impact of Oriental Styles on Western Art and Decoration*; and Dawn Jacobson, *Chinoiserie*.

4. In Flaubert's *Dictionnaire des idées reçues*, under the rubric "Japon," one reads "Tout y est en porcelaine" (Everything there is in porcelain).

5. For a discussion of the influence of Japanese art on European artists, see Colta Feller Ives, *The Great Wave: The Influence of Japanese Woodcuts on French Prints*; Lucille R. Webber, *Japanese Woodblock Prints: The Reciprocal Influence Between East and West*; Siegfried Wichmann, *Japonisme: Japanese Influence on Western Art in the 19th and 20th Centuries*; and Jacques Dufwa, *Winds from the East: A Study in the Art of Manet, Degas, Monet and Whistler 1856–86*.

6. For a detailed discussion and description of the 1931 colonial exhibition, see Herman Lebovics, *True France* and Panivong Norindr, *Phantasmatic Indochina*.

7. Several large format books reproducing the articles and illustrations of the periodical known as *Les Grands dossiers de l'Illustration* are now available. Each book is organized around a theme or a country; there is one on Indochina and one on China with numerous fascinating drawings and illustrations of anthropological, social, political and historical scenes.

8. As examples of this category of critical works, one can cite Gilbert Gadoffre, *Claudel et l'univers chinois*; François Trotet, *Henri Michaux, ou, la sagesse du vide*; Anne-Marie Grand, *Victor Segalen: le moi et l'expérience du vide* and Abdelkebir Khatibi, *Figures de l'étranger dans la littérature française*. One also finds the same kind of approach in the study of the role of the Orient in English-speaking writers. One example is Beongcheon Yu, *The Great Circle: American Writers and the Orient* which examines the religious and philosophical influence of China, Japan and India on writers such as Ralph Waldo Emerson, Henry Thoreau, Walt Whitman, Ernest Fenollosa, T.S. Eliot, and Ezra Pound.

9. For a detailed account of French colonial history, see the three-volume *Histoire de la France coloniale*.

10. For a detailed discussion of the status of Shanghai in the 1920s, see Nicholas Rowland Clifford, *Spoilt Children of Empire*.

11. See, for example, "Bichon chez les nègres" (70–73), "Grammaire africaine" (155–161), "La Grande famille des hommes" (195–198), and the discussion of *Paris-Match*'s picture of an African soldier saluting the French flag in "Le Mythe, aujourd'hui."

12. It is only quite recently that critical studies have taken up the colonial and exotic problematics within the Asian works of the authors I discuss here. Some of them are Yvonne Y. Hsieh, *Victor Segalen's Literary Encounter with China: Chinese Moulds, Western Thoughts* which examines Segalen's adaptation of Chinese material and his representation of China and her people and *From Occupation to Revolution: China through the Eyes of Loti, Claudel, Segalen, and Malraux (1895–1933)*; Chris Bongie, *Exotic Memories: Literature, Colonialism and the Fin de siècle* which includes a discussion of Segalen; Geoffrey Harris, *De l'Indochine au R. P. F.: une continuité politique* and *Malraux: A Reassessment* on Malraux; Lisa Lowe, *Critical Terrains* and Roger Célestin, *From Cannibals to Radicals*, each of which has a chapter on Barthes; Panivong Norindr, *Phantasmatic Indochina* which

looks at the Asian novels of Malraux and Duras; Martine Antle, "Panoptisme et bureaucratie coloniale dans *Un barrage contre le Pacifique*"; and Pascale Bécel, "*LeVice-Consul*: Colonial Mimicry and 'Partial Writing'" and "From *The Sea Wall* to *The Lover* Prostitution and Exotic Parody."

13. In *Exotisme et création*,Vincenette Maigne traces the lexicological genealogy of the term "exotic." While the word is in usage as early as 1548 in Rabelais's *Quart livre*, it was not included in the dictionaries until the late seventeenth century. In fact, it was listed for the first time in Furetière's *Dictionnaire universel* (1690).

14. Besides Malleret, see also the works of Marius-Ary Leblond and Roland Lebel for a detailed exposition of the tenets of colonial literature.

15. While not numerous, there is certainly more critical work on French colonial literature in France than in the United States. I list here some of the book-length studies on exotic and colonial literatures in the field.The earlier ones include Louis Cario and Charles Régismanset, *L'Exotisme-la littérature coloniale* (1911); Roland Lebel, *Etudes de littérature coloniale* (1929) and *Histoire de la littérature coloniale en France* (1931); Pierre Jourda, *L'Exotisme dans la littérature française depuis Chateaubriand*; Marius-Ary Leblond, *Après l'exotisme de Loti: le roman colonial* (1926); Louis Malleret, *L'Exotisme indochinois dans la littérature française depuis 1860* (1934); Eugène Pujarniscle, *Philoxène ou de la littérature coloniale* (1931); Pierre Martino, *L'Orient dans la littérature française au XVIIe et au XVIIIe siècle*; Raphaël Barquisseau, *L'Asie française et ses écrivains* (1947).The number of critical works during the years immediately following decolonization decreased while starting in the eighties there has been a resurgence of interest in colonial and exotic literatures in France. Aside from a few studies which appeared in the seventies such as Martine Astier Loutfi, *Littérature et colonialisme* (1971) and Hubert Gourdron et al. eds. *Roman colonial et idéologie coloniale en Algérie* (1974), most of the critical works appear in the last twenty years: Alain Calmes, *Le Roman colonial en Algérie avant 1914* (1984); Francis Affergan, *Exotisme et altérité* (1987); Patrick Laude, *Exotisme indochinois et poésie* (1990); Bernard Hue ed., *Indochine-Reflets littéraires* (1992); Jean-Marc Moura, *Lire l'exotisme* (1992); Denys Lombard ed., *Rêver l'Asie: exotisme et littérature coloniale aux Indes, en Indochine et en Insulinde* (1993);Alain Quella-Villéger, *Indochine: un rêve d'Asie* (1995); Alain Ruscio, *Amours coloniales* (1995); and Henri Copin, *L'Indochine dans la littérature française des années vingt à 1954* (1996). Critical work in English devoted to the study of French colonial and exotic literature has been quite scarce until recently. Some examples areWilliam Leonard Schwartz, *The Imaginative Interpretation of the Far East in Modern French Literature 1800–1925*;Alec Hargreaves, *The Colonial Experience in French Fiction*; and Hugh Ridley, *Images of Imperial Rule*. In the last ten years or so, inspired by Said's *Orientalism*, a number of studies (such as those by Miller, Lowe, Behdad, or Norindr) discuss the works of certain French canonical writers in the light of Orientalist or Africanist discourses.

16. Eugène Pujarniscle, himself a colonial novelist, speaks of the prejudice readers (probably referring to a metropolitan readership) conceive vis-à-vis colonial literature: "We should not let this error spread among the general public that colonial literature is an easy genre, a second-class literature" (172). Pujarniscle's remark is all the more sur-

prising given the fact that it was made in a book written in 1931, a period which witnessed the crowning of a number of colonial writers by the (then) prestigious Académie Française and the Académie Goncourt. For example, Claude Farrère's *Les Civilisés* (1905) and Henri Fauconnier's *Malaisie* (1930) were awarded the Prix Goncourt. Louis Bertrand, one of the founders of the Algerianist school, was elected to l'Académie Française in 1926 to replace Maurice Barrès.

17. This description comes from Martine Mathieu in her introduction to *Le Roman colonial*.

18. This occultation of the colonial past is found not only in literary studies, but in other domains as well. In his preface to Yves Benot's *Massacres coloniaux 1944–1950: la IVe République et la mise au pas des colonies françaises*, François Maspero notes the marginalizing of the history of the West's colonial expansion in general historical writings such as *L'Histoire de l'Europe* by Jean Carpentier and François Lebrun or *L'Histoire de la civilisation française* by Georges Duby et Robert Mandrou (V). A similar omission has also been observed in theoretical writings. In *Race and the Education of Desire*, Ann L. Stoler interrogates both the repression of the empire in Michel Foucault's *History of Sexuality* and the silence of Foucauldian scholars on this lacuna: "How do we reckon both the book's categorical effacement of colonialism and our overwhelming silence about Foucault's at once conventional and idiosyncratic handling of racism in it?" (viii).

19. For a discussion of the complex development of French colonial politics under the Third Republic, see Raoul Girardet.

20. One of the best known fictional female characters who was shipped to the colonies (in her case North America) is Manon Lescaut. Many of the communards were also exiled to the colonies after 1870. Louise Michel, for example, was deported to New Caledonia where she remained for eight years.

21. This suspicion is, in fact, mutual. The colonials were also highly critical of the metropolitans, in particular of their interference in colonial affairs of which they were totally ignorant. For a discussion and illustration of the conflictual relations between colonials and metropolitans, see Gilles de Gantès's doctoral thesis on the French presence in Indochina, chapter 2; and *L'Aile de feu* by Jeanne Leuba.

22. See Louis Althusser, "Ideology and Ideological State Apparatuses."

23. The debates surrounding the politics of assimilation exemplify the difficulty of definitively deciding what stands are pro- or anti-colonial. While the granting of French citizenship to even a limited number of "natives" who passed the "évolués" test was considered by many colonialists as too liberal and injurious to the settlers' interests, this same politics of assimilation was also strongly criticized by the colonized themselves. An illustrative instance of this is the Blum-Violette Bill in 1936, which was rejected by both the Algerian settlers as well as the Etoile nord-africaine under Messali Hadj's leadership. For details of the Blum-Violette bill, see John Ruedy, *Modern Algeria*, pp. 141–143.

24. The novels of Louis Bertrand, Robert Randau, Ernest Psichari, or Herbert Wild exemplify the colonialist position.

25. Boehmer's description of "colonial literature" seems to coincide with the position of Said who, in *Culture and Imperialism*, discusses at great length the relation of works by Jane Austin and Dickens to the empire.

26. For a detailed development of Said's idea of the "wordliness" of the texts, see his *The World, the Text, and the Critic*.

27. As examples of texts that make up the cultural baggage of the average French bourgeois, Barthes does cite *One Thousand and One Nights*.

28. Said's use of "American" or "European" as referring to some kind of monolithic essence may simplify the highly complex issue of cultural identities, especially in relation to minority American/European groups. Here I adopt the terms in the sense of "strategic essentialism" as defined by Spivak.

29. This inability to identity with the textual implied reader is notably shared by François Cheng, also a non-Western reader of French Orientalist texts. Commenting on Victor Segalen's Chinese works, Cheng asks: "Had it ever occurred to Segalen that he might be read by a Chinese reader?" (133–134).

30. I borrow the word "malestream" from Cornell West, *Prophetic Reflections: Notes on Race and Power in America*.

31. For a detailed discussion of the notion of "habitus," see Bourdieu, *Outline of a Theory of Practice*.

32. The nature of the relation of a post-colonial subject to the two cultures is determined by a great many factors such as his/her society, class, gender, education, and generation, as well as personal circumstances. Hence, one should be cautious of not typifying the experiences of post-colonial intellectuals functioning in the West, many of whom belong to the elite class in their own countries, and extending them to all their fellow compatriots back home. There is an excellent discussion of these issues in Ella Shohat and Robert Stam's analysis of colonial spectatorship in Eurocolonial cinema. In their study, they point out the multiple registers that constitute the spectatorship which is fashioned by the cinematic text, the technical apparatuses, the ambiant discourses and ideologies, as well as the multiple gender, race, nation, class and age identities and identifications of a given actual spectator.

33. This term "interpellate" is borrowed from the work of Althusser. For details, see "Ideology and Ideological State Apparatuses."

34. This cultural alienation of the colonized has been masterfully analyzed by Frantz Fanon in *Peau noire, masques blancs*.

35. This exclusion of women colonial and exotic works continues to inform even recent critical works. A few exceptions are Lowe's *Critical Terrains*, which devotes a chapter on the Tel Quel group and Julia Kristeva; Behdad's *Belated Travelers* which devotes one chapter on Isabelle Eberhardt and one on Lady Anne Blunt; and Norindr's *Phantasmatic Indochina*, which has a chapter on Duras.

36. For a discussion of the genderizing of colonial space, see Anne McClintock, *Imperial Leather*, in particular chapter I.

37. My own research on the presence of French women in the colonies also reveals that the literature promoting colonial female emigration lays a great stress on the civilizing influence of women in the colonies. See my article "Engendering French Colonial History: The Case of Indochina."

38. For a detailed discussion of heteroglossia, see Bakhtin, *The Dialogical Imagination*, in particular the essay entitled "Discourse of the Novel," and *Le Marxisme et la philosophie du langage*.

39. For critical discussions of the monolithic character of Said's Orientalism, see Dennis Porter, "Orientalism and its Problems"; Robert Young, *White Mythologies. Writing History and the West* in particular chapter 7 "Disorienting Orientalism"; Ahmad, *In Theory: Classes, Nations, Literatures*, in particular the chapter entitled "*Orientalism* and After"; and Behdad, *Belated Travelers*.

40. It would be productive to compare the colonial experience of Duras to that of Marie Cardinal who grew up in French Algeria. Like Duras, Cardinal also expresses ambivalent feelings towards France (especially in *Les Mots pour le dire, Au pays de mes racines,* and *Les Pieds-noirs*).

41. The expression is taken from Mary Louise Pratt in her *Imperial Eyes*.

CHAPTER 2. SEGALEN'S "QUEXOTIC" QUEST

1. Since there is no close English equivalent that can convey the polyvalent connotations of the word "Divers" whose meaning is quite far from that of "diverse" or "diversity," I decide to keep the French word.

2. For a detailed biography of Segalen, see Henry Bouillier, *Victor Segalen*.

3. For a listing of all Segalen's Chinese writings, see *Oeuvres complètes: cycle chinois, cycle archéologique et sinologique*.

4. For a detailed discussion of the tensions between colonialism and Segalen's exoticist project, see Bongie, in particular 110–118.

5. The Orphic myth is a salient intertext in Segalen's work as Orpheus represents for him "le comble de l'exotisme." The short story entitled, "Dans un monde sonore," for instance, written for *Mercure de France* in 1907, is a modern version of the Orphic myth, and he later collaborated with Debussy on the drafting of the opera *Orphée-Roi*. There is, as well, the critical study on the Orpheus-inspired paintings of Gustave Moreau, *Gustave Moreau, maître imagier de l'orphisme*. All these texts are assembled in volume I of Segalen's *Oeuvres complètes*.

6. Such a schizophrenic approach is hardly unique to Segalen. In fact, it is a conventional practice among a certain class of Western intellectuals to isolate a cultural tra-

dition which they genuinely appreciate from the people of that culture. Such is, for example, the attitude of the American poet, Ezra Pound, in whose work, as Shuhsi Kao points out, the Chinese reference is limited exclusively to Chinese classical civilization. Another example of such a separation of a cultural heritage from its people was cited by Wole Soyinka in his Nobel Laureate Address in which he recounted the encounter of the famous German Africanist, Leo Frobenius, with the artistic heritage of the Yoruba people (cf. in Gates 23–24).

7. Segalen undertook three archeological missions in 1909, 1914 and 1917. Out of these trips, he produced an important text on ancient Chinese sculptures, *Chine. La grande statuaire*.

8. What attracts Segalen's sensibility as an *exote* about the steles is not only their antiquity (the earliest ones dating back to the Chou dynasty circa 1000 B.C.), but also their imagined immutability that transcends all historical contingency. The steles owe this transcendance not simply to their stony materiality, but, more importantly, to the use of the "Wen" (a form of codified written Chinese) in the engraving of messages on the slabs: "Le style ne doit pas être ceci qu'on ne peut pas dire car ceci n'a point d'échos parmi les autres langages et ne saurait pas servir aux échanges quotidiens: le Wên. . . . Enchaînés par des lois claires comme la pensée ancienne et simples comme les nombres musicaux, les caractères pendent les uns aux autres, s'agrippent et s'engrainent dans un réseau irréversible, réfractaire même à celui qui l'a tissé. Sitôt incrustés dans la table—qu'ils pénétrent d'intelligence,—les voici, dépouillant les formes de la mouvante intelligence humaine, devenus pensées de la pierre dont ils prennent le grain" (*Stèles* 28) (The style of the inscription must be such that it cannot be mistaken for an ordinary language, for it has no echo among other languages and cannot be used for daily intercourse. It is called Wen. . . . Connected by laws as limpid as the thought of the ancients and as simple as musical numbers, the characters hang from each other, grip, and mesh in an irreversible network, refractory even to the man who wrought it. No sooner are they embedded in the slab—which they suffuse with intelligence—than lo! they slough off the forms of man's shifting intellect and become the thought of the stone whose grain they take) (n.pag.). Thus protected from all human fortuitousness, the steles serve as the perfect embodiment and embalment of the absolute Other.

9. The term "metanarrative" is not used in Jean-François Lyotard's sense of "grand récit," but in the narratological sense of a self-reflexive narrative as defined in Gerald Prince's *Dictionary of Narratology*.

10. This fascination with maps as a metaphor of possession and control of the Other is a common motif in Western colonial literature. For example, Conrad's Marlow admits to having "a passion for maps" (20), while Malraux's Claude spends the long hours in the ship cabin staring at maps.

11. In "Mémoires de pierre, la structure intertextuelle de *Stèles*," Lina Zecchi gives an excellent analysis of Segalen's use of the apophatic technique.

12. In "Textual Analysis of a Tale of Poe," Barthes states the importance of proper names: "A proper name should always be examined carefully, for the proper name is, one might say, the prince of signifiers, its connotations are rich, social and symbolic" (88).

13. In many respects, the character of Leys is amazingly similar to that of Kipling's Kim who, born of Irish parents but totally assimilated into Indian culture, is given the role of mediator between the British and the Indians.

14. It may be of interest to point out here that Segalen more than once alludes to the homosexual penchant of Maurice Roy, the real life counterpart of René Leys. In *Annales secrètes d'après Maurice Roy*, Segalen suggests that Roy served as "mignon" to Kouang-Siu to explain the former's access to the Palace (*Oeuvres complètes* vol. 2 577).

15. For a discussion of the doubling process in *René Leys*, see Marc Gontard, *Victor Segalen: Une esthétique de la différence* and Gérard Macé, *Ex libris*.

16. This play on "exhôte" and "exote" is taken from Cheng's "Espace réel et espace mythique."

17. In "La Nature des pronoms," Emile Benveniste argues that the main difference between, on the one hand, the first and second person pronouns, and, on the other, the third person pronoun, is that the latter indicates a "non person" (256).

18. Paul Féval, Père (1817–1887) is an author of the genre "roman populaire," who wrote *Les Mystères de Londres* (1844) and *Bossu* (1858).

19. Loti was, in fact, in Peking right after the sacking of the Forbidden City by Western powers during the 1900 Boxer rebellion. He wrote *Les Derniers jours de Pékin* (1902) which is based on his stay in the Chinese capital.

CHAPTER 3. THE OTHER IN MALRAUX'S HUMANISM

1. The First World War had also changed the relation between the metropole and her dominions when the latter were called upon to send men and resources in the defense of the "motherland" against the Axis powers.

2. In the 1910s, the Third Republic introduced in elementary schools illustrated readers that praised the "good work" of the French in the colonies. In the 1920s, the coverage of colonial history increased to twenty five percent of the history curriculum at the secondary level. For details, see *Histoire de la France coloniale*, vol. 2 and Dominique Maingueneau, *Les Livres d'école de la République 1870–1914*.

3. Besides the "presse coloniale," which was exclusively devoted to colonial news, from 1910 onwards, even the mainstream publications, such as *La Revue des deux mondes*, *Le Journal des débats* or *Le Temps*, increased their coverage of colonial questions. The 1920s saw the production of numerous colonial movies, including the highly popular *L'Atlantide* by Jacques Feyder, and beginning in the 1930, there were weekly broadcasts of radio talks on colonial issues. For details, see *Histoire de la France coloniale*, vol. 2.

4. André Gide in *Voyage au Congo* (1927) and *Retour du Tchad* (1928) and Louis-Ferdinand Céline in *Voyage au bout de la nuit* (1932) are among those who wrote critically about the colonial system.

5. See Robert Aldrich, *Greater France: A History of French Overseas Expansion*.

6. In "Sources et genèse de l'oeuvre" of *Le Règne du malin*, Jean-Claude Larrat notes that, while it is not possible to date in a precise way the composition of this unfinished novel, different sources indicate that Malraux had been working on the book since the 1920s and continued the project all through the 1930s.

7. Besides his biographers, such as Jean Lacouture, the critics who discuss Malraux's novels in relation to colonial politics at great length are Geoffrey Harris, *De l'Indochine au R. P. F.: une continuité politique* and Norindr.

8. A few examples of these critical studies are Jeanne Delhomme, *Temps et destin*; Edward Gannon, *The Honor of Being a Man: The World of André Malraux*; Charles D. Blend, *André Malraux: Tragic Humanist*; Joseph Hoffmann, *L'Humanisme de Malraux*; Gerda Blumenthal, *André Malraux: The Conquest of Dread* and Violet M. Horvath, *André Malraux. The Human Adventure*.

9. Besides the famous essay of Leon Trotsky on *Les Conquérants*, examples of such critical studies are Lucien Goldmann's *Pour une sociologie du roman*, James Greenlee's *Malraux's Heroes and History*, and the works by Harris.

10. An example of this reading is Walter G. Langlois, "André Malraux and the Cultural Lessons of Asia."

11. Examples of this aesthetic reading of the Asian reference in Malaux are Tadao Takemoto, *André Malraux et la cascade de Nachi: la confidence de l'univers* and Michel Temman, *Le Japon d'André Malraux*.

12. Malraux does not indicate the time this conversation took place, but Roger Stéphane states in *Malraux* that the two authors met probably in the spring of 1928 (28 n.).

13. Much ink has been spilled concerning the reasons for Malraux's first Indochinese trip. While his detractors put financial gain (projected sale of the Khmer statues in the West) as among his primary motives, his exegetes focus more strongly on loftier causes such as his aesthetic and intellectual interest in Asian cultures. Most of his biographers devote at least one chapter to his Indochinese adventure. For detailed documentation, see the works of Langlois, Vandegans, Lacouture, Clara Malraux, and Axel Madsen.

14. The expression is from Jean-René Bourrel's article, "L'Exotisme dans l'oeuvre d'André Malraux," which lists as Malraux's Orientalist sources the works of Claudel, Loti, Segalen, Arthur Gobineau, St. John Perse as well as *Le Botin de l'étranger, Journal des voyages*, various colonial reviews and travel narratives by Marco Polo (108–110). Another book that deals with the same subject is that of Vandegans.

15. The representation of the Oriental world as frozen in time has itself a long genealogy in the European vision of the East. In her survey of the representation of

India in the West, Catherine Weinberger-Thomas traces the trajectory of this vision back to the eighteenth century: "Immutability, stagnation, impermeability to history: these flaws of Indian society . . . before being denounced by Marx who read Hegel, were already found in the arguments of Montesquieu speaking on the despotic principle of government" (24).

16. Some of the postwar French intellectuals who sought spiritual inspiration from Eastern religions or philosophies are Romain Rolland, Jean Grenier, and Jean Paulhan, who was editor of *La Nouvelle Revue Française* in the 1920s.

17. For detailed accounts of Malraux's political activities in Indochina narrated from two different perspectives, see Langlois, *André Malraux: The Indochina Adventure* and Harris, *De l'Indochine au R.P.F.*

18. See Christiane Moatti, "Le Motif du Japon," Takemoto, and Temman.

19. René Caillié, born in 1799, set sail for Senegal on the Méduse in 1816. Having survived shipwreck, he became in 1828 the first Frenchman to visit Tombouctou.

20. Camille Douls disguised himself as a Muslim (learning Arabic, studying the Koran and being circumcised) in order to live among the Moors in Sahara in the 1880s.

21. An example is the *Inventaire*, which Claude consults several times for information on the statues. This is, in fact, the *Inventaire descriptif des monuments du Cambodge*, established by E. Lunet de Lajonquière under the commission of l'Ecole française d'Extrême-Orient in 1907 and 1908. For more details, see "Aux sources de *La Voie royale*" in Malraux, *Oeuvres complètes*, vol. 1.

22. I discuss in detail the parasitic relation of the adventurers to the colonial order in "Reading the Colonial in Malraux's Asian Novels."

23. The idea of knowledge or claim to knowledge as a form of or justification for power and control has been developed at great length by Foucault, especially in *Power/Knowledge. Selected Interviews and Other Writings. 1972–1977*. This complicity between knowledge and control is especially rampant in colonial situations as Chinua Achebe points out in his article "Colonialist Criticism": "To the colonialist mind it was always of the utmost importance to be able to say: 'I know my natives,' a claim which implied two things at once: (a) that the native was really quite simple and (b) that understanding him and controlling him went hand in hand—understanding being a precondition for control and control constututing adequate proof of understanding—" (7). In *Orientalism*, one of Said's main theses is precisely how knowing the Orient confers upon Europe her right of control and domination.

24. In *Spoilt Children of Empire: Westerners in Shanghai and the Chinese Revolution of the 1920s*, Nicholas Clifford gives a detailed account of the events leading to the Shanghai insurrection that constitutes the main action of *La Condition humaine*. In a footnote, Clifford offers an interesting comment on Malraux's casting European characters as leaders of the insurrection: "Malraux's account diminishes the Chinese role: the Franco-Japanese Kyo Gisors and the Russian Katov lead the Communist forces in Shanghai, the

French banker Ferral negotiates Chinese loans to the Guomindang, and Chiang's European police chief Konig takes charge of the repression. In his suggestion that the Chinese were followers, not leaders, apparently by themselves capable of neither revolution nor counter-revolution, Malraux incongruously reflects a common Western view of the day" (327). In her *From Occupation to Revolution*, Hsieh also discusses the problematic representation of the role of the Chinese in the revolution in *Les Conquérants* and *La Condition humaine*.

25. In his portrayal of the Chinese scholar, Tcheng-Daï, as a selfish and obtuse old man, Malraux merely reproduces the colonial stereotyping of those native intellectuals who resisted Western hegemony. One finds the same criticism of Annamite intellectuals as living in an obsolete world in Malleret's survey of French Indochinese literature (102).

26. See my article, "The Cultural Other in Malraux's Asian Novels."

27. This mental and cultural transplantation which Malraux's European protagonists bring to the Chinese was a very common colonial practice as Jean-Paul Sartre explains in his preface to Fanon's *The Wretched of the Earth*: "The European elite undertook to manufacture a native elite. They picked out promising adolescents; they branded them, as with a red-hot iron, with the principles of Western culture; they stuffed their mouths full with high-sounding phrases, grand glutinous words that stuck to the teeth ... these walking lies had nothing left to say to their brothers; they only echoed. Indeed, Europe could believe in her mission; she had hellenized the Asians; she had created a new breed, the Greco-Latin Negroes" (7).

28. The comparison I draw between Malraux and Pascal is not fortuitous as it is well known that Malraux was a great admirer of the author of *Les Pensées*.

29. The strategy of turning the Other into one's own foil for the sake of self-glorification can be read as an instance of what Spivak calls the "epistemic violence of imperialism." In her article, "Three Women's Texts and a Critique of Imperialism," Spivak analyzes Charlotte Brontë's *Jane Eyre* to the effect that Bertha (Rochester's creole wife) is made "to act out the transformation of her 'self' into that fictive Other, set fire to the house and kill herself, so that Jane Eyre can become the feminist individualist heroine of British fiction" (215). In other words, the epistemic violence of imperialism entails "the construction of a self-immolating colonial subject for the glorification of the social mission of the colonizer" (251).

30. In his evocation of the Cambodian jungle and its dangers, Malraux reproduces a great many of the topoi of Indochinese colonial adventure stories as laid out by Malleret in his survey of Indochinese colonial literature (68–69). For further discussion of the role of the jungle in colonial adventure narratives, see Catherine Champion, "L'Imaginaire tropical: le paysage indien dans les romans populaires français, 1860–1920."

31. It would be interesting to compare Clara Malraux's narrative of the Banteaï-Sre excursion in her *Nos vingt ans* to Malraux's fictionalized version of the same trip in

La Voie royale. Clara Malraux never once mentions the Mois, whose diabolization plays such an important role in Perken and Claude's metaphysical epic.

32. In *Antimémoires,* Malraux twice evokes the link between the two characters: "I have not forgotten David de Mayrena, whose legend, very much alive in the Indochina of the 1920s, is in part at the origin of *La Voie royale*" (303) and "in many respects, the character of Perken came out of Mayrena" (359).

33. Besides the different sources on real life Mayrena that Larrat gives in the Pléiade, Gerald Hickey also provides useful information on him in *Sons of the Mountain* and *Kingdom in the Morning Mist.*

34. Malraux did publish sections of the novel in the different editions of *Antimémoires.* In *Oeuvres complètes III,* Larrat provides a detailed table that indicates the editions of *Antimémoires* in which parts of *Le Règne du malin* have appeared.

35. Even physically, Mayrena shares a certain resemblance with the Cervantesque knight: they are both bearded and very tall with long limbs. On a few occasions in the narrative, Malraux shows his character in a typically Quixotic pose with his silhouette projected against the starry night sky: "Mayrena était debout le long du bastingage de gauche, la barbe sur fond d'étoiles" (Mayrena was standing along the left ship rail, his beard against the stars) (998) and "Au-dessus des têtes, le grand bras de Mayrena monta vers les étoiles" (Above their heads, Mayrena's long arm rose towards the stars) (1000).

36. Larrat points out that Malraux consulted a great many ethnographic works on the Mois in writing the novel.

CHAPTER 4. DURAS ON THE MARGINS

1. During the colonial era, the French settlers in Indochina used to refer to themselves as Indochinese and the locals as Annamites.

2. The book is briefly discussed in Vircondelet's biography of Duras and James Williams, *Erotics of Passage.* It is mentioned in the "Repères biographiques" (294) in Christiane Blot-Labarrère, *Marguerite Duras.* A detailed account of the circumstances under which the book was written is to be found in Laure Adler's excellent biography on Duras (see in particular 135–140). According to Adler, the book was commissioned by Georges Mandel, then minister of the colonies, in his efforts to propagandize the nation's imperial achievements. The book's co-author, Philippe Roques, was Duras's immediate supervisor in the ministry of colonies, a trusted collaborator of Mandel. In her biography, Adler notes that in later years, Duras tried very hard to "'forget' this book and deliberately omit it from all her bibliographies. She did not like . . . to be reminded of its existence" (139).

3. For a good summary of the major critical trends in recent Durassian scholarship, see chapter one of Williams, *Erotics of Passage.*

4. This information is taken from Vircondelet's biography of Duras.

5. There exits an abundant literature by former settlers who write nostalgically about the colonial "good old days" after their return to the metropole. Besides *L'Empire français*, another example is *Notre Indochine* by Antoine and Madeleine Jay. More interesting still is Cardinal's *Pieds-noirs* in which the author evokes not only her own idyllic *Pied-noir* childhood in Algeria, but also a romanticized history of the whole *Pied-noir* community. See my article on Cardinal and Algeria.

6. Marie Legrand arrived in Indochina in 1905, probably to accompany her first husband, a certain Mr. Obscur, who died in 1907. She then met Henri Donnadieu, a widow with two children. The two married in the colony in 1909. Duras mentions her mother's first husband very briefly in both *L'Amant* (113) and *L'Amant de la Chine du Nord* (164). In her biography on Duras, Adler provides very interesting information on Mme Donnadieu and her life in Indochina, in particular, the episode of the Chinese lover. For information on the history of colonial settlement of women, see my article "Engendering French Colonial History: The Case of Indochina."

7. In "L'Imaginaire tropical: le paysage indien dans les romans populaires français, 1860–1920," Champion notes that, in the Western imaginary, bananas have been for a long time perceived as the fruit of paradise (114).

8. Terms such as "colonialists" and "colonizers" used here are borrowed from Albert Memmi's work, *The Colonizer and the Colonized*. Memmi defines the colonialists as those colonials who wholeheartedly support the colonial system, whereas the "colonizer" refers to the colonial who does not embrace the colonial ideology.

9. For a personal account of the horrendous condition in the rubber plantations in Indochina, see the autobiography of Tran Tu Bing, *The Red Earth*.

10. For a critical analysis of Malraux's political activities in Indochina, see Harris.

11. The maintenance of social hierarchy among whites is, in fact, much more stringent in the colonies than in the metropole. For details, see my article "Engendering French Colonial History."

12. Historically, as early as in the 1880's, the Indochinese peasants already joined the scholar-gentry in their fight against the French. For details, see David G. Marr, *Vietnamese Anti-colonialism 1885–1925* and Joseph Buttinger, *Viet-Nam: A Political History*. For a history of French expropriation of Vietnamese peasants, see Ngô Vinh Long, *Before the Revolution: The Vietnamese Peasants Under the French*.

13. It would be interesting to compare Ma to Isak Dinesen in *Out of Africa* in which the narrator plays the same role of protector of the natives on her Kenyan farm.

14. In *L'Amant de la Chine du Nord*, the Chinese lover told the narrator of his relations with white women in Paris (145).

15. The notion of the "seme" used here has been introduced by Barthes in *S/Z* as one of the five codes which govern our reading of a text. The function of the semic code is to create semantic units on the basis of literary models and cultural stereotypes.

16. For an analysis of the importance of the rhetorical convention based on the commanding view and the panoramic vista in colonial and travel writings, see Pratt, *Imperial Eyes* and David Spurr, *The Rhetoric of Empire*.

17. In *Narratologie*, Mieke Bal gives an interesting analysis of this same passage in terms of the "grillage" and distancing motifs.

18. See Foucault, *Madness and Civilization*.

19. In *Welcome Unreason*, Raynalle Udris points out the effect the Indians have on the Europeans in *Le Vice-Consul* for whom the former "represent a silent, passive, almost occult threat . . . their number, inconceivable for an Occidental mind, carries in its very indifferentiation the threat of its inhumanity. The only way the natives can be apprehended is therefore through abstraction as 'la horde dolente' or 'le nid de fourmis'" (98). In this portrayal of the horrors of India or India as horror, Duras in fact reproduces a certain Orientalist image of India established by a long line of travel narratives that revel in detailed accounts of horrific Indian practices. For details, see Weinberger-Thomas.

20. One of the early critics who has extensively analysed this aspect of the Vice-Consul is Marcelle Marini in her *Territoires du féminin*.

21. Colonial societies tend to turn a blind eye to concubinage between white men and native women, in particular during the period when white women were not allowed to accompany their husbands to the imperial outposts. In fact, an exotic romance involving a European man and a native woman is a sine-qua-non element in many colonial novels as exemplified by the work of Loti.

22. See Norindr for a discussion of these *errances* in *L'Amant*.

23. See, for example, Catherine Rodgers, "Déconstruction de la masculinité dans l'oeuvre durassienne."

24. Germaine Brée, "A Singular Adventure."

25. See Hélène Cixous and Michel Foucault, "A propos de Marguerte Duras" and Danielle Bajomée, "Duras et le désir d'éternité."

26. See Aliette Armel, "La Force magique de l'ombre interne."

27. In "Le Corps et le texte," Madeleine Borgomano investigates "the relations of the body with the text and of the text with the body in the Durassian work" (49). Her thesis is that writing for Duras is "un acte du corps" (an act of the body) (50). See also Marini, "L'Autre corps."

28. Lol V. Stein and Anne-Marie Stretter are the other two characters also associated with the Durassian "lieu de l'écrit."

29. See Benveniste, "La Nature des pronoms."

30. The term "Durasie" is from Claude Roy.

31. See Trista Selous, *The Other Woman*.

32. In *L'Amant*, Duras speaks of the fear that the mad woman of Vinh-Long causes her as a child. The mad woman is one of the many incarnations of the beggar woman in *Le Vice-consul*. For a detailed discussion of the genesis of the "mendiante," see Borgomano, "L'Histoire de la mendiante indienne."

33. For a discussion of the geographical metaphors of writing, see Rosello's article and Borgomano, *Une Lecture des fantasmes*.

34. For a detailed discussion of the situation of Vietnamese women during the French rule, see Paul Grace et al., eds., *Vietnamese Women in Society and Revolution 1. The French Colonial Period*. Their plight has also been represented in fictional works such as Nguyen Hong, *Days of Childhood* and Ngo Tat To, *Quand la lampe s'éteint*.

CHAPTER 5. ANOTHER BARTHES

1. Besides their opposing stands vis-à-vis the De Gaulle government, Barthes is quite critical of the reforms Malraux made in the national theaters. For details, see his "Tragédie et hauteur" in *Lettres nouvelles* April 22 1959, reprinted in volume one of *Oeuvres complètes* (814–815).

2. For a discussion of culturalism, see Dirlik, *The Postcolonial Aura* and chapter two in this book.

3. On more than one occasion, Barthes himself relates his "mythologue" practice to the work of the eighteenth-century philosophers. For example, in an interview with *L'Express* in 1970 after the publication of *Empire*, he explicitly refers to Voltaire as one of his precursors in his contestation of what he calls "the naturalness of the sign": "c'est un très vieux combat dont certaines formes paraissent maintenant un peu archaïques, mais au XVIIIe siècle, qui a eu l'idée de relativiser les croyances de la France de l'époque en les comparant à celles des Chinois, des Persans, des Hurons, des gens comme Voltaire les menaient déjà" (*Grain* 95) (this struggle is an old story, and some of the forms it has taken may seem a bit archaic now, but in the eighteenth century people like Voltaire were already fighting away, trying to 'relativize' contemporary French beliefs by comparing them to those of the Chinese, Persians, Hurons, and so forth) (98). It is interesting to recall that in the article "Le Dernier des écrivains heureux," Barthes is much more critical of Voltaire's stereotyping the Other in his tales.

4. The phobia for the "plein" runs through Barthes's work in which fullness is linked to everything he dislikes, as he explains to Guy Scarpetta in "Digressions": "Tout d'abord, ce que nous abhorrons dans le *plein*, ce n'est pas seulement l'image d'une substance ultime, d'une compacité indissociable; c'est aussi et surtout (du moins pour moi) une *mauvaise forme*: le plein, c'est, subjectivement le souvenir (le passé, le Père), névrotiquement la répétition, socialement le stéréotype (il fleurit dans la culture dite de masse, dans cette civilisation endoxale, qui est la nôtre)" (*Grain* 112–113) (To begin with, what is abhorrent in *fullness* is not only the image of an ultimate substance, an indissoluble compactness; it is also and above all (at least to my mind) a *bad form*: subjectively, fullness

is remembrance (the past, the Father), while its neurotic form is repetition, and its social form is stereotype (flourishing in so-called mass culture, in this endoxal civilization of ours)) (117–118).

5. Barthes already criticizes the pretentiousness of French cooking in "Cuisine ornementale" in *Mythologies* (144–146).

6. "Nappage" and its related term "nappé" are some of the numerous culinary metaphors which Barthes routinely uses to spice up his writings. In contrast to Barthes "the individual" who, according to Louis-Jean Calvet's biography *Roland Barthes*, adores any dish prepared with a sauce coating, Barthes "l'écrivain" abhors the "nappé" in writing. Fleeing anything that "takes," "holds," or "congeals," Barthes privileges whatever breaks the "nappé" such as the fragment.

7. Many of Barthes's articles on theater are reprinted in the first volume of his complete works.

8. Reprinted in his *Oeuvres complètes* vol. 1, 500–501.

9. For a detailed discussion of the use of fragment in Barthes, see Ginette Michaud, *Lire le fragment. Transfert et théorie de la lecture chez Roland Barthes*.

10. It is interesting to note that the word "fix," from which "fixity" comes, has many meanings some of which translate Barthes's fears even more closely than the French term "figé." According to the *American Heritage Dictionary*, "to fix" can mean any of the following conditions, which are all the threats Barthes sees in the bourgeois order: 1. To put into a stable or unalterable form; 2. To make a substance nonvolatile or solid; 3. To kill and keep (a specimen) intact for microscopic study; and last but not the least 4. To spray or castrate.

11. For a detailed discussion of the semiotic, see Kristeva, *Revolution in Poetic Language*.

12. The parallelism between Barthes's Japan and Stendhal's Italy has also been commented on by Yoshiko Ishikawa in "La Passion du Japon" and Knight, *Barthes and Utopia*.

13. For a discussion of the inconsistencies between the early and late Barthes on the subject of the Other, see Célestin.

14. Besides Knight and Chambers, Lawrence Schehr makes the same criticism of Barthes's Moroccan text in *Alcibiades at the Door*.

15. There are several fragments in *Roland Barthes* which develop his idea of paradoxa. See in particular "Doxa/paradoxa" (75/71) and "Paradoxa" (143/140).

16. In one interview in which he speaks of his book on Japan, Barthes mentions the need to include in the theory of the text a reflection on seduction (*Grain* 151/159). He brings up the seduction theme again in *Sur la littérature* in which he explains to Maurice Nadeau that "le texte est un espace séducteur, et que, par conséquent, il faut se poser des problèmes de séduction quand on écrit" (48) (the text is a seductive space and consequently, one must ask the questions of seduction when one writes).

17. In her book on Barthes, Knight also discusses this preface to Loti's novel, which she reads in terms of the Barthesian notion of utopia.

CONCLUSION

1. One example that comes in mind is the works of the post-colonial Algerian writer, Assia Djebar, in which we find a very pronounced dialogic intertextuality with Orientalist writers and painters such as Delacroix and Fromentin, as well as colonial historical narratives.

2. In "Named for Victoria, Queen of England," Achebe recalls how he came to write about Africa: "At the university I read some appalling novels about Africa (including Joyce Cary's much praised *Mister Johnson*) and decided that the story we had to tell could not be told for us by anyone else no matter how gifted or well intentioned" (38).

WORKS CITED

Achebe, Chinua. *Hopes and Impediments*. New York: Anchor-Doubleday, 1989.

———. "Named for Victoria, Queen of England." *New Letters* 40 (Oct. 1973). Rpt. in Achebe 30–39.

———. "Colonialist Criticism." *Morning Yet on Creation Day*. New York: Anchor-Doubleday, 1975. Rpt. in Achebe 68–90.

———. "An Image of Africa: Racism in Conrad's *Heart of Darkness*." *Massachusetts Review* 18.4 (1977). Rpt. in Achebe 1–20.

Adler, Laure. *Marguerite Duras*. Paris: Gallimard, 1998.

Affergan, Francis. *Exotisme et altérité: essai sur les fondements d'une critique de l'anthropologie*. Paris: Presses Universitaires, 1987.

Ahmad, Aijaz. *In Theory: Classes, Nations, Literatures*. London: Verso, 1992.

Aldrich, Robert. *Greater France: A History of French Overseas Expansion*. Basingstoke: Macmillan, 1996.

Althusser, Louis. "Ideology and Ideological State Apparatuses." *Lenin and Philosophy, and Other Essays*. Trans. B. Brewster. New York: Monthly Review Press, 1971. 127–188.

Amin, Samir. *Eurocentrism*. Trans. Russell Moore. New York: Monthly Review Press, 1989.

Andreucci, Christine. "*René Leys*: la parole et le secret." *Victor Segalen*. Vol. 1. 161–172.

Antle, Martine. "Panoptisme et bureaucratie coloniale dans *Un barrage contre le Pacifique*." *L'Esprit créateur* 34.1 (1994): 83–91.

Armel, Aliette. "La Force magique de l'ombre interne." Vircondelet, *Marguerite Duras* 11–24.

Bajomée, Danielle and Ralph Heyndels, eds. *Ecrire dit-elle: imaginaires de Marguerite Duras*. Bruxelles: Université de Bruxelles, 1985.

Bajomée, Danielle. "Duras et le désir d'éternité." Vircondelet, *Marguerite Duras* 249–272.

Baker, Houston Jr. and Patricia Redmond, eds. *Afro-American Literary Study in the 1990s*. Chicago: Chicago UP, 1989.

Bakhtin, Mikhail. (V.N.Volochinov) *Le Marxisme et la philosophie du langage*. Paris: Minuit, 1977.

———. "The Problems of Speech Genres." *Speech Genres and Other Late Essays*. Eds. Caryl Emerson and Michael Holquist. Trans. Vern W. McGee. Austin: Texas UP, 1986. 60–102.

———. *The Dialogical Imagination: Four Essays*. Ed. Michael Holquist. Trans. Caryl Emerson and Michael Holquist. Austin: Texas UP, 1992.

Bal Mieke. *Narratologie: essais sur la signification narrative dans quatre romans modernes*. Paris: Klincksieck, 1977.

Barquisseau, Raphaël. *L'Asie française et ses écrivains*. Paris: Jean Vigneau, 1947.

Barthes, Roland. *The Eiffel Tower and Other Mythologies*. Trans. Richard Howard. New York: Hill and Wang, 1979. Partial trans. of *Mythologies*. Paris: Seuil, 1957.

———. *Critical Essays*. Trans. Richard Howard. Evanston: Northwestern UP, 1972. Trans. of *Essais critiques*. Paris: Seuil, 1964.

———. *Empire of Signs*. Trans. Richard Howard. New York: Hill and Wang, 1982. Trans. of *L'Empire des signes*. Paris: Champs-Flammarion, 1984.

———. *S/Z*. Trans. Richard Miller. New York: Hill and Wang, 1974. Trans. of *S/Z*. Paris: Seuil, 1970.

———. "Change the Object Itself." *Image-Music-Text*. Trans. Stephen Heath. London: Fontana, 1977. 165–169. Trans. of "Changer l'objet lui-même." *Esprit* 4 (1971): 613–616.

———. "Pierre Loti: *Aziyadé*." *New Critical Essays*. Trans. Richard Howard. New York: Hill and Wang, 1980. 105–121. Trans. of "Pierre Loti: 'Aziyadé'." *Le Degré zéro de l'écriture* suivi de *Nouveaux essais critiques*. Paris: Seuil, 1953 and 1972. 170–187.

———. *The Pleasure of the Text*. Trans. Richard Miller. New York: Hill and Wang, 1975. Trans. of *Le Plaisir du texte*. Paris: Seuil, 1973.

———. *Roland Barthes by Roland Barthes*. Trans. Richard Howard. London: Papermac, Macmillan 1977. Trans. of *Roland Barthes par Roland Barthes*. Paris: Seuil, 1975.

———. *Alors la Chine?* Paris: Christian Bourgois, 1975.

———. "Inaugural Lecture, Collège de France." Trans. Richard Howard. in *A Barthes Reader*. Ed. Susan Sontag. New York: Hill and Wang, 1982. 457–478.

———. "On échoue toujours à parler de ce qu'on aime." *Tel Quel* 85 (1980): 32–38.

———. *The Grain of the Voice: Interviews 1962–1980*. Trans. Linda Coverdale. New York: Hill and Wang, 1985. Trans. of *Le Grain de la voix: entretiens 1962–1980*. Paris: Seuil, 1981.

———. "Textual Analysis of a Tale of Poe." *On Signs*. Ed. Marshall Blonsky. Baltimore: Johns Hopkins UP, 1985. 84–97.

———. *Incidents.* Paris: Seuil, 1987.

———. *Oeuvres complètes.* Vol. 1. Ed. Eric Marty. Paris: Seuil, 1993. 3 vols.

Barthes, Roland and Maurice Nadeau. *Sur la littérature.* Grenoble: Presses Universitaires de Grenoble, 1980.

Baudrillard, Jean. *De la séduction.* Paris: Galilée, 1979.

Bécel Pascale "*Le Vice-Consul*: Colonial Mimicry and 'Partial Writing'." *Cincinnati Romance Review* 13 (1994): 218–227.

———. "From *The Sea Wall* to *The Lover* Prostitution and Exotic Parody." *Studies in 20th Century Literature* 21.2 (1997): 417–432.

Behdad, Ali. *Belated Travelers. Orientalism in the Age of Colonial Dissolution.* Durham: Duke UP, 1994.

Bellour, Raymond. *Le Livre des autres.* Paris: Union Générale d'Editions, 1978.

Benjamin, Walter. "The Work of Art in the Age of Mechanical Reproduction." *Illuminations.* Ed. Hannah Arendt. Trans. Harry Zohn. New York: Schocken Books, 1969. 217–251.

Benveniste, Emile. "La Nature des pronoms." *Problèmes de linguistique générale.* Vol. 1. Paris: Gallimard, 1966. 251–257.

Besnard-Coursodon, Micheline. "Signification du métarécit dans *Le Vice-consul* de Marguerite Duras." *French Forum* 3.1 (1978): 72–83.

Betts, Raymond F. *The False Dawn: European Imperialism in the Nineteenth Century.* Minneapolis: Minnesota UP, 1975.

Bhabha, Homi. "Of Mimicry and Man: The Ambivalence of Colonial Discourse." *October.* 28 (1984): 125–133. Rpt. in *The Location of Cuture.* New York: Routledge, 1994. 85–92.

———. "Between Identities." *Migration and Identity.* Eds. Rina Benmayor and Andor Skotnes. Oxford: Oxford UP, 1994. 183–199.

Blend, Charles. *André Malraux: Tragic Humanist.* Columbus: Ohio State UP, 1963.

Blot-Labarrère, Christiane. *Marguerite Duras.* Paris: Seuil, 1992.

Blumenthal, Gerda. *André Malraux: The Conquest of Dread.* Baltimore: Johns Hopkins UP, 1960.

Boak, Denis. *André Malraux.* Oxford: Clarendon Press, 1968.

Boehmer, Elleke. *Colonial and Postcolonial Literature: Migrant Metaphors.* Oxford: Oxford UP, 1995.

Bongie, Chris. *Exotic Memories: Literature, Colonialism and the Fin de Siècle.* Stanford: Stanford UP, 1991.

Booth, Wayne. *The Rhetoric of Fiction*. Chicago: Chicago UP, 1961.

Borgomano, Madeleine. "L'Histoire de la mendiante indienne. Une cellule génératrice de l'oeuvre de Marguerite Duras." *Poétique* 48 (1981): 479–493.

———. *Duras: une lecture des fantasmes*. Petit Roeulx, Belgique: Cistre, 1985.

———. "Le Corps et le texte." Bajomée and Heyndels 49–62.

Bouillier, Henry. *Victor Segalen*. 2nd ed. Paris: Mercure de France, 1986.

Bourdieu, Pierre. *Outline of a Theory of Practice*. Trans. Richard Nice. Cambridge: Cambridge UP, 1977.

Bourrel, Jean-René. "L'Exotisme dans l'oeuvre d'André Malraux." *Revue André Malraux* 18.2 (1986): 105–123.

Brantlinger, Patrick. *Rule of Darkness: British Literature and Imperialism, 1830–1914*. Ithaca: Cornell UP, 1988.

Brée, Germaine. "A Singular Adventure: The Writing of Marguerite Duras." *L'Esprit créateur* 30.1 (1990): 8–14.

Buttinger, Joseph. *Viet-Nam: A Political History*. New York: Frederick A. Praeger, 1968.

Calmes, Alain. *Le Roman colonial en Algérie avant 1914*. Paris: L'Harmattan, 1984.

Calvet, Louis-Jean. *Roland Barthes 1915–1980*. Paris: Flammarion, 1990.

Cardinal, Marie. *Les Pieds-noirs*. Paris: Belfond, 1988.

Cario, Louis and Charles Regismanset. *L'Exotisme—la littérature coloniale*. Paris: Mercure de France, 1911.

Célestin, Roger. *From Cannibals to Radicals: Figures and Limits of Exoticism*. Minneapolis: Minnesota UP, 1996.

Chambers, Ross. "Pointless Stories, Storyless Points. Roland Barthes between 'Soirées de Paris' and 'Incidents'." *L'Esprit créateur* 34.2 (1994): 12–30.

Champion. Catherine. "L'Imaginaire tropical: le paysage indien dans les romans populaires français, 1860–1920." Lombard 43–63.

Chen, Xiaomei. *Occidentalism: A Theory of Counter-Discourse in Post-Mao China*. Oxford: Oxford UP, 1995.

Cheng, François. "Espace réel et espace mythique." *Regard, espaces, signes* 133–152.

Cixous, Hélène and Michel Foucault. "A propos de Marguerite Duras." *Cahiers Renaud-Barrault* 89 (1975): 8–22.

Cixous, Hélène and Catherine Clément. *The Newly Born Woman*. Trans. Betsy Wing. Minneapolis: Minnesota UP, 1986.

Clifford, James. *The Predicament of Culture: Twentieth-Century Ethnography, Literature and Art*. Cambridge, Mass: Harvard UP, 1988.

Clifford, Nicholas Rowland. *Spoilt Children of Empire: Westerners in Shanghai and the Chinese Revolution of the 1920s.* Middlebury: Middlebury Press, 1991.

Coblence, Jean-Michel. "Pékin et Shanghai: clichés littéraires de l'entre-deux-guerres." *Revue d'esthétique* 5 (1983): 97–109.

Copin, Henri. *L'Indochine dans la littérature française des années vingt à 1954.* Paris: L'Harmattan, 1996.

Courtot, Claude. *Victor Segalen.* Paris: Henri Veyrier, 1984.

Dabydeen. David. *The Intended.* London: Secker & Warburg, 1991.

Delhomme, Jeanne. *Temps et destin; essai sur André Malraux.* Paris: Gallimard, 1955.

Derrida, Jacques. *Of Grammatology.* Trans. Gayatri Spivak. Baltimore: Johns Hopkins UP, 1976.

Dinesen, Isak. *Out of Africa.* New York: Vintage Books, 1972.

Dirlik, Arif. *The Postcolonial Aura: Third World Criticism in the Age of Global Capitalism.* Boulder, Colo.: Westview Press, 1997.

Doubrovsky, Serge. "Une écriture tragique." *Poétique* 47 (1981): 329–354.

Dufwa, Jacques. *Winds From the East: A Study in the Art of Manet, Degas, Monet and Whistler, 1856–86.* Stockholm: Almqvist & Wiksell International, 1981.

Duras, Marguerite. *The Sea Wall.* Trans. Herma Briffault. New York: Farrar, Straus and Giroux, 1967. Trans. of *Un Barrage contre le Pacifique.* Paris: Gallimard, 1950.

———. *The Vice-Consul.* Trans. Eileen Ellenbogen. London: Hamish Hamilton, 1968. Trans. of *Le Vice-consul.* Paris: Gallimard, 1966.

———. *India Song.* Trans. Barbara Bray. New York: Grove Press, 1976. Trans. of *India Song.* Paris: Gallimard, 1973.

Duras, Marguerite and Xavière Gauthier. *Les Parleuses.* Paris: Minuit, 1974.

Duras, Marguerite and Michelle Porte. *Les Lieux de Marguerite Duras.* Paris: Minuit, 1977.

Duras, Marguerite. "Rencontres des Cahiers Renaud-Barrault." *Cahiers Renaud-Barrault* 91 (1976): 3–26.

———. "Interviews du 12 avril à Montréal et du 18 juin 1981 à Paris." *Marguerite Duras à Montréal.* Eds. Suzanne Lamy and André Roy. Montréal: Spirale, 1981. 55–71.

———. *L'Homme Atlantique.* Paris: Minuit, 1982.

———. *The Lover.* Trans. Barbara Bray. New York: Pantheon Books, 1985. Trans. of *L'Amant.* Paris: Minuit, 1984.

———. *The North China Lover.* Trans. Leigh Hafrey. New York: The New Press, 1992. Trans. of *L'Amant de la Chine du nord.* Paris: Gallimard, 1991.

Eco, Umberto. *The Role of the Reader: Explorations in the Semiotics of Texts*. Bloomington: Indiana UP, 1979.

Ehrmann, Jacques. "L'Emprise des signes." *Semiotica* 1 (1973): 49–76.

Etiemble, René. *L'Europe chinoise*. 2 vols. Paris: Gallimard, 1988.

Fanon, Frantz, *Peau noire, masques blancs*. Paris: Seuil, 1952.

———. *The Wretched of the Earth*. Trans. Constance Farrington. New York: Grove Press, 1963.

Farrère, Claude. *Les Civilisés*. Paris: Librairie Paul Ollendorff, 1905.

Felski, Rita. *The Gender of Modernity*. Cambridge, Mass: Harvard UP, 1995.

Fetterley, Judith. *The Resisting Reader: A Feminist Approach to American Fiction*. Bloomington: Indiana UP, 1978.

Foucault, Michel. *Madness and Civilization: A History of Insanity in the Age of Reason*. Trans. Richard Howard. New York: Vintage Books, 1965.

———. *Language, Counter-Memory, Practice: Selected Essays and Interviews*. Ed. Donald F. Bouchard. Trans. Donald F. Bouchard and Sherry Simon. Ithaca: Cornell UP, 1977.

———. *Power/Knowledge: Selected Interviews and Other Writings, 1972–1977*. Ed. Colin Gordon. Trans. Colin Gordon, Leo Marshall, John Mepham, Kate Soper. New York: Pantheon Books, 1980.

Gadoffre, Gilbert. *Claudel et l'univers chinois*. Paris: Gallimard, 1968.

Gannon, Edward. *The Honor of Being a Man: The World of André Malraux*. Chicago: Loyola UP, 1957.

Gantès, Gilles de. "Coloniaux, gouverneurs, et ministres. L'influence des Français du Viêt-Nam sur l'évolution du pays à l'époque coloniale 1902–1914." Diss. Université Paris VII, 1994.

Gates, Henry Louis, Jr. "Canon-Formation and the Afro-American Tradition." Baker and Redmond 14–39.

Gauthier, Xavière. "Existe-t-il une écriture féminine?" *Tel Quel* 58 (1974): 95–97.

Girard, René. *Deceit, Desire and the Novel: Self and Other in Literary Structure*. Trans. Yvonne Freccero. Baltimore: Johns Hopkins UP, 1976.

Girardet, Raoul. *L'Idée coloniale en France de 1871 à 1962*. Paris: La Table Ronde, 1972.

Glissant, Edouard. *Le Discours antillais*. Paris: Seuil, 1981.

Goldmann, Lucien. *Pour une sociologie du roman*. Paris: Gallimard, 1964.

Gontard, Marc. *Victor Segalen: une esthétique de la différence*. Paris: L'Harmattan, 1990.

Gourdron, Hubert, Jean-Robert Henry & Françoise Henry-Lorcerie. *Roman colonial et idéologie coloniale en Algérie*. Spec. issue of *Revue algérienne des sciences juridiques, économiques et politiques* 11.1 (March 1974).

Grace, Paul et al. eds. *Vietnamese Women in Society and Revolution. The French Colonial Period*. Trans. Ngo Vinh Long. Cambridge, Mass.: Vietnam Resource Center, 1974.

Grand, Anne-Marie. *Victor Segalen: le moi et l'expérience du vide*. Paris: Klincksieck, 1990.

Greenlee, James. *Malraux's Heroes and History*. Dekalb: Northern Illinois UP, 1975.

Ha, Marie-Paule. "The M(Other)land in Marie Cardinal." *Romance Quarterly* 3 (Fall 1996): 206–216.

———. "The Cultural Other in Malraux's Asian Novels." *The French Review* 71.1 (1997): 33–43.

———. "Reading the Colonial in Malraux's Asian Novels." *Revue André Malraux Review* 26.1–2 (1996–97): 27–40.

———. "Engendering French Colonial History: The Case of Indochina." *Historical Reflections/ Réflexions Historiques* 25.1 (1999): 95–125.

Hargreaves, Alec. *The Colonial Experience in French Fiction: A Study of Pierre Loti, Ernest Psichari, and Pierre Mille*. London: Macmillan, 1981.

Harris, Geoffrey T. *De l'Indochine au R.P.F.: une continuité politique*. Toronto: Paratexte, 1990.

———. *André Malraux: A Reassessment*. New York: St Martin's Press, 1996.

Hickey, Gerald Cannon. *Sons of the Mountains: Ethnohistory of the Vietnamese Central Highlands to 1954*. New Haven: Yale UP, 1982.

———. *Kingdom in the Morning Mist: Mayrena in the Highlands of Vietnam*. Philadelphia: Pennsylvania UP, 1988.

Histoire de la France coloniale. 3 Vols. Paris: Armand Colin, 1991.

Histoire des littératures 3. Paris: Pléiade-Gallimard, 1958.

Hoffmann, Joseph. *L'Humanisme de Malraux*. Paris: Klincksieck, 1963.

Horvath, Violet M. *André Malraux: The Human Adventure*. New York: New York UP, 1969.

Hsieh, Yvonne Y. *Victor Segalen's Literary Encounter with China: Chinese Moulds, Western Thoughts*. Toronto: Toronto UP, 1988.

———. *From Occupation to Revolution: China Through the Eyes of Loti, Claudel, Segalen, and Malraux (1895–1933)*. Birmingham Al.: Summa Publications, 1996.

Hue, Bernard, ed. *Indochine—reflets littéraires*. Rennes: Presses Universitaires de Rennes, 1992.

Hugo, Victor. *Les Orientales. Poésie 1*. Paris: Seuil, 1972.

Hulme, Peter. *Colonial Encounters: Europe and the Native Caribbean, 1492–1797.* London: Methuen, 1986.

Impey, Oliver R. *Chinoiserie: The Impact of Oriental Styles on Western Art and Decoration.* London: Oxford UP, 1977.

Ishikawa, Yoshiko. "La Passion du Japon." *Magazine littéraire* Oct. 1993: 70–72.

Ives, Colta Feller. *The Great Wave: The Influence of Japanese Woodcuts on French Prints.* New York: Metropolitan Museum of Art, 1974.

Jacobson, Dawn. *Chinoiserie.* London: Phaidon Press, 1993.

JanMohamed. Abdul. *Manichean Aesthetics: The Politics of Literature in Colonial Africa.* Amherst: Massachusetts UP, 1983.

Jarry, Madeleine. *Chinoiserie: Chinese Influence on European Decorative Art 17th and 18th Centuries.* New York: Vendore Press, 1981.

Jay, Antoine and Madeleine Jay. *Notre Indochine 1936–1947.* Paris: Les Presses de Valmy, 1994.

Johnson, Barbara. "Responses." Baker and Redmond 39–44.

Jourda, Pierre. *L'Exotisme dans la littérature française depuis Chateaubriand.* Vol. 2. Paris: Presses Universitaires de France, 1956.

Kao, Shuhsi. "Ecriture et imaginaire idéogrammatique chez Segalen." *Victor Segalen.* Vol. 1 57–79.

Khatibi, Abdelkebir. *Figures de l'étranger dans la littérature française.* Paris: Denoël, 1987.

Knight, Diana. "Barthes and Orientalism." *New Literary History* 24.3 (1995): 617–633.

———. *Barthes and Utopia: Space. Travel, Writing.* Oxford: Clarendon Press, 1997.

Kristeva, Julia. *Revolution in Poetic Language.* Trans. Margaret Waller. New York: Columbia UP, 1984.

Lacan, Jacques. *Ecrits.* Paris: Seuil, 1966.

Lacouture, Jean. *André Malraux.* Trans. Alan Sheridan. New York: Pantheon Books, 1975.

Langlois, Walter. *André Malraux: The Indochina Adventure.* New York: Praeger, 1966.

———. "André Malraux and the Cultural Lessons of Asia." *Revue André Malraux Review* 24. 1/2 (1992–1993): 29–40.

Laude, Patrick. *Exotisme indochinois et poésie—étude sur l'oeuvre poétique d'Alfred Droin, Jeanne Leuba, et Albert de Pouvourville.* Paris: Sudestasie, 1990.

Lebel, Roland. *Etudes de littérature coloniale.* Paris: Peyronnet, 1928.

———. *Histoire de la littérature coloniale en France.* Paris: Larose. 1931.

Leblond, Marius-Ary. *Après l'exotisme de Loti: le roman colonial.* Paris: Vald Rasmussen, 1926.

Lebovics, Herman. *True France: The Wars Over Cultural Identity, 1900–1945*. Ithaca: Cornell UP, 1992.

Leuba, Jeanne. *L'Aile de feu*. Paris: Plon, 1920.

Lombard, Denys, Catherine Champion and Henri Chambert-Loir eds. *Rêver l'Asie: exotisme et littérature coloniale aux Indes, en Indochine et en Insulinde*. Paris: Editions de l'Ecole des Hautes Etudes en Sciences Sociales, 1993.

Lombard, Denys. "La Littérature exotique comme miroir nécessaire." Lombard, Champion & Chambert-Loir 11–18.

———. "Prélude à la littérature 'indochinoise'." Lombard, Champion & Chambert-Loir 119–139.

Loti, Pierre. *Aziyadé* suivi de *Fantôme d'Orient*. Paris: Gallimard, 1991.

Loutfi, Martine Astier. *Littérature et colonialisme: l'expansion coloniale vue dans la littérature romanesque française, 1871–1914*. Paris: Mouton, 1971.

Lowe, Lisa. *Critical Terrains: French and British Orientalisms*. Ithaca: Cornell UP, 1991.

Macé, Gérard. *Ex Libris: Nerval, Corbière, Rimbaud, Mallarmé, Segalen*. Paris: Gallimard, 1980.

Madsen, Axel. *Silk Roads: The Asian Adventures of Clara and André Malraux*. New York: Pharos Books, 1989.

Maigne, Vincenette. "Exotisme: évolution en diachronie du mot et de son champ sémantique." *Exotisme et création: actes du colloque international*. Lyon: L'Hermes, 1985. 9–16.

Maingueneau, Dominique. *Les Livres d'école de la République 1870–1914 (discours et idéologie)*. Paris: Le Sycomore, 1979.

Malleret, Louis. *L'Exotisme indochinois dans la littérature française depuis 1860*. Paris: Larose, 1934.

Malraux, André. *The Temptation of the West*. Trans. Robert Hollander. Chicago: Chicago UP, 1992. Trans. of *La Tentation de l'Occident*. Paris: Grasset, 1926.

———. "André Malraux et l'Orient." *Les Nouvelles littéraires* July 1926:2 Rpt. in *Mélanges Malraux Miscellany* 17.1/2 (1985): 53–54.

———. *The Conquerors*. Trans. Stephen Becker. New York: Holt, Rinehart and Winston, 1976. Trans. of *Les Conquérants*. Paris: Grasset, 1928.

———. *The Royal Way*. Trans. Stuart Gilbert. New York: Vintage Books, 1935. Trans. of *La Voie royale*. Paris: Grasset, 1930.

———. "Reply to Trotsky." *Nouvelle Revue Française* 211 (April 1931). Rpt. in *Malraux: A Collection of Critical Essays*. Ed. R. W. B. Lewis. Englewood Cliffs: Prentice Hall, 1964. 20–24.

———. *Man's Fate*. Trans. Haakon Chevalier. New York: Random House, 1934. Trans. of *La Condition humaine*. Paris: Gallimard, 1933.

———. *Antimémoires*. Paris: Gallimard, 1972.

———. *Le Règne du malin. Oeuvres complètes*. Eds. Marius-François Guyard, Jean-Claude Larrat and François Trécourt. Vol. 3. Paris: Pléiade-Gallimard, 1996. 3 vols. 970–1116.

Malraux, Clara. *Nos vingt ans*. Paris: Grasset, 1986.

Marini, Marcelle. *Territoires du féminin avec Marguerite Duras*. Paris: Minuit, 1977.

———. "L'Autre corps." Bajomée and Heyndels 21–48.

Marr, David G. *Vietnamese Anti-Colonialism 1885–1925*. Berkeley: California UP, 1971.

Martino, Pierre. *L'Orient dans la littérature française au XVIIe et au XVIIIe siècle*. Paris: Hachette, 1906.

Maspero, François. Préface. *Massacres coloniaux 1944–1950: la IV République et la mise au pas des colonies françaises*. By Yves Benot. Paris: Edition la Découverte, 1994. i–xvi.

Mathieu, Martine. Présentation. *Le Roman colonial*. Paris: L'Harmattan, 1987. 9–11.

McClintock, Anne. *Imperial Leather: Race, Gender, and Sexuality in the Colonial Contest*. London: Routledge, 1995.

Memmi, Albert. *The Colonizer and the Colonized*. Trans. Howard Greenfeld. New York: The Onion Press, 1965.

Michaud, Genette. *Lire le fragment: transfert et théorie de la lecture chez Roland Barthes*. Québec: Hurtubise, 1989.

Miller, Christopher. *Blank Darkness: Africanist Discourse in French*. Chicago: Chicago UP, 1985.

Mills, Sara. *Discourses of Difference: An Analysis of Women's Travel Writing and Colonialism*. London: Routledge, 1991.

Mitterand, Henri. *Littérature textes et documents XXe siècle*. Paris: Nathan, 1989.

Moatti, Christiane. "Le Motif du Japon dans 'La Condition humaine' d'André Malraux." *Mélanges Malraux Miscellany* 16.2 (1984): 74–99.

Moura, Jean-Marc. *Lire l'exotisme*. Paris: Dunod, 1992.

Ngo, Tat To. *Quand la lampe s'éteint*. Trans. Le Lien Vu and G. Boudarel. Hanoi: Editions en Langues Etrangères, 1959.

Ngô, Vinh Long. *Before the Revolution: The Vietnamese Peasants Under the French*. New York: Columbia UP, 1991.

Ngugi wa Thiong'o. *Decolonising the Mind: The Politics of Language in African Literature*. London: James Currey, 1986.

Nguyen, Hong. *Days of Childhood* (1938) in *The Light of the Capital: Three Modern Vietnamese Classics*. Trans. Greg Lockhart and Monique Lockhart. Kuala Lumpur: Oxford UP, 1996.

Norindr, Panivong. *Phantasmatic Indochina: French Colonial Ideology in Architecture, Film, and Literature.* Durham: Duke UP, 1996.

Parry, Benita. "Problems in Current Theories of Colonial Discourse." *Oxford Literary Review* 9.1–2 (1987): 27–58.

Porter, Dennis. "Orientalism and its Problems." Williams and Chrisman 150–161.

Pratt, Mary Louise. *Imperial Eyes: Travel Writing and Transculturation.* New York: Routledge, 1992.

Prince, Gerald. *A Dictionary of Narratology.* Lincoln: Nebraska UP, 1987.

Psichari, Ernest. *Terres de soleil et de sommeil. Oeuvres complètes.* Paris: Conrad, 1948. 185–294.

Pujarniscle, Eugène. *Philoxène ou de la littérature coloniale.* Paris: Firmin-Didot, 1931.

Quella-Villéger, Alain. "Dire l'indicible Indochine." *Indochine: un rêve d'Asie.* Ed. Alain Quella-Villéger. Paris: Omnibus, 1995. i–xx.

Réal, Elaine. "Structures du récit dans 'René Leys'." *Victor Segalen* Vol. 1 139–147.

Regard, espaces, signes, Victor Segalen. Colloquium organized by Elaine Formentelli. Paris: Asiathèque, 1979.

Ridley, Hugh. *Images of Imperial Rule.* London: Croom Helm, 1983.

Robert, Marthe. *The Old and the New: From Don Quixote to Kafka.* Trans. Carol Cosman. Berkeley: California UP, 1977.

Rodgers, Catherine. "Déconstruction de la masculinité dans l'oeuvre durassienne." Vircondelet *Marguerite Duras* 47–68.

Roques, Philippe and Marguerite Donnadieu. *L'Empire français.* Paris: Gallimard, 1940.

Rosello, Mireille. "Amertume: l'eau chez Marguerite Duras." *Romanic Review* 74.4 (1987): 515–524.

Roy, Claude. "Duras tout entière à la langue attachée." *Le Nouvel Observateur* 31 August 1984: 66–67.

Ruedy, John. *Modern Algeria: The Origins and Development of a Nation.* Bloomington: Indiana UP, 1992.

Ruscio, Alain. *Amours coloniales: aventures et fantasmes exotiques de Claire de Duras à Georges Simenon.* Bruxelles: Edition Complexe, 1996.

Said, Edward. *Orientalism.* New York: Vintage Books, 1979.

———. *The World, the Text, and the Critic.* Cambridge, Mass: Harvard UP, 1983.

———. *Culture and Imperialism.* New York: Knopf, 1993.

Sartre, Jean-Paul. Préface. Stéphane, *Portrait de l'aventurier.* 9–29.

———. Preface. Fanon, *The Wretched of the Earth.* 7–26.

Schehr, Lawrence. *Alcibiades at the Door: Gay Discourses in French Literature.* Stanford: Stanford UP, 1995.

Schor, Naomi. *Reading in Detail: Aesthetics and the Feminine.* New York: Routledge, 1989.

Schwartz, William Leonard. *The Imaginative Interpretation of the Far East in Modern French Literature 1800–1925.* Paris: Champion, 1927.

Segalen, Victor. *Stèles, peintures, équipée.* Paris: Plon, 1955.

———. *Essai sur l'exotisme.* Paris: Fata Morgana, 1978.

———. "Une Orange exprimée, un grand vide." Rpt. in *Regard, espaces, signes.* 89–90.

———. *Les Immémoriaux.* Paris: Seuil, 1985.

Segalen, Victor and Henry Manceron. *Trahison fidèle.* Paris: Seuil, 1985.

Segalen, Victor. *Stèles.* Paris: Orphée/La Différence, 1989.

———. *Steles.* Trans. Michael Taylor. Santa Monica: The Lapis Press, 1987.

———. *René Leys.* Trans. J. A. Underwood. London: Quartet Books, 1990. Trans. of *René Leys. Oeuvres complètes.* Ed. Henry Bouillier. Vol. 2. Paris: Laffont, 1995. 2 vols. 453–572.

Victor Segalen: colloque international, 13 au 16 mai 1985. 2 vols. Ed. Yves-Alain Faure. Pau: Université de Pau et des Pays de l'Adour, 1985.

Selous, Trista. *The Other Woman: Feminism and Femininity in the Work of Marguerite Duras.* New Haven: Yale UP, 1988.

Sharpe, Jenny. *Allegories of Empire: The Figure of Woman in the Colonial Text.* Minneapolis: Minnesota UP, 1993.

Shohat, Ella and Robert Stam. "From the Imperial Family to the Transnational Imaginary: Media Spectatorship in the Age of Globalization." in *Global/Local Cultural Production and The Transnational Imaginary.* Eds. Rob Wilson and Wimal Dissanayake. Durham: Duke UP, 1996. 145–170.

Spivak, Gayatri Chakravorty. "Three Women's Texts and a Critique of Imperialism." *Critical Inquiry* 12.1 (1985): 234–261.

———. "Can the Subaltern Speak?" in *Marxism and the Interpretation of Culture.* Eds. Cary Nelson and Lawrence Grossberg. Urbana: Illinois UP, 1988. 271–313.

———. *The Post-Colonial Critic: Interviews, Strategies, Dialogues.* Ed. Sarah Harasym. New York: Routledge, 1990.

Spurr, David. *The Rhetoric of Empire: Colonial Discourse in Journalism, Travel Writing and Imperial Administration.* Durham: Duke UP, 1993.

Stamelman, Richard. *Lost Beyond Telling: Representations of Death and Absence in Modern French Poetry.* Ithaca: Cornell UP, 1990.

Stéphane, Roger. *Portrait de l'aventurier: T. E. Lawrence, Malraux, von Salomon*. Paris: Saggittaire, 1950.

———. *Malraux: premier dans le siècle*. Paris: Gallimard, 1996.

Stoler, Ann L. *Race and the Education of Desire: Foucault's History of Sexuality and the Colonial Order of Things*. Durham: Duke UP, 1995.

Takemoto, Tadao. *André Malraux et la cascade de Nachi: la confidence de l'univers*. Paris: Julliard, 1989.

Temman, Michel. *Le Japon d'André Malraux*. Arles: Editions Philippe Picquier, 1997.

Tran, Tu Binh. *The Red Earth: A Vietnamese Memoir of Life on a Colonial Rubber Plantation*. Trans. John Spragens Jr. Ed. David G. Marr. Athens, Ohio: Ohio University, Center for Southeast Asian Studies, 1985.

Trotet, François. *Henri Michaux, ou, la sagesse du vide*. Paris: Albin Michel, 1992.

Trotsky, Leon. "La Révolution étranglée." *La Nouvelle revue française* 211 (April 1931): 488–500.

Udris, Raynalle. *Welcome Unreason: A Study of 'Madness' in the Novels of Marguerite Duras*. Amsterdam: Rodopi, 1993.

Valéry, Paul. *Variété I*. Paris: Gallimard, 1924.

Vandegans, André. *La Jeunesse littéraire d'André Malraux; essai sur l'inspiration farfelue*. Paris: Jean-Jacques Pauvert, 1964.

Vircondelet, Alain. *Duras: A Biography*. Trans. Thomas Buckley. Normal, IL: Dalkey Archive Press, 1994.

———. ed. *Marguerite Duras*. Paris: Ecriture, 1994.

Viswanathan, Gauri. *Masks of Conquest: Literary Study and British Rule in India*. New York: Columbia UP, 1989.

Webber, Lucille R. *Japanese Woodblock Prints: The Reciprocal Influence Between East and West*. Provo: Brigham Young UP, 1979.

Weinberger-Thomas, Catherine. *L'Inde et l'imaginaire*. Paris: Ecole des Hautes Etudes, 1988.

West, Cornell. *Prophetic Reflections: Notes on Race and Power in America*. Monroe: Common Courage Press, 1993.

Wichmann, Siegfried. *Japonisme: Japanese Influence on Western Art in the 19th and 20th Centuries*. New York: Harmony Books, 1981.

Williams, James. *The Erotics of Passage: Pleasure, Politics, and Form in the Later Work of Marguerite Duras*. New York: St Martin's Press, 1997.

Williams, Patrick and Laura Chrisman, eds. *Colonial Discourse and Post-Colonial Theory: A Reader*. New York: Columbia UP, 1994.

Williams, Raymond. *Marxism and Literature*. Oxford: Oxford UP, 1977.

Yeager, Jack. *The Vietnamese Novel in French: A Literary Response to Colonialism*. Hanover: New England UP, 1987.

Yoshioka, Hiroshi. "Samurai and Self-Colonization in Japan." in *The Decolonization of Imagination: Culture, Knowledge and Power*. Eds. Jan Nederveen Pieterse and Bhikhu Parekh. London: Zed Books, 1995. 99–112.

Young, Robert. *White Mythologies: Writing History and the West*. New York: Routledge, 1990.

Yourcenar, Marguerite. *With Open Eyes: Conversations with Mathieu Galey*. Trans. Arthur Goldhammer. Boston : Beacon Press, 1984.

Yu, Beongcheon. *The Great Circle: American Writers and the Orient*. Detroit: Wayne State UP, 1983.

Zecchi, Lina. "Mémoires de pierre, la structure intertextuelle de *Stèles*." *Victor Segalen* Vol. 1 385–397.

INDEX

Achebe, Chinua, 62, 93, 122
Adamov, Arthur, 101
adventure
   and colonies, 51
   as a response to European crisis, 51
Affergan, Francis, 17, 91
Aldrich, Robert, 54
Althusser, Louis, 9
Amin, Samir, 2–3
Andreucci, Christine, 33

Bakhtin, Mikhail, xii, 16, 69, 121
Bal, Mieke, 82, 83
Balzac, Honoré de, 12, 95
Barthes, Roland
   the *atopique* in, 105
   on colonialism, 6
   criticism of Doxa in, 99, 103, 104
   criticism of the West in, 18
   criticism of Western theater in, 101–102
   and Duras, 97, 113
   and Gide, 109
   and Loti, 96
   and Malraux, 98, 100
   and Orientalism, xii, xiv, 18, 108, 117
   the Other in, xiii, xiv, 17, 107, 113, 116, 120
   science of signifier in, 102–103
   and seduction, 111, 138n. 16
   and Segalen, 16–17, 96, 97, 113
   and Stendhal, 107–108
   third space in, xiv, 116
   and Voltaire, 96, 98, 108, 137n. 3
   Alors la Chine?, xiv
   critique of the metaphor of penetration in, 110–111
   L'Empire des signes, xiv
   comparison between Western and Japanese cultures in, 100–102
   decenteredness in, 105–106
   emptiness in, 111–112
   haiku in, 103–104
   Japanese signs in, 99–100
   the maternal in, 106–107
   the Orient in, 96
   Orientalism in, 97
   philosophical exoticism in, 98
   La Chambre claire, 107
   Incidents, xiv, 108, 113
   Mythologies, 6, 100, 102, 108
   "Qu'est-ce que la critique?", 15
   "Pierre Loti 'Aziyadé'", 27–28, 114–116
   Plaisir du texte, 29, 95, 105, 117.
   Roland Barthes par Roland Barthes, 104, 105, 109, 116
   S/Z, 18, 24
   codes in, 11, 12, 95–96
Baudelaire, Charles, 97, 121
Baudrillard, Jean, 111
Bellour, Raymond, 99, 102
Benjamin, Walter, 70
Benveniste, Emile, 90

Besnard-Coursodon, Micheline, 93
Betts, Raymond, 51
Bhabha, Homi, 62, 116, 121
Boak, Denis, 49
Boehmer, Elleke, 10
Bongie, Chris, 14, 34, 115–116
Booth, Wayne, 11
Borgomano, Madeleine, 88
Bouillier, Henry, 23, 30, 32
Bourdieu, Pierre, 12, 121
Bourrel, Jean-René, 57
Bovarysm, 26, 40–41
Brecht, Bertolt, 101, 102
Breton, André, 122
Brooke, James, 51
Bugeaud, Thomas Robert, 72
Burton, Richard, 53

Caillié, René, 53
Camus, Albert, 9
Cary, Joyce, 7, 122
Célestin, Roger, 14
Cervantes, Miguel de, 26
Césaire, Aimé, 122
Chambers, Ross, 108, 113, 116
Chen, Xiaomei, 3
China, 1, 3
    and Enlightenment thinkers, 4
    and Europe, 29–30
chinoiserie, 5
Chivas-Baron, Clotilde, 14
civilizing mission, 120–121
Cixous, Hélène, 89
Claudel, Paul, 5, 6, 122
Clifford, James, 3
Coblence, Jean-Michel, 30
colonial discourse, xi, 119
colonial literature, 10, 125–126nn. 15, 16
    versus colonialist literature, 10
    critics of, 7–10
    in France, 47
    gender bias of critics of, 14–15
    relation of exotic literature to, 6–7

colonial propaganda, 5, 47, 130nn. 2, 3
colonials, metropolitan views of, 8
Columbus, Christopher, 91
Condé, Maryse, 121
Confucius, 4
Conrad, Joseph, 7, 9, 14, 93, 122
Courtot, Claude, 21
culturalism, 28, 98, 128–129nn. 6, 8

Dabydeen, David, 122
Dé-Tham, 68
Derrida, Jacques, 25, 39
dialogism, xii, xiii
Dickens, Charles, 10
Dirlik, Arif, xi, 18, 24, 28, 113, 121
Donnadieu, Marguerite. *See* Duras, Marguerite
Donnadieu, Marie. *See* Legrand, Marie
Doubrovsky, Serge, 104
Douls, Camille, 53
Duras, Marguerite
    and the archaic feminine, 92
    and Barthes, 97, 113
    and the civilizing mission, xiv, 73
    and colonialism, xiv, 6, 80
    dehistoricizing the Other in, 93
    and *écriture féminine*, 87–88
    and Indochina, xiv, 71, 92–93
    and Loti, 114
    and Malraux, 71, 76, 82
    as *métisse*, 121
    and Orientalism, xii, 18
    and the Other, 16–17, 120
    transgression in, 94
    L'Amant
        class/race/gender contradictions in, 79–80
        interracial relations in, 86–87, 94
    L'Amant de la Chine du Nord, 86–87, 92, 93, 94
    Un Barrage contre le Pacifique, xiv
        autobiographical elements in, 74
        class conflict in, 77

colonial maternalism in, 78
critique of colonial exploitation
  in, 75–76
and *L'Empire français*, 76
race relations in, 77–78
L'Empire français, xiv
  civilizing mission in, 72–73
  in the Durassian corpus, 73–74
  genesis of, 134n. 2
Le Vice-consul, 16
  colonial society in, 80–81, 83
  the cultural Other and the beggar
    woman in, 91
  the exotic in, 80
  fissuring of the white world in,
    84–86
  the Other writing and the beggar
    woman in, 87–89, 90
  representation of Indians in, 81–82

East, 4, 5
  usages of term, 2–3
  and West, 1–2
Eberhardt, Isabelle, 14
Eco, Umberto, 12, 15, 16
Erhmann, Jacques, 98, 111
Etiemble, René, 4
Eurocentrism, 3
Europeanness, 2
the exotic
  decoding of, 13
  seme of, 12–13
exotic literature
  critics of, 7–8
  gender bias of critics of, 14–15
  relation of colonial literature to, 6–7

Far East. *See* East
Farrère, Claude, 8
Felski, Rita, 92
Fénelon, François, 4
Ferry, Jules, 8, 73
Fetterley, Judith, 11, 15

Flaubert, Gustave, 8, 26
Foucault, Michel, 83, 94
Fournier, Christiane, 14
French feminist movement, 89
Freud, Sigmund, 34
Fromentin, Eugène, 12

Gallieni, Joseph-Simon, 72
Garnier, Francis, 51
Gauguin, Paul, 51
Gaultier, Jules de, 21, 25, 26, 40
Gauthier, Xavière, 87, 89
Gautier, Judith, 5, 14
Gautier, Théophile, 1, 5
Gide, André, 109
Girard, René, 26, 29
Girardet, Raoul, 8
Glissant, Edouard, 27, 122
Goldmann, Lucien, 58
Goncourt, Edmond & Jules, 5

Harry, Myriam, 14
heteroglossia, 121
  and off-center reading, xiii
Hoffmann, Joseph, 57, 58
Hugo, Victor, 2, 114
hybridity, 23–24, 121

Illustration, 5

Japan, 5
Johnson, Barbara, 3
Jones, William, 19

Kao, Shuhsi, 28
Kipling, Rudyard, 1, 3, 7, 9
Knight, Diana, 96, 108
Kristeva, Julia, 5

Lacan, Jacques, 34
Lamy, Suzanne, 71
Larrat, Jean-Claude, 67, 68–69
Lautréamont, Comte de, 121

Lawrence, T.E., 51
Legrand, Marie, 74
Leibniz, Gottfried Wihelm von, 4
Leuba, Jeanne, 14
Lombard, Denys, 7, 9
Loti, Pierre, 5, 12, 14, 25, 57, 96
    archaism in, 27–28
    and exotic literature, 41, 45, 114–115
    Julien Viaud, real name of, 115
Loutfi, Martine Astier, 6, 9, 10
Lowe, Lisa, 108
Lyautey, Hubert, 72

Mallarmé, Stéphane, 121
Malleret, Louis, 7, 14
Malraux, André
    adventure-heroes in, 51–53
    and Barthes, 98, 100
    and China, 48, 50
    and the civilizing mission, xiii
    and colonialism, xiii, 6
    and cultural *métissage*, 62–63, 121
    and Duras, 71, 76, 82
    and the East, 49–50
    and eroticism, 57–58
    and history, 48, 51
    and humanism, xiii, 48
    and Indochina, 48
    and Japan, 50, 98
    metaphysical reading of, 57
    and Orientalism, xii, xiii, 18, 48–49
    and the Other, xiii, 16–17
    and Segalen, 47
    and the West, 17–18
    La Condition humaine, 50, 52, 59
        representation of the Chinese revolution in, 132–133n. 24
        "white man's burden" in, 60–61
    Les Conquérants, 50, 51–52
        genderizing China in, 59
        representation of Chinese in, 61–62
        "white man's burden" in, 60–61

Le Règne du malin, xiii, 48, 56
    contradictions in, 68–69
    genesis of, 67
    heteroglossia in, 69
    humanism of Mois in, 69–70
    Mayrena and Don Quixote, 67, 134n. 35
    and *La Voie royale*, 67–68
La Tentation de l'Occident, 48–50, 59–60
La Voie royale, 16, 52
    adventurer-heroes in, 51–55
    end of adventuring in, 55–56
    representation of Mois in, 64–66
Manceron, Henry, 26
Marini, Marcelle, 87, 90, 92
Martino, Pierre, 7
Massignon, Louis, 19
Mathieu, Martine, 9
Mayrena, David de, xiii, 53, 54
    biography of, 66–67
    Marie Charles David, real name of, 66
McClintock, Anne, 120
Mei, Lan-Fang, 102
Memmi, Albert, 78
Michaux, Henri, 5, 6
Mills, Sara, 15
Mitterand, Henri, 8
Montaigne, Michel de, 102
Montesquieu, Charles de Secondat, 4, 98
Morand, Paul, 57
Moura, Jean-Marc, 7, 14, 98

Occidentalism, 3
Odend'hal, Prosper, 53
Orientalism, xi–xiii
Orientalization
    of Orientalists, 18–19
    self-, xi–xii
Orwell, George, 7

Pascal, Blaise, 63
Paulhan, Jean, 5
Polo, Marco, 4

Ponge, Francis, 113
Porte, Michelle, 71, 80
Porter, Dennis, 17
post-colonialism
   and colonial and exotic literatures, 11–14
   and its intellectuals, 127n. 32
   studies of, 4, 121
Psichari, Ernest, 51

Quella-Villéger, Alain, 7

reading
   heteroglossic, xiii, 16
   and ideology, 15
   off-center, 16–17
Réal, Elaine, 39
Rhodes, Cecil, 51
Rimbaud, Arthur, 122
Robert, Marthe, 26
Roques, Philippe, xiv, 72
Rosello, Mireille, 88
Rousseau, Jean-Jacques, 4, 39
Rushdie, Salman, 121, 122

Said, Edward, 10, 121
   criticism of, 17
   criticism of Orientalism in, xi, 11, 18, 97
   cross-disciplinary approach of, 10–11
Saint-John Perse, 5, 6, 122
Sarraut, Albert, 47
Sartre, Jean-Paul, 63
Saussure, Ferdinand de, 99
Schor, Naomi, 106
Segalen, Victor
   Anély, Max, pseudoname of, 23
   and Barthes, 16–17, 96, 97, 113
   and China, 21–22, 23, 26, 27–28
   and colonialism, xiii, 6, 23–24
   and cultural mixing, 23–24
   and exoticism xiii, 7, 22, 23–24
      Bovarysm, relation to, 25–26
   commodification of, 24
   and *Divers*, 21, 24–25
   and the Orphic myth, 25, 128n. 5
   and Quixotism, 26
   and Loti, 27, 41–42, 45, 114
   and Malraux, 47
   and Orientalism, xii, 18
   and the Other, 16–17, 24–25, 119
   and the West, 17–18
   Essai sur l'exotisme, 7, 13, 24–25, 26, 41
   Les Immémoriaux, 21, 23
   René Leys, xiii
      and *Aziyadé*, 41–42
      castration in, 35–36
      cultural *métissage* in, 36–37
      ellipsis in, 33, 34, 40
      and exotic literature, 26, 41, 45
      inside as absence in, 32
      language of the inside, 31, 33–34
      mediated desire in, 29
      narrative structure of, 29, 39
      narrative subversion in, 42–44
      Peking in, 29–31
      pénétration chinoise in, 38–39
      reversal of narrative roles in, 43–44
      strategic redemptive failure in, 22
      use of pronouns in, 32–33, 38
Senghor, Léopold, 122
Shohat, Ella, 13
Showalter, Elaine, 87
Sollers, Philippe, 5
Spivak, Gayatri, 18, 49
Stam, Robert, 13
Stamelman, Richard, 107
Stendhal, 107–108
Stéphane, Roger, 48, 51, 63
Stoler, Ann, 15, 120

Telquelians, 5
Trollope, Anthony, 10

Udris, Raynalle, 87

Valéry, Paul, 2, 48
Vandegans, André, 47, 57
Viaud, Julien. *See* Loti, Pierre
Vircondelet, Alain, 71, 73
Viswanathan, Gauri, 120
Voltaire, 1, 4, 96, 98, 108

West
    and construction of the Other, xi
    and East, 1–2
    and Orientalism, 11
    spiritual crisis in, 51
    usages of term, 2–3
Williams, Raymond, 17

Yoshioka, Hiroshi, xi–xii
Young, Robert, 18
Yourcenar, Marguerite, 2, 5

www.ingramcontent.com/pod-product-compliance
Lightning Source LLC
Chambersburg PA
CBHW021759230426
43669CB00006B/128